HICKORY WIND

THE LIFE & TIMES

GRAM PARSONS

HICKORY WIND
THE LIFE & TIMES OF
GRAM PARSONS

 OMNIBUS PRESS

London / New York / Paris / Sydney / Copenhagen / Madrid

Ben Fong-Torres

★ ————— PERMISSIONS ————— ★

Permissions

Permissions

To Barry Fong-Torres
in loving memory

★ ——— ACKNOWLEDGMENTS ——— ★

Trying to nail down a life story like that of Gram Parsons was like trying, to take a fine line from Donovan, to catch the wind.

I was fortunate that so many people who knew Gram cared enough about him to join me in the chase. All of the more than one hundred who agreed to be interviewed know they have my gratitude, but I wish, in particular, to thank the following family and friends:

Avis Johnson, Gram's sister; Gretchen Carpenter, his widow, and Nancy Parsons, the mother of his daughter, had to overcome often painful memories to go through their lives with Gram again, but they did it, in the hope that his story would be told fairly. My hope is that they do not feel let down.

Tom Kelly Connor and Pauline Wilkes, Gram's uncle and aunt in Tennessee, were as gracious as they were helpful, and I especially appreciated some vital telephone calls they made to other family members. In Florida, aunt May Snively and cousin Rob Hoskins were equally hospitable.

In Waycross, Georgia, Jack and Roger Williams at the *Journal-Herald* gave me my first bearings. Childhood friends Dickey Smith, Henry Clarke, and Daphne Delano Brown and family friend Edmund Pedrick added vivid colors to the emerging portrait. Billy Ray Herrin, a singer-songwriter and an avid fan of Gram's, led me to the biggest and most emotional surprise I encountered in Gram's boyhood town.

In Winter Haven, writers Billie Ellis and Velma Daniels pro-

Acknowledgments

vided valuable information on both the city and the Snively family. For details on Gram's high-school years, I am indebted to classmates Marium Jones Roberts and Dennis Hupp, and to Robert Hubbard and Joe Dyess, two of his teachers at the Bolles School in Jacksonville.

Gram's first musical adventures were sorted out by numerous friends in Florida, among them Jim Stafford, Kent LaVoie, and Dick McNeer. I especially thank Gram's loyal friend, Jim Carlton, for the use of his tapes and scrapbooks and Patricia Johnson Carter, Gram's high-school sweetheart and first female singing partner. From Gram's folk group, the Shilos, Paul Surratt, Joe Kelly, and manager Buddy Freeman were extremely helpful.

Gram's brief time at Harvard and with the International Submarine Band were illuminated most brightly by the Rev. Jet Thomas, his adviser at Harvard, by producer Suzi Jane Hokom, and by Sub Band members Bob Buchanan, Jon Corneal, and John Nuese.

In California, Gram quickly became a Byrd, a Flying Burrito Brother, and a friend of the Rolling Stones. For memories about the fast lane on which Gram skated, I thank Keith Richards, who called as soon as he returned from a Stones tour of Europe to help me make my deadline; Michelle Phillips, who recounted her day into nightmare with Gram at Altamont; Roger McGuinn, who hired Gram into the Byrds; and Chris Hillman, a fellow pioneer in the fusion of country and rock. Others who provided candid assessments and valuable insights were musicians Barry Tashian, Bernie Leadon, Chris Ethridge, Michael Clarke, and Gene Parsons; Eve Babitz, artist and writer; Andee Cohen, photographer; Pamela DesBarres, number one fan; Eddie Tickner, manager; Terry Melcher and Jim Dickson, producers, and Tom Wilkes and Michael Vosse of A&M Records.

A pivotal moment for Gram was his discovery of Emmylou Harris. I regret that she declined to be interviewed for this book, but am grateful that, in a previous and lengthy series of visits with me, she was so open and articulate that I am confident that her role in his life—and his role in hers—are accurately represented here.

I was fortunate that several people who knew her well, and who worked with her and Gram, were so helpful. They included Tom Guidera, her bass player and boyfriend in Washington, D.C., when she was hired by Gram; Jock Bartley, guitarist on the Fallen Angels tour; and Rodney Crowell, Emmylou's first singing partner in her Hot Band.

I think of the founders and members of the Gram Parsons Memorial Foundation—Mark Holland and John Kravet in Tampa, Fredda and Mary Lee Joiner in Memphis, and Thor Martinsen in Norway—as exactly the kind of people Gram hoped to reach. They

Acknowledgments

were generous with their help, and it is largely because of them that Gram's work continues to reach lovers of "cosmic American music." The GPMF welcomes inquiries: Write to Fredda Joiner at 1719 Faxon Avenue, Memphis, Tennessee 38112. Mark has turned his collection of Gram Parsons memorabilia into an archive of sorts, and it is open to the public by appointment: 3109 Ola Ave., Tampa, Florida 33603.

I never had the opportunity to personally interview Gram, so published and recorded conversations with him were crucial to my efforts. I relied especially on interviews conducted by Bud Scoppa, Jay Ehler. Stanley Booth, Cameron Crowe, Judith Sims, Jan Donkers, and the late Chuck Casell.

In every reference to "I" and "me," the actual words should be "we" and "us." My research assistant was Holly George-Warren, a GP fan, guitarist, writer, and researcher in New York. On our trips to Georgia, Florida, and Tennessee, she proved to be more a partner than an assistant. Time and again, she came up with just the right fact, recollection, or question in an interview; she called on her North Carolina roots to charm strangers into opening their doors to us; she served as driver and storyteller extraordinaire through our miles together, and, after each trip, she transcribed myriad tapes and continued to help and inspire. Gram had the perfect working partner in Emmylou. I was similarly blessed.

Hickory Wind was inspired by another appreciator of Gram's music, Irwyn Applebaum, president of Pocket Books, who contacted my friend and agent, Sarah Lazin. I thank them for their faith, and I especially thank Sarah for her counsel and encouragement.

I am grateful, too, to Leslie Wells for her sensitive as well as skillful editing; to Nancy Hoffman for her editorial assistance; to Robert Oermann and Mary Bufwack for their hospitality in Nashville, and to the Country Music Foundation and John Sherraden at Hatch Show Print in Music City. For all-around friendship, inspiration, and help, I thank Bob Barnes, Paula Batson, Cynthia Bowman, Susan Brenneman, Fiona Campbell, Tom Gericke, Connie Hillman, Martha Hume, Judd Klinger, Greil Marcus, Barr Nobles, the Oakland A's, Jane Rose, Pat Sullivan, Joel Selvin, Karen Thorsen, and Timothy White.

I also need to acknowledge some mentors who taught me journalism in the best way—by example. I will never forget Eileen Murphy at Oakland High School; Jerry Werthimer at San Francisco State; Gordon Lew, publisher of *East-West*, in Chinatown, and John Burks, David Felton, Ralph J. Gleason, Chet Flippo, and many others at *Rolling Stone* magazine. Editor Jann Wenner gave me the best job I ever had. Jann's lessons and kindnesses remain with me.

Acknowledgments

This book is dedicated to my brother Barry, who, like Gram, died at a too-young age, but it is for my entire family, and especially Dianne, whose love, patience, advice, and support got me singing—in my best Elvis voice, of course—the last lines of "Return of the Grievous Angel":

Twenty thousand roads I went down, down, down
And they all led me straight back home to you

CONTENTS

Contents

HICKORY WIND

THE LIFE AND TIMES
OF
GRAM PARSONS

Gram Parsons sounded almost reverent one hazy winter afternoon in the first month of the last year of his life.

He was rehearsing for a tour with a patched-together band called the Fallen Angels, and he was sitting in a junkyard of a house, more a compound than a home. Gram, a young man of great wealth, was staying in a shack in the back.

He was talking about death and drugs and about his favorite place on earth, a wilderness just two hours east of Hollywood, in the Mojave.

"I spend a lot of my time up at Joshua Tree in the desert, just looking at the San Andreas Fault. And I say to myself, 'I wish I was a bird drifting up above it.'"

The Joshua Tree Inn was the kind of place you went to mainly to be away from someplace else.

The rooms in this low-slung, Spanish-style desert motel were small, and they looked about like what you might expect a half-decent jail cell would look like, with their cinder-block walls and exposed overhead pipes—just right for hanging yourself.

Gram Parsons didn't care about decor. He liked Joshua Tree for the national monument, minutes away by motorcycle. There he could get high and commune with the trees, the birds and the stars—and whatever else was up there.

He used to go there with Chris Hillman when they were in the Byrds and the Flying Burrito Brothers together; he went there to make a movie with Michelle Phillips; he went there with the Rolling Stones. Keith Richards, the bad-boy Stone, had become a buddy of Gram's, and they'd take turns sitting in a barber's chair someone had put on top of a mountain. They'd stay up all night, zonked out of their minds, looking for, and sometimes spotting, flying saucers.

In town, he could lounge around either of two taverns, or grab some Sauza Conmemorativo tequila and Jack Daniels and head back to the motel.

Best of all, Joshua Tree was far from Los Angeles, where Gram had just gone through the most unnerving summer of his life.

He was separated from his wife of two years, Gretchen, and he had begun divorce proceedings. Their house had been nearly destroyed by a fire. He'd lost several close friends—a guitarist, an actor, and a dealer among them—within the year.

He'd also completed work on the best album he'd ever made.

With both his record and his marriage close to the finish line, he needed to get away from L.A.

On September 18, 1973, his second day in the desert, Gram was truly a free man. He was with a female companion, Margaret Fisher, who, like so many of Gram's past women, was a beautiful blonde. Better yet, Michael Martin, who'd been his "valet" on his tour early that year, had gone back to Los Angeles to replenish his supply of marijuana.

Gram wasted little time making a connection with a heroin dealer in town. Before scoring, he drank heavily at lunch with Margaret and with Michael's friend, Dale McElroy. Neither woman drank; they sat and watched Gram chain-drink Jack Daniels, then drove him back to the Joshua Tree Inn.

There he found his drug connection and, in a room next to the owners' apartment, he added morphine into his already overloaded system.

Dale was in her room when Margaret knocked on her door, frantic.

"You gotta come with me!" she shouted. She told Dale to get some ice cubes from a nearby machine.

In Gram's room, Dale found Gram on the floor. He had turned blue. Margaret took down Gram's jeans and underwear and inserted several of the ice cubes into his rectum.

As Dale watched in amazement, Gram came to life.

Margaret had employed a trick well known among junkies for reviving an overdose victim. Dale didn't know what Gram and Margaret had been doing until she looked into Margaret's eyes. They were like pinwheels. Margaret told Dale that they'd been booting up morphine.

Gram got up, looked down at his pants and then at the two women. "Gee," he said, "what're you girls doing with my pants down?"

As Gram made his way back to his own room, Margaret Barbary, one of the proprietors of the motel, saw him. Gram was pale and puffy, and she'd seen enough rock musicians to recognize a person under the influence of drugs.

"Gram, you look terrible," she said with genuine concern.

Gram managed a smile. "I'll be all right," he said, and made his way into Room 8.

Prologue

There he spent another hour or two with Margaret before she left to get some food for them. She stopped in Dale's room and asked her to look in on Gram.

"He's sleeping," she said, "but you never know. . . ."

"What do you mean?" said Dale, instantly reminded of the scene a few hours before.

"Just go in and sit with him," said Margaret. "Just be with him; cool him out."

As Margaret drove off in Gram's Jaguar, Dale fetched a book and went to Room 8. Within fifteen minutes, she noticed that his breathing had become labored. There was a rattle in it; she might have heard the sound of regurgitation. Panicked, and with no telephone in the room and no help nearby, Dale got on top of Gram. She'd never taken first-aid training, so she improvised, pounding him, pumping him, trying to get his breathing back into rhythm. Failing that, she tried mouth-to-mouth resuscitation. Whatever she was doing, it wasn't enough.

A few minutes later, Margaret returned, but Gram, as far as Dale could tell, was already dead.

Moments later an ambulance arrived, but the crew judged Gram too far gone for them even to attempt resuscitation efforts. They rushed him to the Hi-Desert Memorial Hospital in Yucca Valley. He arrived at 12:15 A.M. He had no pulse, and after a few attempts at restarting his heart, he was pronounced dead at 12:30. He was two months shy of his twenty-seventh birthday.

Keith Richards was halfway around the world on tour with the Rolling Stones when he got the news a few days later. He was in the bathroom backstage at a stadium in Innsbruck, Austria, when horn player Bobby Keyes approached.

"Hey, man, I got something bad to tell you," said Bobby, who'd done his share of jamming with Gram in country music clubs around Los Angeles. "Gram just croaked out in Joshua Tree."

Keith was shocked. "I said, '*what?*' Because I always had a feeling—it was like with Otis Redding—you would think there were many many more years, that it was only a beginning. And then the hard bit comes in. You say, 'Well, he was just too good to get old.' Just to soften the shock on yourself."

But there was no getting around it. "I was shattered for ages."

By the time Keith was getting the word about his friend, the story had taken a macabre twist. The Associated Press put this on its wires on September 22:

LOS ANGELES—The body of Gram Parsons, who once sang with the Byrds rock musical group, was stolen and possibly burned, police said on Friday.

The casket was taken from Los Angeles International

★ 3 ★

Airport Thursday while awaiting transportation for burial. A casket containing a partially burned body was found 200 miles away near the Joshua Tree National Monument on early Friday, authorities said.

Authorities said they believed but were not certain the body was that of Parsons, 27, who was pronounced dead at a hospital early Wednesday. He had been stricken at a motel in the desert town of Joshua Tree. An autopsy was performed, but it was inconclusive, and authorities were awaiting further laboratory results to determine the cause of death.

A green Western Airlines body bag was found beside the burned casket, sheriff's deputy Larry Smith reported. Authorities found the body after being alerted by campers that "a log was burning near the monument."

The body was Gram's, and the man who tricked it away from the airport and set it on fire was Philip Clark Kaufman, Gram's friend, road manager, and, as it said right on Gram's albums, his "executive nanny."

Besides being a musician, Gram Parsons was a pawn in a southern family deeply embedded in alcohol, suicides, betrayals, and good money gone bad. In death, he was of great value to his stepfather, a New Orleans native who knew just enough about Louisiana laws to realize that if he could prove Gram to be a resident of that state—dead or alive—he could inherit Gram's money. The stepfather made a claim on the body and made plans to ship Gram to New Orleans, where he had no real family or friends.

That's when Phil Kaufman stepped in.

Phil was no stranger to aberrant behavior. His résumé included a stay at a prison called Terminal Island in California for smuggling marijuana. One of his fellow inmates was a starry-eyed would-be singer named Charles Manson, and once they both were released, the two remained friends, although Phil went on to be nanny to the Stones and to Gram Parsons.

A few days after the discovery of the coffin, sheriffs arrested Phil and another man and charged them with grand theft. The two were let go after paying $750—the cost of the casket.

And so it was that the album Gram was proudest of was a posthumous release; that his intended cover photo—of him and his luminous singing partner, Emmylou Harris, straddling a motorcycle—was scotched by his estranged wife; and that, like all his albums, this one didn't sell.

Gram, whose soulful but sometimes frail voice evoked a bro-

Prologue

ken heart, and who wrote songs as if he had one, never had any luck with his recording career, with the International Submarine Band, the Byrds, the Flying Burrito Brothers, or on his own. But through his efforts—sometimes ragtag and botched; other times brilliant but too far ahead of their time—he became identified as a pioneer, perhaps *the* pioneer of country-rock. Although he did champion the idea of hippies playing country music for a rock-and-roll audience, and of bringing longhairs and rednecks together without barroom brawls, he was never comfortable with the phrase.

In late 1972, having completed the first solo album, *GP,* he wrote to Frank Murphy, a buddy from his prep-school days in Jacksonville, Florida.

"Yeah, my music is still country—but my feeling is there is no boundary between 'types' of music. . . . I see two types of sounds—good ones & bad ones—or—ones y'like—ones y'don't. Maybe I should say there's plenty boogie on *GP*—I keep my love for variations even tho' I've some sort of 'rep' for starting what (I think) has turned out t'be pretty much of a 'country-rock' (ugh!) plastic dry-fuck. Excuse the strong language. But these record company thugs are the ones most responsible for what goes down . . ."

Not long after his death, Emmylou became a star on her own. Wherever she went, she talked up Gram, placing him as a musical pioneer in a league with Hank Williams and Jimmie Rodgers. After reading some of her clippings and recalling the reviews Gram got for his last album, she made a rueful comment. "People talk a lot about Gram Parsons, and they write a lot about Gram Parsons, but you never hear Gram Parsons on the radio."

Unlike most biographies of pop music artists, this is one without a built-in, subconscious sound track of familiar tunes.

Except to those who own Gram Parsons' records, this is a narrative that will, I hope, encourage, rather than recall, listening to the man's work.

That's what Elvis Costello, one of the princes of the punk/new wave scene was trying to do when he wrote the liner notes for a 1982 British reissue of the best of Gram's two solo albums:

In the Byrds and the Flying Burrito Brothers, Gram Parsons . . . helped create a Frankenstein's Monster: country-rock. But his first Warner Bros. album, *GP,* paid no allegiance to this style. With an impressive backup band, it was a traditional sounding album, mercifully free of gimmicks like fuzz-tone steel guitar. . . . But most importantly, it featured some of the finest duet singing ever put on a record.

. . . I'd be the last to romanticise his death, and I wish he had avoided his apparent self-destruction and continued to make music as great as this.

But it's hard to deny the irony of hearing the beautiful "Hickory Wind" accompanied by the mock-adulation of a phony audience track—a bitter little comment on scant commercial success.

The year before, I had written about Gram for *Esquire* magazine. In 1981, few people—even among music lovers—knew who he was. It was my job to explain why *Esquire* would make room for an article about him.

"Even though he never cracked the chart, he's in the air everywhere these days," I wrote. "There're nine albums out that feature Parsons in some prominent way; there are the records by Emmylou Harris, protegee and keeper of the flame; there are songs about him by the Stones, the Eagles, and Poco.

"And you can hear him in other musicians as well—people who preceded him, like Willie, Dolly, Bobby Bare, and Delbert McClinton, and those who followed him, like the New Riders of the Purple Sage, the Dirt Band, Rockpile, Carlene Carter, Rosanne Cash, Lacy J. Dalton, and Kris Kristofferson."

James Ring Adams, writing in *The Wall Street Journal* in 1987, noted the swelling ranks of musicians influenced by Gram. Among the top ten selling albums in the country was *Trio*, an acoustic set featuring Emmylou Harris, Linda Ronstadt, and Dolly Parton. In addition, he listed Chris Hillman and his new group, the Desert Rose Band (although Chris was every bit the country-rock pioneer that Gram was); Rodney Crowell (Emmylou's first musical partner after Gram); Ricky Skaggs (who replaced Crowell in Emmylou's band); Sid Griffin and his Long Ryders (Griffin put together a series of interviews and essays in book form in 1985); Elvis Costello (who recorded two of Gram's songs on his album, *Almost Blue*); and Tom Russell, a New York–based singer who wrote "Joshua Tree" for Gram.

Others would add to the list such seventies artists and groups as Jimmy Buffet, Commander Cody and the Lost Planet Airmen, Asleep at the Wheel, the Amazing Rhythm Aces, and Firefall, as well as Lone Justice, REM, and the Kentucky Headhunters. Tom Russell noted Gram's impact on the Eagles, Poco, and other bands and concluded: "When you consider that Parsons turned the above artists on to country music, then consider the millions of people *they* reached, you begin to realize the importance of Gram Parsons."

Prologue

In 1982, Sid Griffin wrote the liner notes for an album of a 1973 radio broadcast of a concert by Gram and his tour band, the Fallen Angels. Sid wrote: "Gram's music remains so powerful that it carries a permanence befit that of Hank Williams, Charlie Parker or Lennon-McCartney. It cut way past skin deep, and close to the bone at that."

My *Esquire* piece, I am sorry to have to admit, was riddled with errors. I relied on a lengthy profile published in 1976 by the rock magazine *Crawdaddy* that, while laying out his story in great detail, bent toward the morbid. As I would learn too late, the *Crawdaddy* piece had been edited without benefit of fact checking and, while it used numerous quotes from Gram, he proved to be one of the least reliable sources on the subject of Gram Parsons.

Gram, it turns out, was quite a story-teller, true to the country tradition. Whether he was putting on an interviewer, regaling a friend, or losing himself in a fantasy world he needed, he wove twists on his life, each so fantastic that they *must* have been true. The family home in Florida was used in *Gone With the Wind*. . . . His dad, whose name was "Coon Dog" Connor, died drunk in jail one Christmas Day. . . . Gram was a theology major at Harvard. . . . The Rolling Stones wrote "Wild Horses" for and about him. . . .

"Gram made up so many strange tales, you didn't know *what* to believe," said his aunt, Pauline Wilkes. His younger sister, Avis, said much the same. "Gram—gosh, Gram never let the truth get in the way of a good story."

I learned that double- and triple-checking, tracking down friends and friends of friends, relatives of relatives, only added to the confusion.

More people remember being friends with Gram than even Gram at the height of braggadocio might have thought to claim. For a man many described as incapable of confiding in people or of having an intimate relationship, male or female, he had many best friends and true loves. At every turn, it seems, he had a musical mentor hipping him to country-rock.

Jim Stafford, who was in the Legends with Gram in Winter Haven, Florida, and who really did teach Gram a few guitar licks, chuckled at how Gram actually became a minor legend, "with this kind of Mondo Gram stuff, guys with Gram rooms, like Elvis rooms."

Jim remembered watching a "This is Your Life" segment on one of his boyhood singing heroes, Roy Rogers. The host, Ralph Edwards, showed the King of the Cowboys a photograph, and as the camera zoomed in, he said: "So, Leonard Slye, here's a picture of you with your prize pig."

Ralph Edwards wasn't making fun of Roy Rogers, said Jim,

"but that's who he was. His name was Leonard and he raised a pig.

"What I'm saying is this: Gram might have evolved into a guy who's got this cult thing going, but I don't think anybody around here *knew* that guy. He *became* that guy. Maybe he's still in the process of becoming something."

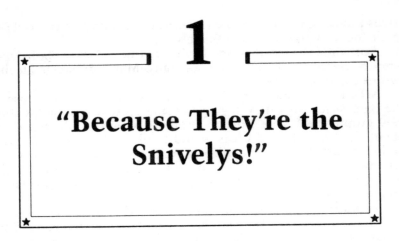

1

"Because They're the Snivelys!"

The chief of the fire department in Waycross, Georgia, used to tell a little story about the time a fire broke out at the country club, in the midst of a New Year's Eve party. "They called the fire truck out there, and Avis (Snively) jumped up on the fire truck and she went to blowing the siren and everything, and they told her she had to stop it.

"And she said, 'Hell, I'll *buy* this damn thing! Nobody's gonna be telling me what *I* gotta do!'"

★

Gram Parsons's mother, Avis, was a Snively. To be a Snively was to be all-powerful in Winter Haven—central Florida—where money grew on orange trees, and the Snivelys grew a good number of those trees.

To be a Snively was to be further enriched with the sale of every crate of Snively Groves oranges, grapefruit, and tangerines; every can of Snively's frozen orange juice concentrate, and every carton of Snively's, Cypress Gardens, or Nu-Zest brand of orange juice or blended orange and grapefruit juice. For Floridians in the citrus industry, the forties and fifties were the boom years, and few made louder noises than the Snivelys.

But while the family was thriving, in one sense, on the sales of wholesome food products, too many of them succumbed to alcohol and its many side effects.

When Gram and Chris Hillman sat around in their house in the San Fernando Valley, trying to come up with a song for their new group, the Flying Burrito Brothers, Gram would tell Chris about the Snivelys and Chris would think of Tennessee Williams and his seamy Southern families racked by sexual trauma, psychoses, and neuroses, drenched in money, liquor, or both. In the Snivelys' case, it was old money, alcoholism, insanity—real or imagined—and greed.

In addition, some of them just weren't very nice.

One family friend insisted that she had nothing but good to say about the Snivelys, especially Papa John, who even played cards with his employees. But when the story got around to bankruptcies and lawsuits within the family, even she had to tell the plain and simple truth. "Liquor destroyed the family," she said.

From Gram's father's side of the family, the Connors, there is a benign, there-but-for-fortune kind of sadness that permeates every thought about Gram and his father Cecil. "It was a hard-living family," said Gram's uncle Tom Connor about the Snivelys. "There are so many tragedies there, so many deaths from alcohol. It's just a horror story."

Rob Hoskins, a cousin of Gram's, sat in his living room in Winter Haven, opened up a hope chest, and brought out a genealogy, in the form of a little book, of the Snivelys and several family photographs in leather frames. He gazed at a sepia picture of his late mother, Evalyn, and recalled her attempts at giving up drinking.

"You have to remember, *alcohol*," Rob said, as if it were a proper name, or an entity like the Devil himself. "My mother . . . Avis . . . Tommy, who was my grandfather's youngest brother . . . his daughter's husband, Tommy's wife . . ."

You'd need the family tree to sort out the ones who *didn't* succumb to drink.

Billie Ellis, society reporter at the *Winter Haven News Chief*, had the Snivelys as one of her main beats. She had plenty of material she could never print. Her first encounter with the family, for example, was in 1957 with Gram's grandparents at Papa John and Dorothy's mansion at Cypress Groves.

As Billie recalled, "She was giving a big party downstairs, and upstairs, he was dying." The reason the rookie reporter knew such a delicate piece of information was simple: Haney, as everyone called Dorothy, was complaining loudly to her guests that "he was taking so long to do it."

"I don't think they were malicious," Billie continued. "They were just that way." She told of some friends who owned an expensive shoe store in town. Various Snivelys would shop there. Or, more accurately, "they would go in and load up with shoes and never pay for them. I asked my friends, 'Why didn't you press them to pay?' 'Because they're the Snivelys,' they said."

It was religion that chased the first Snively from Switzerland to America. Johann Jacob Schnebele, born in 1659, was a Mennonite. Devout Mennonites—the only kind there seemed to be—practiced not so much dogma as discipline. The Mennonite church considered itself a world unto its own, abstained from the vanities of the outer world, and refused civic and military duties. They became the objects of persecution not only by the dominant Catholics but also by Protestants.

In his late fifties, with his son Jacob in tow, Schnebele fled to America, to the province of William Penn, which proved friendly to Mennonite refugees. Here he built a stone house for his family near Cornwall.

Jacob, born in 1694, moved south to Greencastle, just above the Maryland state line. He had five children by his first marriage and fourteen by his second. One of his seven sons, Andrew, Americanized his name and had fourteen children of his own.

And so the Snivelys began.

It was John Andrew Snively who would take the family to Florida. The fifth of eleven children, John was born in 1888 and lived in Altoona, Pennsylvania, where he made do without a college education and held an office job with the Pennsylvania Railroad. In 1911, he married Dorothy DeHaven of Akron, Ohio, and they honeymooned in Florida, where Dorothy's recently widowed aunt lived. Florence Inman and her husband had been among the earliest settlers in the Winter Haven area in the 1880s, when the town was nothing but sand trails and a few families camped on its outskirts. They had been drawn to the area for its climate. Now, her husband having just died, Florence implored "Haney" and her new husband to move to Winter Haven.

The newlyweds found themselves in a town studded with lovely lakes, a town just beginning to take advantage of its plentiful citrus groves. John began working, caring for other people's groves, selling fertilizer, and making groves for himself. He knew the value of real estate, and in 1924, he acquired a twelve-acre grove and organized a company to develop 4,000 lots that eventually became Inwood and Eloise Woods, where he also built the Eloise Woods Water Works. He kept seventy-seven prime acres for himself, and the property, originally swamp lands lined with beautiful cypress trees, with an inspiring view of Lake Eloise, would in 1942 become the site of his mansion. The larger, surrounding property later became Cypress Gardens, Winter Haven's most enduring tourist attraction.

Snively's acquisitions, combined with hard work and a good business sense, paid off. By June 1950 Snively Groves had added a juice plant, a sectionizing plant, a tangerine unit, a warehouse, and a frozen concentrate plant. On June 16, 1950 a fire wiped out all of these facilities.

John Snively rebuilt, and by 1953 business was booming; Snively Groves became the largest shipper of fresh fruit in Florida, growing 20 percent of Florida's citrus and jockeying for top position with one competitor.

Before his first orange crops came up, and while he was selling fertilizer, Snively started a family. In 1915 his only son, John Snively, Jr., was born. Four years later, the Snivelys had their first daughter, Evalyn. After another four years, Haney gave birth to another daughter, Avis.

"Avis was extremely attractive and very bright," said Gram's aunt Pauline. "The whole family was bright."

But Gram's mother was spoiled as a child, said her own daughter, also named Avis. (Gram's sister was called "Little Avis," while their mother, naturally, was "Big Avis.") "Avie could do no wrong, and everybody did everything for her."

Avis attended boarding schools in Virginia and Washington, D.C., before enrolling at the University of Alabama. "She was just as smart as she could be," said Gram's aunt May. Asked what Avis studied, May laughed, as if this was a silly question. Avis obviously didn't need a career.

While John Snively, Jr., joined the family business in 1939, at age twenty-four, Avis and Evalyn whiled away their time, awaiting marriage and families.

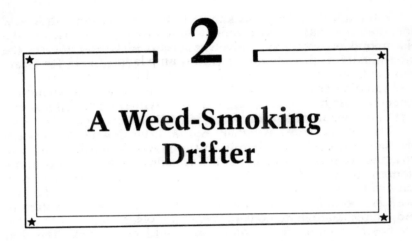

2

A Weed-Smoking
Drifter

Gram had just turned twelve when his father died. He probably didn't learn that his father killed himself until many years later. As an adult, Gram tried to patch up his father's reputation by reinventing him, placing him on the highest pedestal he could dream up: that of a musician who never got his due.

Gram came up with a story that his dad, known to his friends as Coon Dog Connor, was a country singer who could've been a contender. To Keith Richards, he portrayed his dad as a weed-smoking drifter, a lovable hobo. As Gram elaborated on the story, his father became a victim.

"My father had never been able to play the music he loved," he once said. "He wasn't allowed to play. A man who played music back then was automatically considered a drunkard who was never going to amount to anything. So my father studied aeronautical engineering and was later a war ace. But he had always wanted to be a musician—and ever since I can remember, there were always musical instruments lying around."

Although Coon Dog was known to have plunked a guitar now and then and had taken a mostly indifferent stab or two at the Hammond organ in the Snively mansion in Winter Haven, the instruments in their home in Waycross, Georgia, were for Gram and Little Avis to play with.

And although the adult Gram knew well the circumstances of his father's death, he chose, at least on one occasion, to tell a writer that Coon Dog had died drunk in a jail cell on Christmas Eve, 1958.

The truth is that his father, Ingram Cecil Connor, Jr., was the product of a well-to-do family in Columbia, Tennessee, and had little use for country music. And if it hadn't been for a war and a woman, he would have earned a degree in engineering from Auburn University and gone on to a life far removed from factory work in Georgia, misery in the midst of a rich and arrogant family, and, finally, enough demons to drive him to suicide.

Cecil Jr. came from some tough and lofty stock. The first known ancestor on his mother's side was Colonel George Reade, born in England in 1608 and married in Yorktown, Virginia. But a family tree traces the line (without details) to King Edward II and, beyond his majesty, to the first king of Spain, Ferdinand the Great.

Eight generations later, William Connor married Sarah Cecil, and they settled in the farm town of Columbia, Tennessee.

In 1887, Willis and Sarah gave birth to Ingram Cecil Connor, Gram's paternal grandfather. Ingram graduated from the Columbia Military Academy and from business school, then went to work as a traveling salesman for a hardware supply company. He met Nancy Kelly, a teacher from Fayetteville, just north of the Alabama border, and they married in 1913. In 1917, they had a son, Ingram Cecil Connor, Jr. Brother Tom followed three years later, and the boys were joined in 1920 by Pauline.

The Connors lived in a handsome house in Columbia. From here, the father made his rounds. He once rejected a promotion that would have required moving to Nashville, just forty miles away. They'd just be lost in the big city, he told his family.

Ingram loved to hunt and fish, and he kept his shotgun and fishing tackle in the back of his car. While he was on the road, he could always pull over whenever the fishing or hunting looked good.

Pretty much everything he killed—squirrel, quail, or fish—went on the Connors' dinner table. And as soon as Cecil and Tom were old enough, they, too, were taught to hunt and fish.

Music was not prevalent in the Connor household. Grandmother played the organ at the Methodist Church, but the family heard music mostly on Saturday nights, on a windup Victrola record player. Other evenings, the Connors listened to the radio—but they tuned out one kind of music: country and western.

A Weed-Smoking Drifter

To them, western music was laughable, the corn-pone outpourings of hillbillies and hayseeds. Much of the community preferred to think of Nashville as the home of Vanderbilt University rather than that of the Grand Ole Opry.

The only time the Connors heard the indigenous music of their home state was in the summer, when the family would vacation at Beaver Dams Springs in the backwoods of middle Tennessee. Sunday nights, local fiddlers would play for square dancing, and since the hillbilly music served a purpose, it was considered all right.

Cecil Jr. was a high-spirited boy. He and his best friend, Van Shapard, were inseparable. They swam and paddled the Connor boys' Indian canoe on nearby Duck River. When Van enrolled at Columbia Military Academy, Cecil enrolled, too.

In high school years, Cecil, Van, and their buddies played popular tunes on ukeleles. For dancing, the favored music was big band and swing music. Schools prohibited dancing, but the kids could always go to downtown lodges and country clubs. During the Depression, they'd gather at the house of someone in the group, turn on the radio, and dance.

In the fall of 1935, Cecil entered the Alabama Polytechnic Institute at Auburn University in Alabama, majoring in mechanical engineering. He hoped to become an aeronautical engineer.

At Auburn, Cecil made excellent grades and joined the campus ROTC during his first two years. When World War II broke out, he decided he had to serve his country, and enlisted in the U.S. Army Air Force. Just two months before he was set to graduate, he upset his parents by announcing that he was going to flight school in Tulsa.

3

Coon Dog and Avis

No one knows for sure how Gram's father got the nickname Coon Dog. But after the war, that's what he called himself, and that's what everybody called him.

His daughter Avis, who refers to her father as Coon Dog today, thought he got the nickname "because he was such a good hunter, or because he was such a good hunter during the war, in dog fights." Or, as Edmund Pedrick, an attorney in Waycross, put it: "Coon Dog was as ugly as a mudfish. He just *looked* like a coon dog."

After taking flying lessons in Oklahoma and Texas and graduating as a Flying Cadet, Cecil enlisted in the Army Air Force in May 1940 as a second lieutenant. In March 1941 he shipped out to Hawaii, where he was stationed at Wheeler Field, the principal base protecting the Pearl Harbor naval station on Oahu.

As part of the 6th Pursuit Squadron of the 18th Pursuit Group, Cecil handled five kinds of fighter planes and, in November, earned a promotion to first lieutenant, putting him in line to become a squadron commander. Meanwhile, Cecil's buddy Van Shapard was serving in China.

Cecil lived off base, sharing in the rental of a grand house near Diamond Head that belonged to the heiress Barbara Hutton. He stayed in touch with his mother, who would relay news to the rest of the family. In 1941, she wrote to Pauline at college:

> Cecil writes that he is taking music now and has been playing "The Pagan Love Song" with a real mean base. He wrote about going hunting for wild pigs and Daddy was so thrilled he took the letter downtown to let his friends read it.

Cecil was asleep in the Hutton house when the Japanese attacked Pearl Harbor at dawn on December 7, 1941. In a letter postmarked December 13, his mother wrote to Pauline that Cecil was all right and that, when the first sirens sounded, he and a fellow soldier threw on their uniforms and rushed to Wheeler Field.

By July 1942 Cecil was a captain and was sent to New Guinea in the Indonesia Sea to serve as an operations officer and fighter pilot. The Japanese wanted New Guinea as a base from which to attack Australia. Back and forth raged battles between the Japanese, who'd landed in May 1942 and American forces, under General Douglas MacArthur, through the duration of the war.

Cecil's military records show that, between the summer of 1942 and the next spring, he flew fifty combat missions over New Guinea and Australia. By 1943 he was made major and was a squadron commander. A decorated hero, he was given a presidential unit citation for "extraordinary heroism in action against an armed enemy," along with an air medal, an Asiatic-Pacific theater ribbon, and an American defense ribbon. But in March he was stricken with malaria and hospitalized in Australia. In July he transferred to Bartow air field in Florida, disqualified from flying and from overseas duty because of his illness.

On his return from Australia, Cecil said little about his experiences, leaving his family with fragmented horror stories.

He told Pauline about his hospital stay and about how enemy bombers would swoop over and strafe the hospitals. Attendants had to grab patients and put them in ditches to wait out the attacks. Cecil—chilled, fevered, and sweating from his malaria—suffered numerous nightmares.

He was, not surprisingly, a changed man. The spirited, spunky boy his childhood friends knew had become a somber young man.

Cecil continued to serve in the air force, assuming officers' duties at Bartow. The base is located just southwest of Winter Haven, and a frequent visitor was John Snively, Jr., son of the citrus baron and a friend of several pilots. John met Coon Dog, and they talked about getting together to do some hunting or fishing. At one point, John mentioned his sister, Avis. John, who was married to May Pate and had two children, set up a double date. By fall of 1944, when Coon Dog was transferred to the Perry army air field in north Florida, he was seeing Avis on a regular basis, and in January they announced their engagement.

They were married March 22 in Winter Haven at the Snively mansion, which had become the natural gathering place for family occasions. Avis was stunning on her wedding day, dressed in a white satin dress with a low bodice. The lanky Major Connor was in full military dress.

In retrospect, it was appropriate that Major Connor was in uniform when he married into the Snively clan. After honeymooning in Daytona Beach, Cecil's dreams of a career in engineering and of starting a family of his own in his native Tennessee would be dashed. He got his orders to report for duty in Waycross, Georgia.

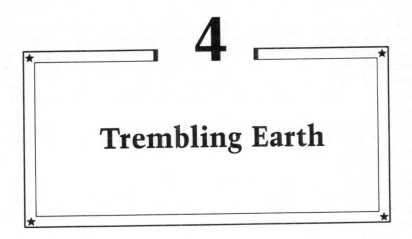

4

Trembling Earth

Gram Parsons spent his childhood in Waycross. This is where he first saw the one great idol of his life, Elvis Presley, and where he had his first girlfriends. But he had no great affection for the town, and understandably so. One friend talked about why Gram wouldn't be nostalgic about Waycross: "Look what happened there. His mother left his father, his father turned into a hopeless alcoholic and burned the goddamned house down. And if Gram went back there, the townspeople would try to kill him."

Gram did go back, and he was mostly amused.

In his high school years, Gram would occasionally visit Waycross to see friends. Soon he'd be at a loss for something to do. Sometimes he'd make his way downtown, plunk himself down on one of the rocking chairs on the front porch of the Ware Hotel, and look at the farmers and railroad workers passing by.

"They all look the same and they all talk the same and they all think the same," he'd say to nobody in particular. And he'd chuckle softly and rock some more, quite satisfied with himself, content in the knowledge that he had someplace else to go.

★

Jerry Wexler, the great record producer (of Ray Charles, Aretha Franklin, and a hall of fame of others) was thinking aloud one night, searching for a song idea for Wilson Pickett. He turned to composer Bert Berns and suggested Waycross as a subject. "I figured there couldn't be any more down-home place than that," he said. "Waycross, Georgia, would have to be the asshole of the world."

Waycross is an easy town to pick on. It's small, it's stagnant, and, for God's sake, it's in the *Deep South*, right on top of the Okefenokee Swamps.

Billy Ray Herrin thought he knew Waycross. He was born and raised there, and when he decided to open up a record shop in 1974, he figured he'd pay tribute to his favorite musician, Gram Parsons, by naming it after one of his favorite Flying Burrito Brothers songs: "Sin City."

He should have known better. The people of Waycross, pop. 20,000, believe in hard work and hard worshiping. There are 140 churches listed in the phone book, and eight cocktail lounges. And two of the bars are out of town.

Not that the local folk reminded anyone of Mennonites. Stanley Booth, a Waycross native who escaped into the wicked world of rock-and-roll journalism—where he later met the Rolling Stones and Gram Parsons—once wrote about his hometown: "There is violence, illicit sex, drunkenness—in a word, sin—in south Georgia, but they have not become behavioral standards."

And they are not to be brandished on a neon sign, the way Billy Ray did with his store.

"I got blackballed by the whole durned town," said Billy Ray. He renamed the shop The Happy Sack.

Waycross, Billy Ray told me, is a railroad town that never lived up to its potential. "The Atlanta Constitution dubbed Waycross the metropolis of south Georgia in 1928. Waycross was going to be what Atlanta was to north Georgia. We were number six in population at that time. At one point we were the size of Savannah and Augusta and Macon—but it stopped growing. From 1928 to the eighties we only gained 10,000 people."

It was slow to grow in other ways, as well. As the 1990s began, Waycross was still a black and white town, as in, "You black folks can live in town; we'll be just fine out here on the outskirts." It's voluntary segregation, and it allows for informal Klan meetings at places like Miss Kitty's breakfast house.

Still and all, it was a peaceable arrangement, and it led Jack Williams, managing editor of the Waycross *Journal-Herald*, to define the town's "reasonably good race relations" with the fact that he had never seen a cross burned inside city limits.

Trembling Earth

This is where Papa John Snively sent his daughter and her chosen man. Snively Groves had opened a box-making factory in Waycross in 1942. The wartime shortage of wood veneer had inspired the company to cut its own, and management chose Waycross, a town in the heart of Georgia's lumber industry, with easy access to Florida by rail and highways.

Some believed that the senior Snively chose Coon Dog to run the factory—at the same time crowning him with the title of Vice President, Box Division—simply because he was from the area. Others thought he sent him to Waycross just to get him out of Winter Haven. O. J. Cowart was superintendent of the plant under Coon Dog. He thought of the new boss as a figurehead.

Coon Dog and his bride arrived in town in 1945 and lived in an apartment—a set of rooms in a large house just down the block from the Cowarts—while they awaited the building of a house of their own in the Cherokee Heights neighborhood, the most handsome section of town.

On November 5, 1946, Avis delivered Ingram Cecil Connor III. She was transported for the occasion to Winter Haven Hospital so that she could be close to her family and, not incidentally, have better medical care than the Snivelys deemed available in Waycross.

Soon the Connors moved into their new house at 1600 Suwannee Drive. There was nothing Snively about the house, a single-level building with red and white brick exterior and a Spanish tiled roof. It was built for comfort, with three bedrooms, three baths, a spacious living room, and, in the rear, a sun room with a terra-cotta tiled floor. A wet bar separated the dining room from the kitchen.

The house seemed designed to give Avis, Coon Dog, and their family a semblance of the suburban life-style that postwar Americans had begun to admire. It rambled. It welcomed sunlight through picture windows. It afforded the children enough room that they could stay out of their parents' way. Gram's even had its own bathroom, and on his door was a brass knocker engraved with his name. Soon after Avis was born, in 1951, she had her own adult-sized room and her own brass plate.

Edmund Pedrick, an attorney whose father was a partner in the Snively Groves' law firm, heard Inez Sheppard, one of the Connors' babysitters, tell how prim and proper Gram Connor was when she first met him, at about age six. He was dressed like a Little Lord Fauntleroy. He was methodical and careful with his possessions. When he first met Inez, he showed her a locked cabinet in the hallway and informed her, "That's where my Daddy keeps his guns. We're not allowed to go near it."

As an adult, Gram said that he was a misfit, at best, in Waycross. But he struck others as a model kid.

Dickey Smith's family moved into Cherokee Heights in 1953,
and the boys met in second grade at Williams Heights school. He
remembered Gram as a good-looking kid with lots of girlfriends.
Gram was also a favorite with the teacher. He was such a good
reader that, for after-lunch readings, the teacher would often let
the seven-year-old Gram do the honors.

Outside the classroom, Gram was known as the kid with the
most, best, and newest toys, crammed into a walk-in closet and
scattered all over his room. Most of Gram's friends don't recall him
flaunting his relative wealth, but he had his moments. "I had
friends who didn't like Gram because they thought he was a patho-
logical liar," said Dickey. "He'd say, 'I wrote this song,' or 'When I
go to Florida, the chauffeur picks us up, and we have yachts.'"

Dickey, tired of his bragging, would offer a weak retort: "Sure
you do." And then one summer Dickey visited Winter Haven. He'd
have breakfast in bed, and go for swims in the family's Olympic-
sized pool. He'd watch Gram shopping for toys by the shelfload,
piling purchases into a Cadillac, and roaring away. Sometimes, the
kid wasn't lying.

Not that life at 1600 Suwannee, where Dickey spent many
Friday nights, was straight out of "I Love Lucy."

From his visits to Gram's, he noticed that Coon Dog and Avis
kept liquor in their house, out in the open. That was rare in the
fifties, and it confirmed his suspicion that Gram's family was . . .
different.

Also quite noticeable were various black servants, including
women who served as maids, cooks, and baby-sitters, and men
who gardened, drove family members the five-hour trips between
Waycross and the Snively homes in Winter Haven, and sometimes
did more. Johnny Barnes sang and played piano around the house,
and Sammy Dixon, a brother of one of the maids who was just a
few years older than Gram, sometimes baby-sat him. When Gram
was old enough, Sammy taught him how to ride a bicycle.

But when Gram played, it was usually with schoolmates and
neighborhood buddies like Dickey Smith and Henry Clarke. Play
often meant pranks. On weekends they'd hide in Gram's garage,
waiting for unsuspecting drivers along the unpaved side streets of
the neighborhood. When a car approached, they'd throw empty tin
cans under the wheels.

As the tires crunched cans, they'd run out, shouting, *"Hubcap!"*
and the driver would screech to a halt, scamper out, and look for
hubcaps.

Other times, one of them would lie down in a vacant lot across the street, and Gram would put a bicycle over him, pour ketchup over his head—and wait for a reaction.

When that got boring, Gram would steal a pack of cigarettes from his parents' supply, grab the sterling silver lighter out of the living room, and sneak down to the woods at the end of Suwannee Drive. After one cigarette and the resulting nausea, they'd ditch the pack and sneak the lighter back into the house.

Gram also liked exploring the Okefenokee Swamps, which began just a few miles south of town, with his father and friends. "Okefenokee, you know, means 'land of the trembling earth,'" Gram said. "And everything down there is mush . . . red shifts and bogs and mud ducts."

The Swamps, Waycross's main claim to fame, is the subject of one of Little Avis's favorite books, *Suwannee River: Strange Green Land*, by Cecile Hulse Matschat. Matschat describes the Okefenokee as "the almost unknown wilderness which is nearly as wild and untamed today as it was thousands of years ago. It is a great gray world of flooded land and water, inhabited by innumerable birds, by huge bears and wild swine, alligators and snakes, and primitive human beings who pole their boats under the cypresses and prowl like wild men."

Back at home, the main events around Gram's social circle were the almost weekly parties he hosted in the spacious back sunroom—commonly known in the south as "the Florida room" because of its large windows and exposure to the sun. At one end of the room was the piano, but Gram rarely played at his own parties. Most Saturdays, a dozen or so friends would gather and dance to Gram's records, even taking lessons in slow dancing and the jitterbug.

Music—in the form of a trumpet, a set of drums, a player piano, and records—quickly became Gram's favorite pastime. But his sister thought that their father needed the music as much as anyone. "I'm convinced that part of Coon Dog's problem is what we now call postwar stress syndrome, and I think the music helped him. He shared that with us." In the evenings, if the kids weren't playing music, they were often listening to it on the radio, on a show called "The Hoot Owl Jamboree."

While Big Avis was the disciplinarian, the one who'd wash their mouths out with soap, Coon Dog was the comforting shoulder to run to. He was the one they'd try to please, often with music.

"If we could pick out a song on piano," Avis said, "we were just the smartest kids in the universe."

By the time he was nine, Gram was taking piano lessons from Bessie Maynard, a grandmotherly type who provided cookies and cake before the instruction.

Gram stayed with her for two or three years, but he was immediately impatient with her methods, preferring to play popular music and improvise. To Mrs. Maynard's dismay, Gram had a great ear, and after hearing a song or a record a couple of times, he could go to the piano and play it.

By the time he was in fourth grade, Gram had written his first song. It sounded like he'd been listening to Jerry Lee Lewis, and it was called, all modesty aside, "Gram Boogie."

Gram's musical head would soon be turned by another instrument: the guitar. On the radio he'd heard Elvis Presley, Buddy Holly, and Carl Perkins, and one day Gram watched a friend, Burnet "Boo" Clarke, playing a Gibson acoustic. He immediately asked to be taught how to play, and although Boo didn't consider himself much of a picker, he showed Gram a few chords and marveled at how quickly Gram learned.

When Elvis himself hit town for a concert at City Auditorium on February 22, 1956, the nine-year-old Gram was front and center. He took two older girls—fourteen-year-old twin sisters named Daphne and Diana Delano. Daphne went with Gram to the stage door to wait for an autograph from Elvis.

Gram, of course, told it a bit more flamboyantly years later. "I went with a couple of twins who wore bobby socks," he said. "He was billed second to Little Jimmy Dickens. Little Jimmy Dickens had some ridiculous hit at that time. I actually just walked up to the front row and the aisle seat was empty. It was a basketball gym that held about 700 people. I just sat down. . . . Finally, he came on, and the whole place just went bonkers and the chicks were all moving down and stuff like that. And I thought, 'Gee whiz!' "

Although Daphne said there was no dressing room, and that they got autographs from Elvis at the stage door, Gram said he marched through Dickens's dressing room, "back into Elvis's, and said, 'Hello there, you're Elvis Presley and I'm the little kid who buys your records and I think you're all right.' And he said, 'Yeah,' and shook my hand. Gave me an autograph . . . made sure I was with the twins."

As nonchalant as Gram might have tried to act, he was like a little girl when it came to Elvis. He was swept away.

"Elvis influenced me tremendously," he said. "If it wasn't for him, I would have probably strayed into country music. I always paid attention to anything that had a steel guitar in it . . . but then all of a sudden, somebody turned me on to Elvis."

Gram never addressed the issue of Elvis's specific musical influence on him. It was Presley, along with his fellow rockabilly musicians at Sun Records in Memphis, who accounted for the first hybrids of three American musical forms: country, rhythm and blues, and rock and roll. Gram was lucky or astute enough to have caught on to Elvis at his purest, before RCA Records began applying Brylcreem to his music.

Every Saturday morning the family driver, Johnny Barnes, would take him and sometimes Little Avis, to the Ware Tire Company, which contained a record shop. They'd pick out a dozen 45s at a time.

After Gram had quickly mastered the latest Elvis tunes, it would be showtime. Gram gathered up friends and neighbors and put on shows, using the circular front stoop of his home as a stage. He, of course, was stage center. He'd put the needle on "Blue Suede Shoes" and lip-sync to the song while his band pretended to play instruments behind him.

Flora DuBose and other neighborhood kids were convinced that Gram, with his slicked-back hair, his well-practiced curled-lip sneer, and, of course, properly propulsive legs, was Elvis come to Suwannee Drive. Equally adoring was Little Avis, who was three or four when she was recruited to back up her brother. She liked Elvis, she said, mainly because Gram liked him.

The boy everyone swore looked just like Elvis actually bore more of a resemblance to Beaver Cleaver—Gram's baby fat stayed with him until he was ten, giving him a round and cheeky face. But he had one feature that might connect him with The King: his dad's hound-dog eyes.

On stage—or, more accurately, on stoop—Gram was all business. If Avis made the mistake of actually hitting the keys of her toy piano, Gram would stop and glare at her. He didn't want any clowning around. Sometimes Avis, trying to compensate for her shyness in front of crowds, would act goofy. "Stop that," Gram would order. "You just straighten up and play."

While Gram, like thousands of other boys around the country, was fantasizing about growing up to be Elvis Presley, his mother was making plans to send him away.

In the spring of 1956, she saw an article in *Harper's Bazaar* about boarding schools, and decided that the Bolles School, a combination prep school and military academy in Jacksonville, Florida, might be perfect for Gram. At the time, Gram was in fifth grade.

Avis didn't take any action until early the next year, when she learned that Bolles accepted boarders for the sixth grade. She applied to have Gram enrolled that fall. The Rev. William Brace, rector of the Grace Episcopal Church and a good friend of the

Connors, wrote a supporting letter. "Gram is a child of unusual talents who will, I am sure, be able to measure up to the intellectual requirements of your school. He has had experience in summer camp so that being away from home will not be a problem. I feel too that there are qualities of leadership here which will emerge in due course."

By August, Avis had sent off $1,605 tuition for Gram in advance—wondering, in an accompanying letter, whether her action was "agreeable"; asking whether Gram should wear plain-toe shoes; and reporting that Gram was "becoming very anxious about school." As for herself: "I do hope your teachers make him get down to business and do the work we know he is capable of doing."

On his arrival at Bolles in September 1957, Gram filled out a cadet questionnaire. He listed reading, spelling, science, and history as his favorite subjects in school; English, arithmetic, and study hall as subjects he liked least. His top three choices for college were West Point, Annapolis, and "Georiga Tech."

Surprisingly, the boy who would be Elvis left music off a long list of favored activities and hobbies that included hunting, fishing, skiing, polo, swimming, baseball, football, shell collecting, and boat racing.

The questionnaire asked for a short essay about "any particularly interesting or unusual experiences in your life, including your hopes for the future." The questionnaire left room for perhaps a dozen lines, and suggested that students continue on the back of the legal-sized page, if necessary.

Gram wrote:

I have crashed through a car window
gone out a mile on a raft alone (7 years old)

Gram never had to bother chasing girls as far as Dickey Smith can remember. "It just seemed like they always showed up. It was like a dream come true."

That was in grammar school. In high school, Jim Carlton, among others, was knocked out by his charisma. "He had what Errol Flynn had; what Gable had; what Elvis had. There were just sparks flying off him."

Later, when he hooked up with the Byrds, the Burritos, and the Rolling Stones, one of the admirers of his style was Keith Richards. "He was a very impressive guy," Richards said. "And what a line he could spin with chicks! I wish I had the scripts!"

Gram's line, as well as Terry Melcher, the record producer who met him in 1969, could figure it, stretched straight back to Waycross. In other words, "He was a little kid. If you make the girls want to mother you, that's the best thing you can do. At least you get the door open."

Just before he entered his teens, Gram's baby fat dropped off, and he turned into a slim and striking teenager, his hazel eyes rendered all the more piercing by dark eyebrows like his mother's. By age eleven he was displaying his form at his Saturday parties, which were sometimes spiced up by "promming," a regional variation on the old spin-the-bottle kissing game. Whoever the bottle paired up wouldn't just have a quick kiss; they'd "prom around the house." Most boys had difficulty coming up with enough conversation to last the circuit; Gram rarely returned without having kissed his promming partner.

By age thirteen Gram had a girlfriend who worked at Cypress Gardens. She was at least a couple of years older than he, and she was one of the hoop-skirted southern belles who graced the Gardens, usually seated on benches at a distance, to be seen but not touched. During breaks Gram would go over and make out with her on a bench, in full view of tourists.

Even today Gram seems to have a hold on many of the girls and women he knew. Patti Johnson, who sang with him and dated him when they attended Winter Haven High, admitted: "After you and I talked, it took me two days to get over it. It is very difficult in a lot of ways, losing somebody you love a lot. Someone you cared so much about when you were young; you carry that differently. Sometimes his music would bring back so many feelings and memories, I almost couldn't listen to it."

Daphne Delano Brown, Gram's childhood buddy, also felt compelled to follow up a conversation with a letter full of memories—of afternoons swimming at the Okefenokee Golf and Country Club in Waycross; of a night spent in the Connors' backyard, lying in hammocks and talking into the night with this articulate and serious little boy.

And then there was Flora DuBose, who knew Gram primarily between third and fifth grade in Waycross. She still has a Valentine's Day card that Gram sent her in grade school. The highlight of third grade was a George Washington play; Flora remembered it mainly because another girl got to be Gram's partner in the minuet. Even then, Flora said, "We all knew that was so special, to be his partner. There was kind of a magic about him."

Flora last saw Gram when they were fifteen. It was one of those sweet summers when young love blooms. She remembered going to the beach; hearing him sing a Peter, Paul, and Mary song; and, most of all, getting her first real kiss from him.

Flora is married now and lives in La Luz, New Mexico, where she is a librarian. "Sometimes I think about him too much," she said with a sigh. "It's so sad."

5

West Point South

The Bolles School was once a luxury hotel, nestled between busy San Jose Avenue and the winding St. Johns River, which intersects Jacksonville. With its sprawling lawns shaded by tall trees draped in diaphanous Spanish moss; its arched, antiqued masonry walkways; and Spanish tiled buildings with fountain plazas, it could easily have been transformed into a monastery or a small college.

Instead, in 1933, it became a prep school for boys who spent half their time playing soldiers.

If Gram truly aspired to West Point, Bolles would have been a sensible stepping stone. Half military and half college prep, the school was frankly schizoid. Mornings were military—rise and shine, fall out, march into breakfast, sit at attention. Cadets then became regular students attending regular classes until afternoon, when the military classes took over.

Gram didn't particularly like the regimen, but he managed to get through his first months without event, for which Avis Connor wrote her thanks to Captain Chuck Sowash in January 1958: "We are delighted with all the school has done for Gram. He seems so happy."

West Point South

Back in Waycross, his father was beginning to feel bridled.

To outsiders, the Connors seemed busy with work and community affairs. Avis, remembered by townspeople as a vivid young woman with plenty of drive, was director of the women's group at the Episcopal church, president of the women's auxiliary to the Okefenokee Golf and Country Club, and an energetic fundraiser for the community concert series. Coon Dog found a way to mix his love of outdoor sports with children by way of the Boy Scouts. He organized and served as scoutmaster of Troop 80—which he named after his own 80th Fighter Squadron. Coon Dog and Gram were in Indian Guides, a father-son camping program sponsored by the YMCA. And, as his father had done with him, Coon Dog took Gram hunting as soon as he thought Gram and his buddies could handle .22 rifles.

But for all their involvements, the Connors were still stuck in Waycross. Avis could, and did, run off to Winter Haven to replenish herself with family gossip and funds; Coon Dog could lose himself in the woods. But they had to come home. To relieve the boredom they turned to a hyperactive social life and, especially, to drink.

On the surface they were simply good hosts. Sally Lanier, Avis's friend for years, said that whenever Avis and Coon Dog were home together, there were bound to be others in the house. Almost every afternoon, she said, they would have people over for drinks and then go out to a club to eat.

The Connors' social circle included doctors, dentists, railroad company executives, and ministers—and, friends and family recall, they *all* drank. To circumvent liquor laws of the fifties, they repaired to clubs and lodges for their drinking or went out of state to get packaged liquor.

Gram's friend Dickey got to know the routine: While the kids played in Gram's spacious room, Coon Dog, Avis, and their friends sat in the living room and drank. They needed no music; "they'd just sit and drink and drink and drink."

Stories circulated about what was going on besides drinking.

Billy Ray, the "Sin City" store owner, tried researching Gram's story in the mid-seventies and conducted several interviews around town. He soon caught wind of something called "the shoe game"—the fifties version of wife swapping. "It was popular among the upper-class. You'd go to a party and the women would lay their shoes in a big pile, and the men would each pick up a shoe, and whatever foot the shoe fits . . ." Billy Ray didn't bother with any further details.

Another story—possibly hearsay—involved Avis and a doctor being caught in bed; another had a family friend making a play for her. Separate from Avis, but in the Connors' circle, there was a dizzying round of pregnancies, separations, traded couples, second marriages, and at least one death.

In short: Sin City.

★

On Sunday, December 21, 1958, Snively Groves put on its Christmas party at the Elk's Club in Waycross. For the first time that anyone could recall, Avis attended along with Coon Dog. The next day, Coon Dog drove his family to the train station and saw them off to Winter Haven, where the family always spent its holidays. He then drove to Baxley, forty miles north of Waycross, where the Snivelys had built a veneer mill to provide more wood for boxes. There he met with the plant supervisor, O. J. Cowart. Each year, Snively Groves delivered baskets of holiday fruit to customers, friends and employees, and Coon Dog promised O.J. that he'd give him a list of recipients the next morning, just before he left for Winter Haven. He then drove back home.

On Tuesday, Coon Dog went to his office in Waycross and signed some checks for his secretary, Edna McIntosh, to distribute. Then he left. In Baxley, O.J. waited until noon before giving up on Coon Dog. He and an assistant took care of the gift baskets. Around five o'clock, his wife called to tell him what had happened.

The Christmas Eve edition of the Waycross *Journal-Herald* carried the story on its front page:

> I. Cecil Connor, prominent Waycross businessman and boy scout leader, was found at his home, 1600 Suwannee Drive, late yesterday afternoon. Coroner J. A. Willis said Connor was found lying across his bed and had been shot in the right temple. A .38 caliber pistol was found near the body. An inquest will be held at a later date upon completion of an investigation, the coroner stated.

In Winter Haven the adults kept the news from Gram and Little Avis until after Christmas Day. Avis then told her children in separate talks.

Gram was devastated; Avis, confused. She couldn't comprehend that Daddy wouldn't be there, especially since he'd told her, just a couple of days before, to be a good girl; that he'd be seeing her soon.

But Tom Connor thought his brother had had no intentions of another Christmas with the Snively clan. He had told Tom that he felt trapped in his job, that he had to get out of the family business.

Around Thanksgiving, Cecil had asked his mother to visit him in Waycross. Tom accompanied her on the trip and found his brother in high spirits. He told Tom that he'd figured out a way to escape the Snively job, and that he'd never been happier. Life with Avis, he said, was wonderful.

Tom would learn later that such sunniness was typical of suicides; that once they'd decided to end things, they felt relief from all pressures.

Coon Dog left no note. But three weeks before his death, he went to a photographer in Waycross and had a color portrait made, with instructions to mail it to his mother. Nancy Connor received the portrait after her son had died.

On December 30, a small headline on page 10 of the *Journal-Herald* read: CONNOR'S DEATH RULED ACCIDENTAL.

Few people outside the coroner's office believed the story. Coon Dog was an expert hunter and military officer who was familiar with carbines, submachine guns, and rifles, and who was considered a sharpshooter with a .45 caliber pistol. He had no reason to be cleaning a gun in his bedroom on the eve of a trip to a family gathering in Winter Haven.

Coon Dog's sister, Pauline, went to the mortuary in Waycross. She told the mortician, "Cecil was my brother. I want to know what happened." He showed her the body. In the right temple was a hole the size of a quarter. Pauline no longer had any doubts that her brother had killed himself.

Coon Dog's suicide came ten months after the death of Papa John Snively, and the company was now in the hands of his son, John Snively, Jr. Still, both Tom and Pauline believe their brother continued to feel desperately trapped in the Snively family.

Gram's cousin Rob thought Coon Dog killed himself because his marriage was failing. He'd heard that from his mother, Evalyn, but had nothing more to go on. But a friend of Avis's, who wanted to remain nameless, said that when first married, Avis seemed proud of Coon Dog's accomplishments and his hopes for the future. In more recent years, she said, Avis had begun to drift away.

One local friend who attended many of Avis and Coon Dog's parties said Avis was having an affair, and he thought this was a factor in Coon Dog's suicide.

Little Avis wasn't shocked by such rumors. "It could've been," she said. "Things were mighty strange around the house."

Edmund Pedrick, the lawyer whose father was an attorney for Snively Groves, didn't think Coon Dog's death was caused by any extramarital affairs.

"My impression is that if there was any problem at all, it was because he was not allowed to forget who had the money."

Hickory Wind

It wasn't that Coon Dog was in any way a poor relation; his own family was solid. But few were as wealthy as the Snivelys. And Avis had a great interest in getting and spending money.

There was also Avis's need to secure her place on the Snively totem pole. As Little Avis recalled, "Mother was always jealous of the relationship between Haney [her mother] and her sister, Evalyn." It was in Avis's interest, then, to visit home as often as possible.

"The going back and forth to Winter Haven wasn't fair to Coon Dog," Little Avis continued. "Mother would go to Winter Haven for every little thing, because that's where her mommy and daddy were."

Coon Dog's body was shipped to Winter Haven and buried in the Snivelys' family plot. At the funeral, his casket was draped with an American flag. And Avis moved with her two children back to the Snively home in Winter Haven.

O. J. Cowart was one of the pallbearers that rainy day. At the cemetery, he remembered seeing Avis emerge from a Cadillac. With the chauffeur holding an umbrella over her, she said a quiet Amen to a spoken prayer, and quickly disappeared into her car.

To the Connors, the Snivelys' feelings were made painfully clear by an event that preceded the funeral: They had a party.

It was a cocktail party at Evalyn Snively's, staged on the night before the funeral. Coon Dog's sister, Pauline, was shocked by the sight that greeted her. "She had a great big tent put up in the backyard and large iron tubs filled with charcoal for warmth, and there were bars set up and waiters in white coats."

Evalyn had had the party planned for some time, and simply decided to proceed, family death or no family death. Many of her guests were the same people who would attend Coon Dog's funeral the next afternoon.

Out of guilt, sentiment, or both, Avis took to carrying a gift Coon Dog had give her, a small wood carving of a hunting dog, curled up in sleep. She kept the dog on her nightstand and carried it with her when she traveled.

Pauline remembered Avis bringing the wooden dog when she and Coon Dog visited her in Columbia but was frankly amazed to hear that she carried the souvenir after his death. After all, as Pauline's husband put it, Avis expressed a "total lack of remorse" over Cecil's death. "There was no . . . grief."

Coon Dog's death naturally shattered the Connor family, but they had another blow coming. Coon Dog's mother, Nancy, had not been able to make the ride from Columbia to Winter Haven. Pauline and her brother, Tom, decided to take their mother to Florida in June, when Gram and Avis would be out of school.

The group first went to the cemetery, then called the Snivelys. Evalyn answered the phone.

"When did you get in?" she asked. Pauline said the family had been in town for about an hour.

"Well," said Evalyn, immediately suspicious. "What have you been doing?" Pauline told her that Mother had wanted to go to the cemetery. "We went, and now we'd like to come out and see you."

Evalyn turned cold. "If you went to the cemetery before you came to see my sister, just don't bother coming," she scolded, and hung up the phone.

Pauline was stunned, and her mother couldn't believe what had happened. Nancy called back and asked to speak with Avis. Evalyn had already conferred with her, and when her mother-in-law told her, "I understand Evalyn says she doesn't want us to come out," Avis could only respond meekly, "Yes, that's right."

The Connors left without seeing Avis or her children, and they would not communicate until six years later, when Gram called his grandmother and grandfather to invite them to his high school graduation.

Gram, meanwhile, was falling apart. In June 1959, Major DeWitt Hooker, superintendent of Bolles, wrote Avis to inform her that "Gram's conduct record over the past year has been so poor that the Discipline Committee has voted that we will be unable to accept him back next fall."

The backbreaker appeared to be a letter Gram had written. After Avis had her brother, John Snively, Jr., call Major Hooker, the superintendent wrote once more to her: "I am enclosing the torn, but legible, letter which Gram admits writing. He told the committee that he wrote it to get his feelings 'off his chest,' and that he intended no one else to see it. However, other little boys did see it, and it was turned over to Captain Sowash. I am sure you can understand that a thing of this kind is a very bad influence upon classmates and cannot be tolerated." Gram's letter has been lost, but one can imagine the kind of resentment toward authority that it expressed.

Gram was on his way back to Winter Haven. Before his next attempt at school, however, Avis tried to soften the blow of Coon Dog's death by taking her children on a cross-country train trip.

The trip lasted the entire summer. The three survivors, along with Robert Owens, a young entertainer who acted as escort and gofer, boarded in Florida, rode to Chicago, and journeyed across the country to San Francisco, and back by way of New York and the East Coast. They visited the Grand Canyon, national parks, and museums; they ate at the finest restaurants and supper clubs, where they were entertained by Nat "King" Cole and Tony Bennett.

For Avis and the kids, Waycross was already a dimming memory. Big Avis made one trip back to Suwannee Drive, picked out what she wanted moved to Winter Haven, and put the house up for sale.

Waycross Sheriff Robert E. Lee and his wife Marie moved in a year later.

When she was looking the house over before buying it, Marie opened the clothes dryer and spotted a note tucked in the door. She said it read: "Whoever finds this note, please take good care of this house, and I hope it brings you as much happiness as it brought me. Love, Gram."

Others around town swore that the note actually concluded: "I hope it brings you more happiness than it brought me."

6
New Family, New Bands

Gram Connor was twelve years old, and his life had been disrupted beyond repair. He began to turn to music. As a kid, he'd learned that it was an easy way to get attention. And right now, that's what he needed. But even as he adjusted to Winter Haven, to a new school, and to new friends, things were happening over which he had no control.

Shortly after moving, Avis met and married Robert Ellis Parsons, a slick salesman who leased heavy equipment for building roads and bridges to clients in Cuba and South America. Parsons was movie-star handsome, and he had lost no time in sweeping Avis Connor off her feet. To most members of her family, however, Parsons had one transparent goal: to get his hands on as much Snively money as he could.

Family members called him "a greedy son of a bitch" and "the biggest schmuck that ever walked the face of the earth." Soon after Gram's friends got a look at him, they joined the chorus. Chris Hillman thought of Parsons as a "slimeball. . . . You had to count your fingers after you shook hands with him."

Whatever moves Parsons made to profit from his relationship with the Snively family, his first was a legal one: He adopted Gram and Avis, ordering new birth certificates in which their names became Gram and Avis Parsons. On the certificate, Gram's father was listed as Robert Ellis Parsons, twenty-one, a salesman from Louisiana; his mother, Avis Snively, twenty-three.

Little Avis thought her mother wanted to erase the idea of her and Gram having ever had any other father. "Maybe she felt ashamed about the suicide, or maybe she felt partially responsible."

For Gram, this rewriting of history meant a new start. At St. Joseph's, a coed school open to students of any religious denomination, Gram was as impressive as he had ever been in Waycross. Jim Carlton met him in January 1960, and when he spoke to me about Gram, he echoed Dickey Smith, Gram's elementary school classmate. The nuns, Jim recalled, often had Gram class-sit for a missing teacher, since Gram could make up stories and keep his fellow students in rapt attention. Sometimes Gram was a little too impressive, and he'd get slugged by jealous boyfriends.

As he did in Waycross, he drew friends to his house. After staying for a short time at the Snively mansion, Avis had found a house on Piedmont Drive. Once again, Gram got a few perks: He had a private entrance to his bedroom; he put a piano in his room and turned it into his own haven.

By 1960, at age fourteen, Gram was still fixated on Elvis, and he knew he wanted to sing. For his eighth-grade class picture, Gram flipped his collar up, à la Presley. But with Elvis in the army and his records coming out in dribs and drabs, Gram began to explore everything from country and mainstream pop to R&B and jazz. He listened to records by Ray Charles and jazz artist James Moody. On the piano, he could range from boogie-woogie to Floyd Cramer and Peter Nero. He and Jim saw Jerry Lee Lewis and Roy Orbison in concert, but Gram also took note of an R&B group, Jake and the Gospel Soul Twisters, whose wild outfits would inspire him in later years. About the only music Gram *didn't* like was that of the blander singers who tried to stand in for Elvis. "I really hated what I heard on the radio—Bobby Vee, Bobby Vinton, and that whole bit," he said. "It was negative inspiration."

One night Jimmy Allen, a fellow teenaged rock-and-roll dreamer, was at Gram's house and heard him playing the piano. He'd met Gram before, at a party, and remembered him as the kid with the new Fender Stratocaster guitar.

Jimmy, who was in the tenth grade at Winter Haven High, gave Gram guitar lessons—followed by rides on Jimmy's small Harley-Davidson motorcycle. Soon he recruited Gram for a band he was forming with drummer Skip Rosser, an eleventh-grader known as "Flat Top." They had another kid, Marvin Clevenger, on bass.

Gram, who was two years younger than Jimmy, impressed him and Flat Top immediately with his singing. Gram suddenly found himself not only in his first rock band, the Pacers, but in a starring role as lead singer.

Gram's potential was obvious. He could read music at the piano, and he was a fast learner on the guitar. Although he had long fingers—so that when he moved from one string to another, he had to skip—he got smoother as time went on.

The Pacers were a Top 40 band, playing whatever hits were current. They played Chuck Berry, Buddy Holly, Ray Charles, the Ventures, Pat Boone (one of Gram's big tunes was "Moody River"), and lots of Elvis.

Gram sang "Heartbreak Hotel," "Blue Suede Shoes," and "I Want You, I Need You, I Love You." Gram's front-stoop Elvis-the-Pelvis imitations were in the past; now he was searching for a style of his own. At their very first gig, at a train depot in Dundee, Florida, a capacity crowd of about fifty teenagers gave him his first taste of stardom. With no room to dance, the kids just stood there, awed by the sight of a live band. The girls, Jimmy remembered, went nuts. And the object of their mania was Gram.

Flat Top, nominal leader of the band, didn't like Gram's moves, minimal as they might have been. Bluenoses—especially in the South—were railing against rock and roll and its usual accomplice, juvenile delinquency; Flat Top wanted the Pacers to play it safe. He even decreed that they dress in matching buttoned-down short-sleeved shirts and black slacks.

Through Gram, the Pacers got work at the Snively mansion and the golf and country club; they also performed at local teen hangouts. A day's or night's work would bring each Pacer between $10 and $25, excellent money in 1960.

But after just a year together, Gram had bad news for the Pacers. He was leaving. The band had just recorded a couple of songs at a nearby studio when Gram announced that he was joining another local band, the Legends.

Flat Top exploded. Outside the studio, he began slapping Gram around. Gram was on the ground, crying, and just as Flat Top was about to hit him with a clenched fist, other members of the band came to Gram's rescue.

Gram didn't take long to bounce back. He became lead singer and rhythm guitarist in the Legends, a band that included Jim Stafford, the fastest guitar in town. Jim, several years older than Gram, was the son of a dry cleaner in Eloise, the part of town built around Snively Groves' packing plant.

Gram had spotted Jim fronting a number of groups floating around the Florida circuit, playing teen centers, sock hops, and battles of the bands. Gram had invited Jim to spend the night a few times. Once he got over his awe at Gram's home, including a maid bearing trayfuls of Canadian bacon and Pepsi-Colas, Jim would pull out his guitar for some informal picking sessions.

As had Jimmy Allen, Jim took note of Gram's long fingers. "He had these fingers that looked like he could wrap them around a Fender guitar neck about a time and a half. He had perfect hands for a piano player, but he really wanted to be a guitar player."

The Legends were a loose group. They were anchored originally by Gram; stand-up bassist Jim Carlton, Gram's friend from St. Joseph's; drummer Lamar Braxton; and Jim Stafford, who carved out a niche as a comic singer-songwriter in the mid-seventies with songs like "Spiders and Snakes," "My Girl Bill," and "I Got Stoned and I Missed It."

In later editions of the band, Lamar would be replaced by Jon Corneal, who later drummed with Gram's International Submarine Band; and when Jim graduated from high school, his spot would be taken by Jesse Chambers, most recently a songwriter and bassist with Ricky Skaggs. Sometimes there were horn players; most times not.

The Legends were a cover band, playing hit songs established by others. Their repertoire included Ray Charles's "What'd I Say," Little Richard's "Rip It Up," Chuck Berry's "Johnny B. Goode," Duane Eddy's "Guitar Man," the Virtues' "Guitar Boogie Shuffle," and the Ventures' "Walk—Don't Run"—plenty of showcases for Jim Stafford's sizzling guitar work. And always there were a couple of spots for Gram's apparent taste for ballads, among them "Ebb Tide," which he performed at the piano; "Harbor Lights"; and the Everly Brothers' "Let It Be Me."

The Legends never made it big, but they felt as if they did. They got plenty of work both in and out of town. And, instead of the typical family station wagon, the Legends had a Volkswagen bus emblazoned with the combo's logo on its sides. It was the largesse of stepdad Bob Parsons, who made it a priority to ingratiate himself with Gram.

In Tampa, the Legends were regulars on WFLA TV's "Hi Time" bandstand show, and they were even named Band of the Year.

Even so, the group wasn't enough to keep Gram busy. Several times he played keyboards with the Rumors, a band fronted by Kent LaVoie, a singer and guitarist who would go on to great pop music success in the early seventies as Lobo.

One night in the spring of 1962, Kent had a gig at the Tiger's Den, almost one hundred miles east of Winter Haven, and hired Jim Stafford and Gram as Rumors for the night. Because he had a bus, Gram was charged with transporting a small Baldwin organ from Kent's house. Gram had learned to duplicate the calliope sound of Freddy Cannon's "Palisades Park" on the organ. Since Gram was still only fifteen, a friend, Doug Wiggins, drove him.

At showtime, with a crowd of 200 waiting, Gram was missing, and the band began without him. After the first set, Gram wandered on to the stage, his hair messed up and shirt bloodied. He was holding his arm, and he kept repeating, in front of the shocked audience: "Wasn't *my* fucking fault!" When Kent asked what happened, Gram shouted: "We hit a fucking cow! We hit a fucking cow!"

Just off stage was a door leading to a lot where the van was parked. The bus was mangled. "It was a little like a slaughter house," said Jim. Doug had a broken foot, but Gram, eager to do his job, went on stage and sang and played "Palisades Park." Four songs in, however, he told Kent that something was wrong with him. At the hospital, he learned that he had cracked several ribs.

In 1962 Gram couldn't help hearing the noise folk music made as it invaded the Top 40 charts, with the Kingston Trio and Peter, Paul, and Mary leading the way. He teamed up with Jim Carlton on bass for comic-relief takeoffs on the Smothers Brothers. And, with Peter, Paul, and Mary in mind, Gram hooked up with friends at Winter Haven High to form a trio called the Village Vanguards.

"We were pretty free-wheelin'," said Dick McNeer, the guitarist of the Vanguards. They picked Patti Johnson, a cheerleader and a girlfriend of Gram's, to be the third member because she could carry a tune, she was pretty, and, best of all, she had long blond hair.

The Vanguards worked a few paying gigs, but their primary function was to perform during the Legends' breaks. Their career, as such, may have peaked in late March 1963, when they placed third in a Kiwanis Club talent show. They sang Woody Guthrie's "This Land Is Your Land" and Peter, Paul, and Mary's "Puff the Magic Dragon."

Patti, who was a year older than Gram, never took the Vanguards seriously. For her, it was just another way to be close to her boyfriend. To get into the group, Patti had to endure an audition—but not for Gram and Dick. She was over at Gram's one afternoon when he told her, "My mother wants you to sing for her." Patti proceeded to perform, *a cappella*, in front of Avis. Through her nervousness, Patti noticed that Gram's mother was extremely intoxicated. Avis offered no reaction to Patti's performance.

Within months of their wedding, Avis was pregnant; she and

Bob Parsons were having troubles, and she had turned to the bottle.

Some friends saw only Avis's nice side. Jim Carlton remembered her as a sweet woman who happened to have a severe drinking problem. Patti had seen her mean side, and flinched when Avis would embarrass her kids in front of visitors. Patti thought Avis was hurting, not only about the past but about Bob Parsons. "She knew Bob wasn't being a completely faithful husband, and that he was using her for her money."

She and Gram wound up doing errands for his parents, including late-night runs across the county line to fetch cases of liquor. One day she skipped school to pick up twenty-five pounds of caviar in Palm Beach.

Gram's friends knew he had problems but rarely found him able to discuss them. Maybe, they thought, he just didn't want to be a drag.

With the adventurous Dick McNeer by his side, Gram soon found other ways to numb his pains. They found a cornucopia of mysterious prescription drugs in Avis's medicine cabinet. The Parsons, Dick said, lived across the street from a doctor who was part of their social circle and apparently kept Avis well stocked.

Dick didn't think Gram relied on drugs to escape troubles. He took them simply because, if he hit on the right one, it made him feel good.

Between them, said Dick, the two racked up more than one hundred absences from school in Gram's junior year. They would make it in for roll call, but if they got bored an hour or two later, they would get into one of their cars and take off.

Gram barely managed to complete most of his classes. He got F's in English, Spanish, and American history, pulled a D in art, and got Incompletes in typing and chemistry.

After Gram failed his junior year at Winter Haven High, Avis pulled strings to get him back into the Bolles School. One family friend, a Bolles alumnus, used his status to get Gram considered for readmission, and on his entrance examination that summer, Gram was listed simply as a tenth-grade student at Winter Haven High, rather than a failed eleventh-grader.

But before his last semester at Winter Haven concluded, he had one more turbulent note to play.

Although rumors bounced around the high school that Gram had gotten Patti pregnant, she said it was a far simpler matter: She and Gram had made plans to elope.

They picked a night when the Legends had a job, a dance at the Women's Club at Lake Howard. At intermission, the Village Vanguards would do a short set, and Gram and Patti would take off and get married.

New Family, New Bands

They had her car packed, complete with a map of Georgia, and were just about to leave the club when her father showed up. He'd been tipped off. "We ran to the car and tried to escape out of the parking lot, and Dad blocked the car," Patti remembered.

The families kept the two apart, the episode put an end to the Vanguards, and she didn't see Gram again that year, with the exception of her senior prom a few months later. Gram was heading back to Bolles in the fall to repeat his junior year; Patti was graduating. Their romance may have soured, but a prom date was a prom date. Patti remembered that Gram was in a foul mood all night and not much fun. He did, however, sing a couple of songs during intermission.

Gram had developed a need to perform. In high school Jim saw Gram carrying his guitar into classrooms. His sister, Avis, said that as soon as Gram walked into a house, he'd look for a piano. Finding one, he'd sit and play. "That was sort of like taking out a cigarette and smoking it," she said. "It comforted him."

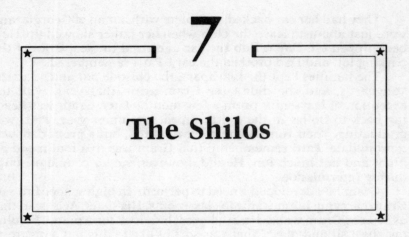

7

The Shilos

Gram's plate was never quite full. Even while he was in the Legends, with the Vanguards on the side, he'd begun wedging in solo folkie performances in and out of Winter Haven. In the fall of 1963 he found his way into a folk group, the Shilos.

At a dinner party hosted by Big Avis a couple of years before, he had met Buddy Freeman, a young horseman who rode in shows with Little Avis. Gram made it clear to Buddy that he had no interest in horses; he was a musician. Buddy told Gram that he knew the owners of the restaurant and asked if Gram might like to play the piano in the nearby lounge.

Immediately after dinner, Gram took a seat at the piano and sang a couple of pop songs. Buddy was impressed by Gram's emotional voice and musicianship; he looked like he belonged on stage. Buddy continued to see Big and Little Avis, and in late 1961, he hosted Gram and a few buddies at his home in Greenville, South Carolina. There Gram had pulled out a guitar at an informal cookout.

Within weeks Buddy began getting phone calls from people wanting to book Gram for musical engagements. Buddy was dumbfounded. He was in the wholesale distribution business; he wasn't a manager. He called Gram to tell him about the calls and suggested that maybe Bob Parsons's secretary could help him.

"Well, why can't you just handle it?" Gram responded.

"I'm not in the business," Buddy replied.

"Well," said Gram, "my mom likes you."

When Buddy continued to resist, Gram told him that Avis would be calling.

One phone call later, Buddy began helping Gram with his bookings as a solo artist, and it didn't take him long to get up to speed. He got Gram an appearance on a Greenville television station, and Gram's singing caught the ear of a deejay, Johnny Batson, who was emceeing a hootenanny competition at the Memorial Auditorium and needed talent. Johnny wanted Gram to appear on the show, but the contest was limited to groups. He asked if Gram could act as a judge and maybe toss in a song or two at intermission—for free.

At that moment, Buddy became a manager. He negotiated a $500 fee—plus expenses—for Gram.

Before the show, Gram met two musicians backstage. They were Paul Surratt and Joe Kelly, two-thirds of a group called the Shilos. The third member, George Wrigley, was in the hospital after getting worked over in a nightclub fight.

Gram had checked the list of groups and he had a question. He had planned to perform a song called "Hills of Shiloh" and wanted to see if the Shilos might be doing the same song.

Paul, the Shilos' banjo player, was immediately struck by Gram, who was tanned and dressed in a flashy blue shirt with a gold medallion hanging from his neck. Here, he thought, was a charismatic guy.

Paul and Joe assured Gram that they wouldn't be conflicting with him. As they chatted, Paul mentioned that he was a fan of the Journeymen, a folk group formed by John Phillips.

"You guys know about the Journeymen?" said Gram.

The three started singing the Journeymen's "Run Maggie Run."

"All of a sudden," said Paul, "it was like six voices! We all just stopped and looked at each other. 'What was *that?*' we said. We got cold chills. And then we sang another one."

Gram invited Joe and Paul to sing with him on stage. Needless to say, Gram, the judge, found the Shilos to be the best group in the house that night, and before evening's end, Gram's wheels were turning. The Shilos, who'd been together in one form or another since junior high–school days, knew that another change was in the works.

Paul was so excited, he never got to sleep that night.

The next day, while Paul and Joe visited George at the hospital to tell them about their new partner, Buddy tried to talk Gram out of his notion. Buddy felt that the Shilos were young and silly, and thought Gram wanted them more for comic relief than as musical partners.

"You're three leagues above them in talent, and socially, I don't see how you all would ever fit together," he told Gram. Besides, he hadn't even met the third member of the Shilos.

Gram was insistent. "I like their music," he said. "And they have good harmony and good instruments."

Buddy soon found himself manager of a new ensemble, Gram Parsons and the Shilos.

Under Buddy's guidance, the group began to make some real money. They had been performing for $25 and $50, with the occasional $75 gig. Buddy began getting them $300 and up, less his 20 percent cut. Because Gram lived in Florida, the group often performed without him; he'd fly into South Carolina only for a few weekend appearances and television shows.

With the better money came better instruments. Buddy went shopping for a new Martin guitar in New York with Gram and Avis. When Gram mentioned he'd like a twelve-string Goya guitar, Avis resisted until Buddy spoke up about his need for professional instruments. Well, said Avis, relenting, "One's going to be for Christmas and one's going to be for his birthday."

Buddy became a taskmaster. He pushed for as many rehearsals as possible. Fearing that Gram, in concert, was getting too hoarse too quickly, he took him—and the rest of the group—to a vocal trainer. And he told them they should learn to apply makeup for their television appearances. The boys refused; they wished Buddy would stick to booking their shows. They had no problem with the higher pay or better engagements.

One booking was actually arranged by Gram: a fund-raising party for a gubernatorial candidate sponsored by his grandmother, at the Snively mansion. Buddy recalled that Haney not only paid the group's regular fee but also passed a china dish around, saying, "Chip in for the band." Her friends came up with more than $1,000 as a tip for the boys.

They were also sent to a studio in Chicago to record songs to promote inland surfing at Cypress Gardens, and for Florida's exhibit at the 1964 World's Fair. Buddy was exasperated by the trip; the boys were under-rehearsed, he thought, and didn't come up with anything original. The closest was "Surfinanny," which resulted from Gram grafting new words on to an old Shilos song, "Raise Some Ruckus Tonight." "Surfinanny" wound up as an unofficial theme song for Cypress Gardens, but neither it nor the boys' rendition of the New Christy Minstrels' "Julie Ann" was exactly right for the World's Fair pavilion.

Buddy thought he knew what the Shilos needed. Inspired by the success of hootenanny revues like the New Christy Minstrels, he figured a way to stretch the Shilos into a two-hour variety show, at the same time giving Gram's vocal cords an occasional rest. He brought in two girls, Kathy Fowler, who specialized in Joan Baez songs, and Marilyn Garrett, a fine soprano who, incidentally, was a cousin of Buddy's. They would sing solo and in various combinations with the Shilos.

The group didn't mind having the girls doing solo spots, but the girls' singing together with them would only confuse the Shilos' identity. They gave in to Buddy only a couple of times.

After their experience in Chicago, Buddy was convinced that the Shilos didn't have enough good, original material; so much so that he turned down a chance for them to audition for the Ed Sullivan show. In the spring of 1964, the show was, more than ever, *the* springboard for pop stars, ranging from Elvis to the Beatles. He never told the boys about the opportunity.

In the summer of 1964, the Shilos spent a month in Myrtle Beach, South Carolina, doing a series of concerts. Without Buddy around, they got kicked out of their hotel for raising too much of a ruckus and moved into a big rented house a block from the beach. Between concerts, lounging around with a houseful of new friends, they came to the conclusion that Buddy was a damper on their music and that he no longer deserved a one-fifth cut of their earnings.

When Buddy visited them one weekend and proceeded to clear the house of what he considered a "bad lot" of kids, his group cut him off. Joe Kelly told him, "You haven't done anything for us this summer, and all you're doing is bitch. So that's *it*."

8

I Wore My Youth
Like a Crown

Five years had passed since Gram had last attended the Bolles School and, ironically, just as America was discovering a little war that wouldn't go away in Vietnam, Bolles dropped its military connections. In 1961, the school decided to concentrate on being a liberal arts-oriented college prep school.

With that decision, the whole world changed for Bolles's 400 boys. The 1965 yearbook reflected a looser mood, its students posing with electric guitars, Beach Boys albums, and rifles as well as books; and listing hobbies such as "sleeping" and "dating blonde girls."

On the surface, the beautiful campus, the high educational standards, and the peer group of mostly well-to-do, southern young men, were a perfect fit for Gram. But Gram carried with him a unique set of challenges.

"It's difficult pinning him down," said Robert Hubbard, head of the English Department and a teacher of and counselor to Gram. The professor was initially impressed with Gram in his English class in the fall of 1963, as he began his repeat of his junior year. "He handed in an extraordinarily good poem. But unfortunately, it was Lawrence Ferlinghetti's."

I Wore My Youth Like a Crown

By now, it was customary for Gram to carry a guitar onto campus and into the classroom. Joe Dyess, who had Gram as an English student in his junior year, remembered the time Gram did a reinterpretation of the old folk song "Barbara Allen" and set it to his own music. Gram's performance had his classmates crying.

Between classes, Gram, guitar in hand, often went to the back of the campus, where a wooden walkway led to the banks of the St. Johns River. Gram would stop short of the walk and sit inside a large stone gazebo, where he would work on his music. Invariably, a crowd would gather, to Gram's quiet satisfaction.

While his teachers and friends perceived Gram to be a loner, one who did not easily confide in others, there was no question that he loved attention and used his musical talent to get it. Gram often performed in the lobby of Bolles Hall, his dorm. The lobby, with its high ceilings set off by hand-painted cypress beams, didn't offer the best acoustics, but it was handsome, and it could hold 200 students at a time. Here, and outside by the fountain, and at the weekly convocation, Gram performed.

As a junior, Gram was in the Debate Club and competed in a National Forensics League debate in Gainesville. Given a topic, a speaker had to improvise for twenty minutes. Gram concocted a hilarious story about his "pet octopus."

Gram's onstage humor was mostly borrowed—he did Smothers Brothers routines word for word—and he liked Shelley Berman, Johnny Carson, Steve Allen, Brother Dave Gardner, and Jonathan Winters.

Frank Murphy, an artist and fellow student at Bolles, thought Gram liked to test people just to see how far he could go. Gram once asked him to make up some cards for him reading, "It's OK, I'm a Musician."

Frank was once hospitalized with an injury. He got a visit from Gram and two other friends. Gram had his guitar in one hand and his case in another. Frank, no fool, was immediately suspicious.

"Gram," he asked, "how come your guitar isn't in your guitar case?"

Gram smiled and opened up his case. It was crammed full of beer. The visit soon became a party, with several other patients in the ward sharing the brew. Numerous other patients complained that they could get no attention: The nurses were all sitting around listening to Gram singing.

Bolles was a boys' school, but girls were never far away. Once, Gram's schoolmate and fellow Waycrossian, Roger Williams remembered, Gram just happened to bring his guitar to a dance at Bartram, a nearby girls' school. When Gram was asked to do a few numbers, he sang Ian and Sylvia's "Four Strong Winds." The girls were crowding the stage apron and swooning. "Every girl in that place just went wild over him," Roger said. In the commotion, Gram lost his guitar. Several days later, the headmaster at Bartram told Bolles officials that the guitar had been found. A girl had been sleeping with it.

Gram was a member of the Centurions, described as a "service club"; actually, it was the closest thing Bolles had to a fraternity. In the 1965 yearbook, the club was credited with presenting a folk concert featuring "the Shilos, a group from Greenwich Village."

Actually, the Shilos spent all of a month in New York, in the summer of 1964.

They had parted ways with Buddy Freeman, and after Gram had gone to spend a week in the Village, the rest of the group joined him. While Paul, George, and Joe took turns sleeping on a decent mattress in an artist's apartment, Gram was sharing a loft on Houston Street with a woman named Zahariah. "Zah" sang at a cabaret, the Cafe Rafio, which became the Shilos' main stage in New York. It was a modest one, shared with Zah and a poet named Normal. Everyone passed the hat.

In their short time in New York, Gram and the Shilos connected with the Journeymen, the folk group whose songs helped bring them together. Dick Weissman, banjo player, singer and songwriter who had just left the Journeymen, remembered cutting five songs with Gram one afternoon at a studio called "6 West 57th," where Peter, Paul and Mary did some of their recording. A friend of Dick's was the engineer; unfortunately, Dick has been unable to locate any tapes from the session.

One day, George spotted John Phillips on the street. John knew Paul Surratt from his backstage visits at Journeymen concerts around the south, and when George told him that he was in a group with Gram Parsons and Paul Surratt, John invited them all to the apartment he was sharing with his girlfriend and fellow singer, Michelle. As a favor, John took the Shilos to the office of Albert Grossman, manager of Bob Dylan and other top-line folk artists. One of Albert's assistants wanted to book the boys at The Bitter End at Christmas, but his enthusiasm faded when he learned that the Shilos were still in high school and too young to sign a contract.

They had missed out on Ed Sullivan; now they'd connected with the heartbeat of the Village folk scene, only to be sent back to school. The month in New York had been exhilarating, but as they headed home, the Shilos knew that they wouldn't get many more chances.

Instead of spending the holidays in the Village, the Shilos worked at a new nightclub that had opened in Winter Haven. It was

I Wore My Youth Like a Crown

called the Derry Down, and it was another effort by Bob Parsons to win Gram over. He had turned a plain downtown warehouse he owned into a teen nightclub that would serve as a showcase for his stepson.

Bob had found the expressway to Gram's heart—at least for the moment. Gram gave the club its name, telling a reporter for the *Tampa Tribune* that he took it from the old folk song "Down Derry Derry Down." He wanted the club to evoke an eighteenth-century English inn. A pass read: "A pub for knaves and rogues, fools and sages, matter not what be their ages." Menu items included Derryburgers and Downdogs; drinks—all nonalcoholic—were given Renaissance names: "A Midsummer Night's Dream," "Falstaff," "Hotspur."

"We were really going to go old English," said Gram to the newspaper, "but the trouble is nobody here understands it. Even Hotspur is pretty far out for Winter Haven."

Jim Carlton, who stayed in touch with Gram after the Legends had dissolved, recorded a couple of the Shilos' sets that were performed at the Derry Down and aired on a local radio station. On the broadcast, Gram did pretty much all the talking, encouraging the radio audience to come on down ("We're right next door to Gilmore Pontiac here on Fifth Street Northwest") and regaling listeners with typical folk-group banter. Fellow Shilos were subjected to well-rehearsed put-downs: "George Wrigley is the genius of our group. He writes all his own songs—and steals everybody else's. . . . We have Paul in the group to remind us that mental illness strikes one out of every four people. . . ."

In the style of folk singers of the day, Gram provided complete and earnest, if occasionally irreverent, credits. Introducing "I May Be Right," Gram said that the song "was written by a friend of ours, Dick Weissman. Dick used to play with a group called the Journeymen, and although the Journeymen had probably the highest potential of any group that was ever recorded, they were a great big flop. We'd like to revive the Journeymen and Dick Weissman in particular by playing their songs."

Without a Buddy Freeman watching over them, the Shilos of late 1964 were undisciplined, prone to muffing both lyrics and instrumental parts. But when they found their common track, they were ringers for the most accomplished groups of their day: the Kingston Trio, the Limeliters, and Peter, Paul, and Mary. On certain songs, it was as if one magically multilayered person was singing, with a voice both sweet and robust at the same time.

Even if Gram was pleased with the chance to perform at Bob Parsons's club, his relationship with his stepfather was strained. According to sister Avis, it seesawed between love and hate. Gram

★ 49 ★

apparently saw Bob as a leech on the Snively fortune. And yet, early on he was attracted by Bob's worldly ways, his playboy style, and his sense of adventure.

Bob was very interested in the Cuban cause, according to Little Avis. One group of exiles, bent on returning and overthrowing Fidel Castro, trained in Polk County. Through his business connections, Bob got to be friends with the leaders, and he and Gram visited one of the training camps. By coincidence, *Life* magazine had a photographer there, but after Big Avis heard about the visit, the pictures never saw the light of day. "Mother," said Little Avis, "had an absolute fit."

Avis had given birth to a baby, Diane, in the fall of 1960, and hired an eighteen-year-old sitter named Bonnie. Everyone, it seems, knew that Bob and the sitter were having an affair. Bob rented a cottage in north Florida every summer, hosted clambakes, and kept Bonnie by his side.

With their marriage having moved so rapidly onto the rocks, Avis turned to alcohol with a vengeance.

Gram knew that things at home were bad, but he had an escape hatch: college. He applied to four schools in February, including Johns Hopkins and Harvard. Years later, Gram flippantly explained his application to Harvard: "I wanted to find out what Tim Leary and Richard Alpert were up to." Gram's counselor, Robert Hubbard, guided him through the entrance exams, as well as the essay that helped him gain admission to Harvard in lieu of a high grade point average and test scores.

"I did a back dive into Harvard," Gram said in 1972. "They were looking to break out of their traditional mode of choosing students, and I was *way* out of the mold." In another interview that year, he said he had no idea how he got in. "I guess they figured they had enough class presidents and maybe they needed a few beatniks." He added: "I was also ready to start thumbing to get out of Waycross. There's an old saying about it: As soon as you learn to walk, you start walkin' out of town." Gram, of course, had been away from Waycross for seven years by the time he applied to Harvard, but he was right about the university's liberated admissions policy in the mid-sixties.

In Jim Carlton's yearbook for 1964, Gram wrote, with a combination of weariness and optimism:

> I have been waiting for God to come to me at my house, piped in on my television, but no one can tell me the right channel to tune in on. We have been like an upside down American flag (a little screwed up perhaps, but stirringly patriotic). Maybe my philosophy has helped

you. I think so from the looks of things. I can't really think of anything nice to say about you that you don't already know. There are too many "good times" for me to remember, so forgive me for not boosting your ego.

Perhaps someday we'll both find out what we want. If so we can't help but get it. In the meantime we must suck knowledge, like cyanide, from an old peach pit. See you in the "Playground of the Stars." Until then—

Sound as ever,
Gram

On a Saturday in mid-March, Gram visited Jim in Winter Haven and, warming up for a recording session the Shilos had planned for the following week, ran through a handful of folk numbers. Jim's tape recorder caught a spirited version of Shel Silverstein's "Hey Nellie Nellie" and a gentle reading of Tom Paxton's "Last Thing On My Mind."

The next Saturday, the Shilos booked an hour at the campus radio station at Bob Jones University, a religious college in Greenville. Paul Surratt saw the session as a last-ditch effort to save the group. His father paid $33.70 for the studio time.

The group was strictly business in the studio. Station WMUU gave them two microphones, and one of them went to amplify Joe's stand-up bass. With no mixing or overdubbing facilities, Gram, singing lead on all nine songs, simply stood close to the mike while the others leaned back and forth to sing their parts.

The resulting tapes, which were released by Sierra Records as *Gram Parsons: The Early Years, 1963–1965*, revealed the Shilos as a group that was playing it safe. They were based on tradition, and when they wrote new songs, those were fit into the folk mode.

Gram squeezed in a solo blues tune he'd written the year before in Greenwich Village for his singer friend, Zah.

"Zah's Blues," with Gram and his guitar backed only by Joe's bass, is a languid echo of the Kingston Trio's after-hours rumination, "Scotch and Soda." His voice is stark; at one point it cracks as he sings about the fragility of love. The lyrics are awkward; it's as if they're just stumbling out from heart to mike:

A baby doesn't know how loneliness can feel
She has her own small world and nothing in it's real
Just spread joy all around and watch the sun comin'
    down
When I was young the world was rich
With spices and parfaits
My heart was filled with pride

* 51 *

Hickory Wind

My head was filled with praise
I wore my youth like a crown
And watched the sun comin' down . . .

But in the spring of 1965, "Scotch and Soda"–type tunes were about as hip as Richard Nixon. The Beatles had changed the content and sound of pop music; along with Bob Dylan, they were in the process of revolutionizing the concepts of albums. They were turning the Top 40 topsy-turvy.

The charts were dominated by the British invasion and by Motown. Bob Dylan was making waves by fusing folk music with rock. In California, Dylan had caught the ears of The Byrds, who recorded his song, "Mr. Tambourine Man." In New York, the leader of the Mamas and the Papas, ex-Journeyman John Phillips, was listening intently to the Beatles.

Gram heard, too, and in late May, with the Shilos' tapes having gone nowhere, he wrote to Paul Surratt:

> i've been thinking. if we want to make it as a group we're going to have to do some serious rearranging. the people want a really different sound, and ours isn't different enough yet . . . for one thing i think we should sing all new music with a few exceptions. i think we should work on my material. i know it will sell. music, believe it or not is during [sic] towards a more—[here Gram typed out a misspelled "aesthetic," then crossed it out and chose an almost antonymous word]—intellectual vein. we should go into serious rehearsals, now i know we've said that before but now it *is* a necessity. i'm sure that my music is going to be as big as dylans, and after my album we will have the advantage of owning my music . . . we are going to have to cash in on this thing dylan's started, and like it or not we'll be associated with him. i still want very much to make it with the shilos. i always have . . .
>
> sound as ever,
> Gram

But by the time Gram wrote that letter, he knew he was headed for Harvard and that the group was finished.

On a fine June morning in 1965, he was down by St. Johns River, preparing to line up for the commencement exercises. Members of his family had come in from Tennessee to watch his final performance on campus.

At 10:30, his English teacher, Joe Dyess, pulled him aside.

The school had recieved a phone call an hour before. After an extended stay at Winter Haven Hospital, Avis Parsons had died.

I Wore My Youth Like a Crown

The teacher gave Gram the news. Gram had known of his mother's poor health and thought her death was just a matter of time. He had told Dyess once that his mother's doctor had warned her, "If you take another drink, it could be your last one." Gram had had every reason to expect that she would drink again.

Robert Hubbard didn't know how Gram was informed about his mother's death. Dennis Hupp, a classmate of Gram's, said nothing was amiss with Gram on graduation day.

But Dyess said the school gave Gram the option to skip the graduation ceremonies, and Gram chose to go ahead.

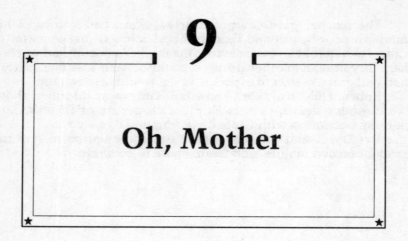

9

Oh, Mother

$\mathbf{A}$mong the Snivelys, the verdict was unanimous: Bob Parsons drove Avis to her death.

Bob had set a clear pattern of working his way into the Snively family: Immediately after their wedding, she was pregnant. He then adopted Gram and Avis. Next, according to several Snivelys, he coerced Avis into filing a $1.5 million lawsuit in 1962 against her own brother, John Jr., and her sister, Evalyn.

The charge, according to Gram's cousin Rob Hoskins, was that they were stealing from her. Actually, said Rob, the citrus industry had suffered two bad years in succession. "We weren't stealing anything; as a matter of fact, we were stealing from everything else to make sure she had plenty of money."

The Snivelys fought the suit, of course, but some of the family admitted that while John Jr. was a good citrus producer, he was not nearly the businessman his father was. A woman who was close to the elder Snively said John Jr. fell short of Papa John's standards of honesty. The son, she said, was spoiled by money and disabled by liquor. And he found himself being sued by his own younger sister. The suit tore the family apart and exposed its financial problems.

Although details are difficult to come by—most of the principals are dead, and family members had sketchy information at best—there are some clear bottom lines: The suit was settled out of court, and Avis received a number of orange groves. But the litigation ultimately cost the Snivelys millions. A direct line could be drawn from the suit to the bankruptcy of much of the family business in 1974. By the mid-sixties, the family had sold its plants to a citrus cooperative that had been formed by Papa John and John Jr. Everything, said Rob, was sold on a distressed market, and property that was sold for $3,200 an acre is now worth five times as much. Meanwhile, the Snivelys' net worth—estimated at $28 million when Papa John died in January, 1958—had shrunk to about $2 million by 1972, according to Avis.

The end result of the lawsuit, as one Snively tallied it: "Papa John had three kids: Avis, Evalyn, and John Jr. Avis's kids get a pretty good income, and Evalyn's kids get a pretty good income, and John Jr.'s don't get nothin'."

Today, several younger Snivelys, including John III and brother Pate, are still in the citrus industry, but only as growers.

On top of the lawsuit and the resulting family traumas, there was the matter of Bob and the baby-sitter.

According to Little Avis, her mother sought psychiatric help just before her death. She seemed to be doing well, the daughter thought, but then her physical health failed. Avis Parsons died of alcohol poisoning, and Rob Hoskins laid the blame on Bob Parsons. "That son of a bitch brought her a bottle of scotch while she was in the hospital," he said. Little Avis restrained her comments but did say that Gram went to the hospital to look up whatever records he could find. "I was satisfied that if Gram thought it was cirrhosis of the liver, it was cirrhosis of the liver."

Little Avis, who attended Gram's graduation exercises with Uncle Tom and his parents, didn't learn of her mother's death until after the ceremonies. She wasn't certain that Gram actually heard the news himself before graduation. But as she talked, she remembered something: When she came down the hotel stairs for the party, Gram embraced her and gave her a long, intense hug.

"Maybe," she thought in retrospect, "he was on the verge of saying something."

Just before the funeral, he fielded phone calls from friends, and Jim Carlton overheard him. Jim, who thought Gram spoke in 2/4 time, said he slowed down even more, into a regal cadence that reminded him of Duke Ellington, as he told friends, "Yes . . . she *had* been declining."

Gram's coolness stunned old friends like Dickey Smith from Waycross. Dickey, who hadn't seen Gram in about four years, went to the house on Piedmont Drive a couple of hours before the funeral and found Gram in bed, strumming idly on his guitar. He had a drink by his bed. He looked up and, without getting off the bed, shook Dickey's hand, then returned to his drink.

"As you can see," he said, "I'm not going to mourn for the rest of my life. I just don't believe in sitting around and moping. Life is going to go on."

Dickey went to the mansion after the funeral and couldn't help noticing how Gram's grandmother, Nancy, appeared to be the only person who was truly mourning.

"I can still see her going up the steps crying and closing the door to her bedroom," said Dickey. "And everyone else stayed downstairs and there were cocktails and hors d'oeuvres."

Avis was hard pressed to remember Bob Parsons grieving—at least outwardly—over the loss of her mother. Apparently, he just wanted to get out of Winter Haven, which suddenly felt much too small, and after a summer at Ponte Vedra, he moved the family fifty miles north to Winter Park, near Orlando.

Gram spent some time at Ponte Vedra that summer. He maintained his ambivalence toward his stepfather; he might never be Coon Dog, but when Gram needed help, Bob was there. Shortly after his mother's death, Gram received greetings from the Selective Service, and Bob Parsons moved right in.

"The Commies will be at the back door before I let Gram go," he vowed. Gram was soon excused on a 4-F, a deferment from military service for physical reasons.

He was free to go off to Harvard.

10

A Harvard Man

Officially, Gram enrolled at Harvard University in September 1965 and withdrew in February 1966.

The truth is that he never entered.

Rev. James E. Thomas, popularly known as "Jet," was an assistant dean in the freshmen dean's office while doing graduate work at Harvard's divinity school. He was seven years older than Gram Parsons when they met. Jet, who came to Harvard from Virginia, was a Baptist, and although he was ordained later, in 1966, he liked to think of himself more as a teacher and "minister at large" than as a Bible thumper.

Gram, whose room on campus was just a short walk from Jet's apartment, became a regular visitor, playing his guitar, singing country tunes, and talking with the young minister about religion (Gram later said he majored in theology at Harvard, explaining, "I was into God then." In fact, as a freshman, it was too early to declare any major).

"I think I was there about four hours and fifteen minutes," said Gram about Harvard, in 1972. "I hardly got my clothes hung up."

"I was turned off by the fact that I had to study all these things

I didn't understand," he said another time. "I lasted four or five months by playing music and having good times."

Although—maybe flippantly—Gram had listed Timothy Leary and Richard Alpert as drawing cards at Harvard, Gram missed the LSD researchers by two years.

He had also missed the peak of Cambridge's folk scene, two or three years earlier. It had been home—or at least a convivial crash pad for open-ended lengths of time—to the likes of Joan Baez, Bob Dylan, Bob Neuwirth, Tom Rush, Richard and Mimi Fariña, Eric Andersen, Geoff Muldaur, and Pete Seeger. The folk scene was centered at places like Club 47, whose owners had to fight off law enforcement and civic officials with one hand while somehow keeping its doors open with the other.

It was a free-wheeling time. Among the students of Harvard, MIT, and Radcliffe, and the surrounding communities of Cambridge and Boston, there were ears open to not only folk (and jazz and blues) but to the deepest roots of folk.

As Paul Arnoldie, a guitarist and self-described "green kid from Wyoming" who spent a life-changing summer of 1962 there put it, "Cambridge was as pure a folk music thing as I'll ever have in my life. There's something nice about folk music—a lot of heartfelt stuff. That's what folk music is—people singing and playing simple stuff really straight."

Groups like the Charles River Valley Boys offered "Olde Timey Mountain Music," string band music that took listeners—many for the first time—to the smokiest hills of Tennessee. But the Boys' repertoire also extended to folk ballads, jug band music, and the country blues of Mississippi John Hurt.

In the fifties, Boston had places like the Mohawk Ranch ("Original Home of West & Hillbilly Shows") and the Hillbilly Ranch. The singing cowboys and cowgirl stars of a local television show, "Hayloft Jamboree," wore white ten-gallon hats, fringed shirts with kerchiefs, and string ties. The cast included, at various times, Ferlin Husky, Webb Pierce, Lester Flatt and Earl Scruggs and the Foggy Mountain Boys, Jack "Cowboy" Clement, Bill Keith, who was such a wizard that he came to be called "the world's foremost nuclear banjoist" and got drafted by one of the fathers of bluegrass, Bill Monroe, to play with him in Nashville and at the Grand Ole Opry.

Bill Keith soon discovered another great picker, a kid from Maine whose entire family, it seemed, was conversant with fiddle, banjo, guitar, and a catalog of country tunes ranging from the Opry's first singing star, Roy Acuff, to its latest, Hank Williams. In 1954, the family moved to Burbank, California, and the sons formed a group called the Country Boys, with Roland White on mandolin, Eric White on tenor banjo, and Clarence White on guitar. It was Clarence who caught Keith's ear. In 1964 Clarence was only eighteen, but picking like he'd taken medication from Doc Watson. After a tour of the Cambridge scene and an appearance at a Newport Folk Festival, the band went through a couple of lineup changes, became the Kentucky Colonels, and settled back in Cambridge.

Clarence, Bill, and others of the early Cambridge music circles would one day figure in the music of Gram Parsons.

★

Gram arrived at a Cambridge that had just been electrified. Even the most dedicated purists couldn't help noticing what the Beatles were doing to Top 40 rock and roll, especially in the album they issued in the winter of 1965, *Rubber Soul*. Those musicians who'd rocked and rolled in their teenage, garage-band years and who'd switched styles as they stumbled and partied their way through school felt a release, a ticket back to the exuberance of those first records of Elvis and Buddy, of Chuck and Little Richard, of Gene Vincent and Eddie Cochran—only mixed, now, with what they'd learned through folk, blues and country. When John Sebastian got the electric flash and formed Lovin' Spoonful, his music combined rock with what he'd been playing and hearing from the jug bands of Cambridge.

How much of this history Gram knew is uncertain. Possibly he knew none of it and didn't have to do any research. After all, Gram had packed rock and roll, pop, R&B, folk music, and more than a bit of the South with him for his trip to Harvard.

Hosting Gram at his apartment, Jet Thomas would mention his love of old-time country music, and Gram would favor him with requests—from ancient Baptist songs to Hank Williams hits like "Cold Cold Heart" and "Your Cheatin' Heart."

Within days of arriving on campus, Gram had a band together. Few people ever heard it, but it had a name—the Like—and Gram wasted no time getting himself some ink. In November a story in a Winter Haven paper was headlined: HAVENITE BRINGS GO GO TO STAID HARVARD YARD.

From all reports, it was just another casual affair of Gram's. And it was a mismatch. The players were mostly students at the Berklee College of Music in Boston. Formally trained in classical music and jazz, they weren't anything but rock and roll.

By the time the article appeared in Winter Haven, Gram was searching around for new musical partners. He soon found Ian Dunlop, a singer, guitarist, and saxophone player who was part of the Refugees, a rock band in Providence. Gram also met a friend of Dunlop's, John Nuese, a guitarist with the Trolls, which included two members—Lowell "Banana" Levenger and Michael Kane—on their way to forming another band, the Youngbloods.

Ian and John had already worked together in a couple of bands, including one called Happy Pantaloon and the Buckles. But they were immediately taken by Gram—and willing to serve as backup musicians to him—when he began telling them that he had connections with Marty Ehrlichman, a talent manager in New York who handled Barbra Streisand. Gram also said that he had a deal with RCA Records.

Gram, with John on guitar and Ian playing bass, and with one holdover from the Like, electric pianist Tom Snow, formed the nucleus of the new, improved, but drummerless Gram Parsons and the Like.

The band initially did mostly Gram's material—primarily because that's what he said his New York connections wanted from him—but without great enthusiasm. Gram was still showing signs of post-folkie syndrome and writing what Ian heard as "very verbose, dripping songs," among them "November Nights," in which he recalled the snow-white frost on his lover's doorway, and how the wind tossed her hair.

Fortunately, he was also writing tunes like "Brass Buttons," a song with sharper images that he played for a fellow folkie he'd met in the Village, Richie Furay. Years later, the song would be recorded by Richie's band, Poco, and by Johnny Rivers as well as by Gram.

> Brass buttons, green silks, and silver shoes
> Warm evenings, pale mornings,
> Bottle of blues . . .

One night in Boston, Ian and John went to see an R&B band that Ian had been told was hot as Chinese mustard. "These guys played seven nights a week and they toured all over the Midwest. . . . I was knocked out." Ian and John sat in with the band for a couple of numbers and afterward learned that the drummer, Mickey Gauvin, was tiring of the road.

With Mickey on board, the Like was all over the place. Ian described Mickey as "an ass-kicking, redneck, hard-working drummer" who, ironically, derided country as "shit-kicking music." Ian himself ranged from fifties-style rock and roll to rhythm and blues. Nuese's heart belonged to rugged, rural country, the bluegrass of Doc Watson and the Stanley Brothers. Add Gram's folk and pop sentiments and Tom Snow's jazz, and the result was a band called the Like whose members were anything but alike.

A Harvard Man

And Brandon deWilde hadn't even entered the scene yet.

Brandon, an actor, met Gram in New York and, while visiting him in Cambridge, became an unofficial member of the band.

He made his first mark at age eight in the Broadway play *Member of the Wedding*, in 1950, and went on to a major role in *Shane* with Alan Ladd. Brandon was the "king of the child actors" in the fifties. He went on to get roles as a troubled young man (in *Blue Denim*, 1959, with Carol Lynley) and as a clean-cut, innocent young man (in *All Fall Down*, 1962, with Warren Beatty and Eva Marie Saint; and in *Hud*, 1963, with Paul Newman and Patricia Neal).

By the time he met up with Gram, Brandon was friends with the young rebels of Hollywood—the Fondas, Dennis Hopper, Bruce Dern, and Jack Nicholson—and he was tiring of the movie business. He could sing and write songs, and he wanted to try music. And, according to John Nuese, he could have done it. Next to his work with Emmylou Harris, he said, Gram's best duet singing was with Brandon. It reminded him of the best harmony duet of the time: the Everly Brothers.

But after Brandon returned to New York, Gram and the Like had to get down to work deciding on a sound. Between Gram and John's common knowledge of country and Ian and Mickey's R&B–rooted rock-and-roll drive, an electric country synthesis emerged. It was a rock-and-roll takeoff from starting points set down by Merle Haggard and Buck Owens, country visionaries based in California.

At a time when the British Invasion and its many soldiers dominated pop music, country music rarely got onto the charts. Gram wasn't concerned with what was selling. In late 1965 he liked the Beatles enough to learn their latest single, "We Can Work It Out." But his heart still belonged to folk music. In one of his trips to New York, he'd met Fred Neil, the reclusive, Florida-based singer-songwriter who wrote "Everybody's Talkin'." Gram began singing his songs.

Gram professed to love country music. He may have been doing nothing more than telling new buddies what they wanted to hear; as Ian noted, Gram always went out of his way to please people. In retrospect, he said, Gram was living in an "emotional vacuum. He was always eagerly reaching out, trying to meet new friends and find people he could trust and relax with."

He may have wound up with the Berklee students for such reasons. But whatever drove him to align himself with country music, he was convincing.

At Harvard, he told Jet that he thought of the best country music as "white gospel" or "white soul music." And he told—and showed—John Nuese enough so that John was convinced he had a musical ally. "Gram and I believed from day one that contemporary country music played by young musicians would eventually be accepted," he said.

Years later, Gram looked back on Cambridge as a watershed—a place and time in which, as he told Judith Simms, "I passed my identity crisis and came back to country music." He credited the musicians he met there with helping him rediscover his native music. "They always had their ears open, and they actually reintroduced me to country music after I'd forgotten about it for ten years. And the country singers like George Jones, Ray Price, and Merle Haggard—they're great performers, but I had to *learn* to dig them. And that taught me a lot."

Just before Thanksgiving, Gram and the Like packed their instruments into a rented car and drove to New York to follow up on his manager's promises. They cut a couple of demo tapes, returned to Cambridge, and waited for the phone to ring. After waiting a whole week, the guys decided that it was time to reevaluate their music—again. They whittled down the list of Gram's songs that they performed, tried turning the ones they did into rock-and-roll songs, and widened their repertoire to include oldies like "Rip It Up," one of Gram's favorites from his days with the Pacers and the Legends.

By the winter of 1965, Gram was still supposedly a Harvard student, although, as far as Jet knew, he spent a lot of time under the influence of what Leary and Alpert had left behind and too little time in classrooms. He was well on his way to flunking out when he saved the university some paperwork by dropping out.

Gram once ascribed his use of LSD to "a juvenile fascination" and confessed that it was the main reason he left school: "I had taken so much of it."

Jet Thomas remembered Gram tripping on LSD on weekends away from the campus, then visiting him, distraught and in tears. He expressed concern about his family, and in particular about his sister, Avis. He told his adviser that he felt helpless in the face of his family history.

After a year in Winter Park, Bob Parsons packed up Bonnie, Little Avis, and Diane and moved to New Orleans. Here, Avis was in misery. Shortly after her mother's death, Bob had married the former baby-sitter, who began bragging to her friends about her sex life with Bob, telling them that he especially liked the fact that she didn't wear much makeup—or any underwear. Bob, the picture of sophistication, and Bonnie, the latter-day hippie, made an intriguing and handsome couple, and they maintained a spacious and attractive house near Audubon Park. They lived the high life, and more than a few friends suspected that they were doing so with money from his dead wife's estate.

A Harvard Man

Avis didn't fit in. She felt like "an odd cog that needed to be thrown out." She repeatedly asked to be allowed to attend high school near Winter Haven, but Parsons wouldn't allow it, fearing that she'd get too close to the Snivelys.

Avis spent most of her time complaining and wishing someone would take her away. She wrote to Gram but found him inconsistent in his responses. Sometimes he could be generous and thoughtful; other times, puzzling, epigrammatic, enigmatic. She knew that he was often too strung out on drugs to act on her behalf.

And yet Gram tried. On November 8 he responded to his sister's distress calls with a letter that looked casual—he typed it out double-spaced on a sheet of Harvard stationery and didn't bother with capital letters—and promised nothing, yet delivered a sense of concern and of wearied wisdom.

i wish there was some one thing i could tell you, some clear advice or magic spell to whisk away all the things that are bothering you right now. i'm not going to speak from the lofty pedestal of age and experience because i'm not *that* old and the problem is obviously not entirely a growing pain. besides, they're not just your concern they're *our* concern, yours mine and diane's, and i'm afraid they will continue for some time yet. the best thing we can do is learn from the past and live our lives the right way so, in time, when we can do something to change things, we will be real people. not sick or haunted by what life has done to us. we have the advantage of seeing definite examples of what can happen when people permit life to tangle them so badly that there is no escape. for us— there is time—life can be real and beautiful if you build it that way—honestly—so there will be no lies or shadows to be afraid of later. so far, none of us have any reason to be ashamed, and i don't think we ever will. but, it's true, it requires a lot of work, knowledge, and love. i know we love each other. maybe we don't say it often enough because we've seen love twisted so many ways, but i hope you've never doubted it. as for knowledge—i can never convey what a blessing a place like harvard is. there are so many wonderful brilliant people here. i just hope you have the chance to go to some really good schools. it may seem unreal and far away but you'll have to start now. you may not particularly adore the school you're in now, but get all you can from it anyway. read on your own. the next time we're together i'll give you some books. good books are always a gas. you like poetry—read allen ginsburg, dylan thomas, e. e. cummings, lawrence ferlinghetti, t. s. eliot, even edgar allan poe has a lot to say. you like plays—read edward albee, arthur miller, tennessee williams, albert camus, find out why shakespeare's tragedies are different from the contemporary tragedies of miller (death of a salesman, after the fall) or williams (the glass menagerie). this way you can learn how great minds work and probably answer a lot of your own questions. these books can teach you more than i could ever hope to. above all—believe in yourself—and in other people—they're the only thing that is real. i'll try to write as often as i can. until then—live your life as you see it—as best you can—give it a solid foundation for the future.

> sound as ever,
> Gram

★

"If you can remember the sixties, you weren't really there."

> —Robin Williams

It could be argued that, whether Gram Parsons remembered the sixties or not, he wasn't really there.

Take the beginning of the decade. For some, the kickoff was the first sit-in by blacks at a Woolworth's counter in South Carolina in February 1960. For many others, it was the assassination of President John F. Kennedy in 1963.

Gram Parsons was still in high school. He and the on-again, off-again Legends had a gig that evening at Bolles, and Jim Stafford was driving up from Eloise for it. Jim had heard the news, of course, but made the drive, listening to radio reports along the way up. When he saw Gram, he told him, "I don't think they're going to have this dance."

And Gram replied, "Don't be silly."

Jim didn't think Gram, who had just turned seventeen, was being flippant. Maybe he was too shocked to think rationally; assassination, after all, was such a *foreign* concept in 1963. Young people, especially, weren't ready for such an event, and didn't know how to feel about it.

At that time, Gram was singing with the Shilos, and he was keeping close tabs on all the best folk singers, chief among them Dylan, who was writing some of his most powerful songs: "Blowin' in the Wind," "A Hard Rain's A-Gonna Fall," "Masters of War."

While the Shilos resisted their manager's requests to do hit

A Harvard Man

folk songs by the Kingston Trio and the Limeliters, they also shied away from message songs. In songwriting, Gram stuck to traditional forms and love songs and showed not a sliver of interest in the politics of the day. Only when he heard, in Dylan, a way to cross over to a wider following by taking up the electric guitar and forging folk-rock, did Gram suggest the same path. Even then, he didn't keep the group together long enough to take it.

The sixties were a time of young people bucking authority and the prevailing political system. They sought social change. They protested for free speech on college campuses; for civil rights everywhere for an end to war, the draft system, the use of nuclear power.

But the sixties were a two-sided coin. There were also the hippies, the "love children" whose quarrels were with established society itself and who chose to live by Timothy Leary's slogan: "Turn on, tune in, drop out."

By the late sixties, more than a few political protesters were digging drugs and rock and roll; more than a few flower children were joining in peace rallies. The two-sided coin was becoming more of a marbled ball.

Gram would wind up in a big house and live communally with a rock band; he did grow his hair long and use drugs; women came and went. Gram, of course, was practicing free love before the price was ever lowered. But he lived his life outside of any movement or trend.

For all the Sturm und Drang of the times, Gram's storms were personal, and they were disturbances he tried to weather by way of money, connections, drugs, and the indifference they afforded him.

No one could recall ever seeing or hearing about Gram being involved in a protest of any sort. In a time that would be defined by such songs and sentiments as "Get Together" and "love one another right now," Gram was in his own world.

In a sense, Gram didn't need the sixties, either as an excuse or as an inspiration for the way he lived.

Still, he struck others as perfectly symbolic of the times. Like a lot of young people, Gram was trying to break through limits and the "normal" way of seeing things. And, if only by his chosen musical direction, Gram was poking at convention.

As Jet Thomas saw it, Gram pulled into focus both the good and bad of the sixties counterculture. "He could be an angel or a devil. He projected a kind of James Dean quality, that of a sort of a cultural outlaw, which he loved, by the way. He was a cultural outlaw doing country music and talking about it as a form of white spiritual music."

And yet Gram wanted to be a star.

11

International Submarine Band

Gram talked about having a deal with RCA—not coincidentally, Elvis's label—but he never made a record for that company.

It was Brandon deWilde who got Gram recording again in New York. Brandon was making a demonstration tape and wanted Gram's band to back him up. With Tom Snow along to play keyboards, the band cut four songs with Brandon singing and playing guitar, but none of them was ever released.

After the sessions, the band decided that they'd be better off staying in New York than trying to make a go of country and R&B in Cambridge.

Gram dropped out of Harvard and, in New York, found his first real home away from home. It was a rambling eleven-room house in the Bronx, on the corner of University Avenue and 195th, in a nice Irish-Italian-Jewish neighborhood. He could have it for about $300 a month, furnished.

The band moved in in January, and the party began. As all young rock musicians did to get a semblance of a recording studio, the guys tacked up egg cartons against the walls of a room—in their case, an attic space—thus creating a rehearsal facility.

International Submarine Band

As the word spread about the rock band that had a big house of its own, visitors gathered, among them members of the Blues Magoos and Barry Tashian, a friend of John and Ian's and leader of the Boston-based rock band, the Remains.

The Remains, at one time New England's biggest rock-and-roll band, were nearing their end. For Barry, the boys in the Bronx were a welcome escape. Here there seemed to be no pressures. It wasn't exactly a hedonistic hippie scene, but there was a lot of freedom. These were young men on the loose, trying to make a go of music and having fun doing it. And marijuana and LSD were readily available.

One evening, Ian was sitting around with Mickey, talking trivia. The subject of the "Little Rascals" series came up, and one or the other remembered an episode in which Our Gang auditioned for a radio show with its slapdash musical ensemble they called the International Silver String Submarine Band. Suddenly they had a new name for the band. Gram was among the first to agree that "the International Submarine Band" sounded hipper than "the Like."

Although their new name conjured up acid rock, and they were beginning to dress in mod and western wear—colorful shirts, bell-bottom pants, and cowboy boots—their music was like nothing Barry had ever thought of playing. The Buck Owens songs and duets dazzled him. He'd heard Buck and his band, the Buckaroos, and thought the Sub Band sounded like them—but with a pronounced rock-and-roll attitude.

Around the neighborhood, the Sub Band could not go unnoticed. One rock fan who worked at the local supermarket made life a lot easier for them. Whenever one of the band members shopped there, the clerk would check through a half-dozen items and ring up, say, twenty-five cents.

One girl in the neighborhood, a fifteen-year-old named Marcia Katz, got so curious about the guys she saw and the music she heard coming from the house that one snowy evening she knocked on the door.

Gram answered, and Marcia asked, "Are you a fraternity?"

"Wait a minute," said Gram, and he disappeared upstairs. A moment later, Brandon deWilde appeared at the doorway, then left. Finally after everyone had taken a look at the young visitor, she was invited in, just in time for a rehearsal.

Marcia became a regular at the house, a combination mascot and little-sister figure who would do occasional chores in exchange for an entree into an exciting new world. "I was like 'good old Marcia,'" she said.

The Submarine Band, in actuality, was still struggling. They continued to work on demo tapes with Brandon; one session produced a version of Buck Owens's "Together Again"; another was pure Sub Band—Little Richard's "Rip it Up," Wilson Pickett's "In the Midnight Hour," and Buck Owens's "Just as Long as You Love Me"—with Brandon on lead vocals. On their own, the Sub Band stuck with high-powered country, finding inspiration from, of all people, Ray Charles. Brother Ray had taken country music into the pop charts in 1962 with his hallmark album, *Modern Sounds in Country and Western Music*, and he had taken a Don Gibson song, "I Can't Stop Loving You," to number one. But "modern sounds," at that point, meant giving country tunes a big-band arrangement. In late 1965, Ray came back with *Country and Western Meets Rhythm and Blues*. This time out, he took Buck Owens's "Together Again" and "I've Got a Tiger by the Tail" and Bill Monroe's "Blue Moon of Kentucky," unleashed the Raelets behind him, mixed in some Percy Mayfield dirty blues and a couple of lush ballads, and redrew the boundaries of music once again. The album was not nearly the success *Modern Sounds* and a follow-up were, but it reached the Bronx.

"I think that record is the key," said Ian. "That was the thing that broke the barriers between all of us, getting into this amalgam of a truer country music, but with a rock or a slight rhythm-and-blues treatment."

The Sub Band learned several of the Ray Charles tunes, but they were still searching for their own sound. Unlike most new bands, they had the luxury of Gram's money, which kept them housed and fed without having to become a Top 40 cover band.

Within a couple of months of arriving in New York, Gram split up with Marty Ehrlichman. He found another mismatch: Monte Kay, who worked with the Modern Jazz Quartet.

With no recording deals in sight, the Sub Band decided to tour, choosing a territory familiar to Gram. For most of the spring, they traveled around central Florida, playing Daytona Beach during spring break, popping into the Derry Down in Winter Haven, and opening several shows for Freddy Cannon. Freddy, whose most recent big hit had been "Palisades Park" in 1962, was riding a theme song from the television dance show "Where the Action Is."

The Florida trip ended on a surrealistic note. The Sub Band somehow wound up in a parade in Cocoa Beach, waving to the folks from the back of a blue Cadillac. When they showed up for the Freddy Cannon show at the Holiday Inn, they found an audience of six people.

Back in New York, the group began getting jobs at night clubs, playing country and R&B and getting mixed reactions. John Nuese heard the mutters of "shit-kicking music" in the audience, and the band tried to brush them off. Gram by now was committed to country.

In April, Monte Kay got the band a recording deal—of sorts. They were hired to cut a promotional single for a Norman Jewison film, *The Russians Are Coming, The Russians Are Coming.* It was an odd match; the film, a comedy about a Russian submarine accidentally running aground off the shore of Nantucket, starred Carl Reiner, Alan Arkin, Eva Marie Saint, Theodore Bikel, Jonathan Winters, and had absolutely nothing to do with rock and roll. The sound track was composed by Hollywood veteran Johnny Mandel.

The Sub Band's version of "The Russians Are Coming" was a sparse instrumental, capably executed but hardly worth the paper it was charted on. It sounded like the pseudo-rock that gurgled under nightclub scenes in movies of the early sixties. On the flip side, the Sub Band got in their country licks with "Truck Driving Man." The performance was competent, but the song, shades of "Act Naturally," was less than challenging.

Issued on the tiny Ascot label, the record made its quick journey to nowhere. Years later, Gram would complain about his experience with Ascot. "Everybody took advantage of us," he told a disc jockey in an interview broadcast in 1972, in the Netherlands. "Truck Driving Man," he said, was their first real shot at mixing country with rock and soul, but "nobody understood it."

Meanwhile, Monte Kay got the Sub Band more work. They opened a concert at Central Park for another band with a name inspired by the Our Gang reels, the Young Rascals. The Rascals were hot enough to draw 15,000 people to the park, giving the Sub Band its biggest audience ever.

Next, Monte got the Sub Band a deal with Columbia Records for a single. Gram came up with two songs: "Sum Up Broke," with words by Gram, music by John, and apparent inspiration from any number of British bands, and "One Day Week," a Parsons composition that borrowed from the Beatles and the Dave Dudley country hit, "Six Days on the Road," but also displayed some lyrical cleverness.

Gram heard "One Day Week" as "a Jerry Lee Lewis number that Jerry Lee Lewis never got a chance to do. It was the same sort of feeling." The Sub Band, he said, were trying to resurrect the sound of early Sun Records rock and roll. "Nobody was into trying to do anything straight from 1953, and a lot of people were doing good-time music." 1966, pop watchers will recall, was the year of such hits as "Hanky Panky" and "I'm a Believer." "When you look back on it," said Gram about the yummy-yummy sounds of that time, "it's sillier than trying to do country music."

Although Columbia apparently made some attempts to promote the band—they were the subject of a find-the-errors contest in the July 1967 issue of the fan magazine *16*—the Sub Band record got lost in the massive Columbia Records shuffle.

The ISB found some solace in the nightclubs of New York. They became regulars at discos like Trude Heller's, where they often went on to play the last set, around 2:30 in the morning; and at Ondine's in midtown.

In the daylight hours they continued to refine their sound. As Ian Dunlop recalled, the failures on Ascot and Columbia served only to firm the Sub Band's resolve to attack country music. In 1966, Buck Owens issued a new album, *Roll Out the Red Carpet for Buck Owens and His Buckaroos*, and its contemporary production caught Ian's ear. Don Rich used effects on his lead guitar that had been absent from most country records; the electric guitar and bass drums sounded heavier, as in a rock band. And Buck challenged country convention by recording R&B classics, including the Drifters' "Save the Last Dance for Me."

With Buck on their side, the Sub Band dug in their heels. Now they explored songs like the Louvin Brothers' "Satan's Going to Have to Learn to Live Without Me Now" and "There's Dust on Mother's Bible."

At their best, they sounded like magic—at least to each other. But, ultimately, performers need acceptance from audiences, and some of the Sub Band members began to tire of being outcasts. They'd play in front of long-haired, folk-rock audiences who made it clear that they were there not for hillbilly gospel but for Phil Ochs's biting songs of social commentary and protest.

At clubs they were often faced with rock fans who had no interest in traditional country music. It simply wasn't hip. As Ian explained, all around them were young white rock musicians exploring black music or mimicking the British bands. Some British groups—led by the Beatles, the Yardbirds, and the Stones—along with American groups like the Byrds, were toying with Eastern sounds.

Ian thought Gram's band was being logical. "We were saying, 'Look, we're just four white guys, and if our roots are anywhere, maybe they're down where they always were—with Elvis and country musicians and stuff like that. That's our roots, man. Forget the Ravi Shankar stuff.'"

Of course, the Ravi Shankar stuff was selling, and the Sub Band stuff wasn't. No matter. The band continued on the country road, but inevitably they found themselves playing to fewer people and getting fewer jobs.

Around Thanksgiving, just as the band members were beginning to sour on New York, Gram went to California, where Brandon deWilde was making a movie. One day early in December, Gram telephoned the Bronx house, and John Nuese answered.

"I'm in love," Gram announced.

When he got back to New York, he took Marcia Katz aside to tell her all about Nancy. Gram had helped Marcia celebrate her sixteenth birthday by taking her to Greenwich Village for dinner and dancing. "It wasn't a date, but it was a date," she said. Gram's idea was to let Marcia know that she wasn't just "good old Marcia."

In her time around the house, Marcia hadn't ever seen Gram with a regular girlfriend. Now he was telling her that he'd met the most beautiful girl ever, that she was coming out to New York, and that he couldn't wait to introduce Nancy to her.

One afternoon, Marcia saw a woman walking down University Avenue, and she knew it was Nancy. Gram was right. "I thought she was the most beautiful person I had ever met. And beautiful inside, too."

Nancy Marthai Ross was a vision in, of, and for the sixties. She was a sylph; lithe, graceful, beautiful, with the kind of eyes that inspired Stephen Stills to compose "Suite: Judy Blue Eyes" for Judy Collins. Nancy knew Stephen, and David Crosby, and Steve McQueen—and she'd been married before she met Gram. That, she says, was when she fell in love.

She was as intense as she was lovely, and she is no less so today. She lives in a modest white wood house near downtown Santa Barbara, one of Hollywood's favorite escapes. The house is identified with brass letters spelling out PARSONS by the front door. On the door, alongside a photo of Gram showing off the back of his Nudie jacket, Nancy has posted a hand-lettered sign reading: WELCOME TO ONE OF GRAM'S MANY MANSIONS. Inside, tokens of Gram are everywhere, and everything not nailed down is shaking to the peak-volume sounds of a gospel song, "Grace," being sung by the Los Angeles Mass Choir, playing on a tape deck.

In the backyard there is a fabric dome tent over a bed that appears to be floating in air.

Is that her occasional boudoir? "Oh," she says, "that's Gram's house."

It is clear that her story is best told by Nancy herself:

I'm from Santa Barbara, California. I was schooled in Europe, Morocco, and Santa Barbara. I grew up with David Crosby here in town. David would pilfer things from the local merchants and stage holdups, play cops and robbers—it was very funny.

I was thirteen when we met. David and I were part of the debutante set. We were the renegades of the debutante scene. I won't tell you what my mother did one Christmas. [A beat.] Yes, I will. She wrapped the Christmas tree in black crepe paper because David and the kids and I were out terrorizing the neighborhood. And then when David brought some friends home, she pulled an unloaded gun on him. My mother wasn't usually like that.

My father was a captain in the Royal Air Force of England and drove over 150 different types of aircraft during the Second World War. You know, another daredevil. Gram's father was a pilot, too. A cosmic connection—definitely!

I married Eleanor Roosevelt's grandson, Rex, at sixteen, seventeen. I was still married to Rex when I was with David. Boy, I sound like a gadfly. But David watched me. The marriage lasted a couple of years. I got an apartment and started designing restaurants for Elmer Valentine of Whisky-a-Go-Go. And I had a flaming—oh, I guess I *am* more of a gadabout than I . . . I had a flaming affair with Steve McQueen—oh, it was just too much. . . .

Eighteen, nineteen. Then David came in a convoy of Porsches. All the Byrds bought the same 911 Porsches. He picked me up and carried me to the Porsche and took me up to his little bachelor apartment, where I drew pentagrams on the wall. That was the beginning of what he had wanted ever since I was a little girl. But I wouldn't sleep with him, and he was just enraged. [As David]: "Why, *everybody* wants to sleep with me!" And that cracked me up, because I grew up with him.

And he thought I wouldn't stay unless he bought a house, so he went and bought a beautiful house on Beverly Glen. That was the best year of my life.

Brandon deWilde, who was a good friend of David's and Peter Fonda's, brought Gram up to our Beverly Glen house one Christmas time. I remember seeing him in the back of Brandon's car as my old 1949 DeSoto Woody came down the driveway and stalled out. And David was a tyrant with me. He'd hand me fifty bucks and expect me to come home with forty. And would want a lot of stuff to show for the other ten. I mean a *real* . . . laying back on his bed, naked, *tyrant*. He got away with it until [hums] dum-de-dum-dum . . . this guy in the back of Brandon's car. I remember thinking to myself, He's got a certain charm, but he looks like a drowning water dog, a coon dog . . . you know, droopy.

And then Gram came up the hill. When I came back from shopping, David was laying there ranting and raving about the money I'd spent, and Susan deWilde slipped me an extra ten so I wouldn't get in that much trouble. And Gram stood in the background, going, "Hmmm." And here comes full-on telepathy. He could hear me and I could hear him, and did we start having a ball! Part of me knew he was going to change my life. And I was *ha-a-appy*. [Choking up] And healthy and young and very, very beautiful, I realize now, inside and out. Filled with light!

Okay, David, ironically enough, left for a Southern tour that night. Well, it's eleven at night, I'm cleaning the house, like all good ladies did while their old man was gone, ship-shape, incense in the drawers, socks with the sandalwood—when, *knock, knock, knock* at the door. There he is.

"How did you get here?"

"Brandon dropped me off."

"What do you need? David isn't here."

[With a southern drawl]: "Ah *know*. . . . I just want you to look at this music."

"Okay."

So he came in and we talked and he showed me his music. He said, "What am I trying to do?" And I said, "Well, okay, get a pencil and a paper and a flow of consciousness."

Now, the telepathy I spoke of before gets blocked whenever Gram did something that wasn't straight from the heart . . . and I started writing on that paper, okay, "Brass buttons, green silks, silver shoes"—flow of consciousness stuff about what he wanted.

And then . . . he backed me up into the kitchen cabinets, which I'd just finished with my psychedelic swirls and pentagrams and stuff, and he said [very Southern], "Listen, I've been lookin' for you for a *looong* time, and I'm gonna take you." And I heard a bell, distantly. And I tried to be brave.

"Don't be silly, I'm David's lady."

By the way, I was supposed to marry David in about three weeks. Cute. And he wouldn't stop staring me in the eyes. Now, for all my flitting about in the loose and free sixties, I was never unfaithful to David. It didn't occur to me.

Gram picked me up and that did it. David had picked me up, and that was wonderful. I like when a man can pick you up. . . . That's important, you know. It's like women and men really *are* different. And every woman in her heart of hearts, unless she's really enraged, wants a man to be able to carry her off, knowing what he's doing while carrying her off. He picked me up, carried me to the big bed, and in the middle of making love and my being unfaithful, he sat up and he said, *"God, I knew it was going to be like this!"* And I just looked at him and laughed.

And I was gone. I was gone.

12

The Trip

Boys, I want to move this band to Los Angeles." Gram didn't need to do a hard sell. The guys were ready. In New York they were going nowhere slow, and they knew that California had clearly become action central for the pop scene.

It wasn't just the Beach Boys and "California Girls," or the early Byrds, whose core group—Roger (then Jim) McGuinn, Gene Clark, and David Crosby—had formed as the Beefeaters in 1964 and had a hit in the spring of 1965 with Dylan's "Mr. Tambourine Man." Nor was it Barry McGuire, who stole some of Dylan's protest thunder with P. F. Sloan's "Eve of Destruction" the same year; or the Monkees or Paul Revere and the Raiders, who reminded everyone that novelty bands could hit the big time; or the San Francisco scene that blossomed like wildflowers with the Jefferson Airplane, the Grateful Dead, Big Brother and the Holding Company, Quicksilver Messenger Service, and, from across the Bay in Berkeley, Country Joe and the Fish.

And it wasn't just that one of his early heroes—John Phillips of the Journeymen—had given up on New York and roared into Los Angeles with the hit song "California Dreamin'." And that the Doors, Buffalo Springfield, Love, the Turtles, the Grassroots, the Association, and others were making their first noises.

The Trip

California was also home for a healthy country scene, and had been since the thirties, when Okies by the thousands migrated to the West Coast from the Oklahoma dust bowl, along with refugees from Texas and New Mexico. It was especially so during World War II, when people from throughout the South came there. All sought work and a better life; all brought with them their taste for the music of their soil.

In the sixties, country music had toeholds in urban and industrial centers like Bakersfield, Sacramento, San Francisco, and San Diego. In Los Angeles, a good number of artists identified with pop and rock music had no trouble demonstrating either their roots in or their love of country music; the Everly Brothers, Glen Campbell, Rick Nelson, Linda Ronstadt, and Michael Nesmith (who wrote "Different Drum," recorded by Linda and her Stone Poneys) come to mind. So does Bobby Darin, the eclectic singer-songwriter who, in 1963, wrote and sang "You're the Reason I'm Living."

There were also numerous musicians and bands who'd plowed the country road with little concern for commercial success: the Gosdin Brothers (Rex and Vern), the Nitty Gritty Dirt Band, the Dillards, and, before they found their way to the Byrds, Chris Hillman of the Hillmen and Clarence White of the Country Boys and Kentucky Colonels, were examples.

Gram, as was typical, had done the spadework. He found a house for the rest of the band on Willow Glen Avenue, off Laurel Canyon Boulevard and just north of Sunset.

He, of course, was in love, and would be living with Nancy.

In Los Angeles, Gram's contacts didn't take long to come through. Brandon deWilde's friend Peter Fonda was starring in *The Trip*, a hippie exploitation film (shot "in psychedelic color") based on the remains of a script by Jack Nicholson.

Peter met Gram and the rest of the Sub Band at Brandon's house, took a liking to them, and talked Roger Corman, the producer, into giving them a role. In April, with the South African emigré trumpet player, Hugh Masekela, producing, the band cut a song by Gram, "Lazy Days." However, Corman rejected it. According to Peter, the producer didn't think the song was "acid" enough.

The Sub Band still managed to get into the film, playing on stage in a key nightclub scene. But between quick cuts of dancing, painted bodies, and light-show effects, there was barely a glimpse of the band. And they were lip-, guitar-, and drum-syncing to music played by the Electric Flag, a San Francisco-based band led by Chicago blues guitarist Michael Bloomfield. (In the film, the music was credited to "The American Music Band," a slogan the Flag used.)

Peter, like Brandon, wanted to be a singer, and when Gram visited Peter at his house, they would play their guitars and sing

Everly Brothers and Buddy Holly songs. Gram sang his "November Nights" for Fonda, and the actor decided to record it. Gram was thrilled. He taught Peter the guitar parts, and a few weeks later, "November Nights" was released on the Chisa label. For the B side, Fonda sang Donovan's hit, "Catch the Wind."

Peter encouraged Gram to stay in Hollywood. "The streets here are paved with gold!" he told Gram.

With the help of Ronnie Herrin, who worked at the Whisky-a-Go-Go, the Sub Band found some work, opening for such bands as Iron Butterfly, Love, and the Peanut Butter Conspiracy. But the gigs were too occasional, and life in L.A. was lazy. Barry Tashian, who'd hung out with the Sub Band in the Bronx, was now hanging out with them at the Laurel Canyon house. Gram would call sometimes and encourage the band to get going. But there was far more talk about playing than actual playing. Instead, the guys would go to flea markets or, on occasion, to the desert.

Gram needed to perform. Soon after arriving in Hollywood, he'd found his way to Nudie's Rodeo Tailors. Nudie Cohen, outfitter to the country stars ever since cowboys got to be stars, regaled Gram with tales about his buddy, Hank Williams. Nudie transformed Gram into a rhinestone cowboy and turned him loose on the country music clubs in and around Los Angeles.

Gram said his ambition "was to go to the honky-tonks and win the talent contests and show them that a guy with long hair could be accepted."

He claimed that it took him two years to win the contest at the Palomino, the best known of the clubs. Every Thursday, Gram drove out to "the Pal" in North Hollywood, sat among the crowd, and waited his turn. "And for two years I was beaten by some yodeling grandmothers and the same guy, who sang 'El Paso' every week."

Sometimes, Bob Buchanan accompanied Gram on stage. Bob was a native of Michigan who'd just left the New Christy Ministrels when he met Gram at a house Fred Neil, the singer-songwriter who Gram had befriended, was renting while recording in Los Angeles. With their affection for Fred as a link, Bob and Gram became fast friends; Nancy helped find Bob an apartment just behind the one she shared with Gram. And Bob joined Gram at the Pal.

As Bob recalls, the person they lost to, every time out, was a man in a wheelchair who sang Johnny Cash. A guy in a chair singing "I Walk the Line" as good as Cash was a hard act to follow, and an impossible one to beat.

Talking to Judith Simms in *Rolling Stone*, Gram portrayed himself as the Clint Eastwood of the guitar-slinging scene. "When things got tough at the Palomino, I went to the tougher ones,"

Gram said. He heard about The Aces, in the city of Industry, twenty-four miles east of Hollywood, out near Richard Nixon country. There, "They keep it going all night long on Saturday and reopen the bar at six in the morning. I started going out there every weekend. The first couple of times I nearly got killed; there I was in my satin bell-bottoms and the people couldn't believe it. I got up on stage and sang, and when I got off, a guy said to me, 'I want you to meet my five brothers. We were gonna kick your ass, but you can sing real good, so we'll buy you a drink instead.' Thank God I'd got on that stage."

But more than anything, Gram was still looking to get his band into a recording studio again.

Lee Hazlewood was a singer, songwriter, arranger, and producer from Oklahoma, with credits ranging from R&B groups like the Coasters to rockers like Duane Eddy. He helped sculpt the tough-girl voice and pose that sent Nancy Sinatra to the top of the charts with "These Boots Are Made for Walkin'" in 1966. By that time, he had his own record label, LHI.

Not long after moving to Los Angeles, the Sub Band connected with LHI through two intermediaries: a manager, Steve Aldsberg, and a friend of Steve's, a singer named Suzi Jane Hokom. Suzi was a girlfriend and employee of Lee's with one production credit: a pop band from Amarillo, Texas, called the Kitchen Sink. Steve took her to the Sub Band's house for a visit, heard them go through a few songs, and liked what they heard. Right away, Gram, who was two years younger than Suzi Jane, stood out. Suzi suggested to Lee that he sign the band.

But before he could, the Submarine Band broke up.

The split had begun even before they moved to Los Angeles, according to Ian. When Gram was visiting in California over the winter, Ian had met with Barry Tashian and the Remains' keyboard player, Billy Briggs. Playing music in the egg-carton room, they began talking about someday putting together a different kind of group. Perhaps anticipating such a possibility, Barry and Billy had followed the Sub Band out to Los Angeles. Ian liked the Sub Band's outlaw, out-of-the-mainstream approach, but after a few months of hardly any work, things were getting stale.

Around the end of May, Gram told the rest of the band that he wanted to focus on traditional country. It was a perfect opening for Ian. While John Nuese stuck with Gram, Ian and Mickey split to go with Barry and Billy in a loose new aggregation.

The new band, said Ian, would play everything the Sub Band

did, plus bebop, western swing, and, apparently, whatever else might occur to them. He came up with an appropriately free-wheeling, mixed-up name: the Flying Burrito Brothers.

The very first lineup actually included Gram, according to Barry. They played songs like "Truck Driving Man" at a tiny club in the San Fernando Valley.

At an audition at a country club in Topanga called the Corral, the Burritos met a band led by Leon Russell, the Oklahoma-born session player and producer. Some of Leon's sidekicks would become regulars in the Burritos as well.

It may not sound as if what the Burritos were doing was that far afield of what Gram wanted. Gram's "cosmic American music," after all, included country and R&B as its main ingredients. The differences, apparently, were in purity and presentation. "They were into small rock clubs and stuff like that," said Gram to a radio interviewer. He wanted to try straight-ahead country. "I can't really sing about anything else," he said.

In a rambling, stoned interview with Chuck Casell of A&M Records in 1972, Gram discoursed on country music. "It's a beautiful, beautiful idiom that's been overlooked so much, and so many people have the wrong idea of it. God, I just can't believe it. When you say 'country music' to people, what some people think, how little they know. . . ."

He praised Merle Haggard and Hank Snow, but, he said, "When they think of these guys, they can't think of anything but bad stuff. They think of a WASP cab driver listening to three-chord music. If they can listen to mountain gospel, if B. Mitchell Reed (a popular disc jockey in New York) can play that to them, they sure ought to be able to kick some shit. Because that's where it comes from, where the whole feeling comes from."

Ian and the first Burritos, meantime, bounced around local clubs. "They would have a different personality every night," said Gram. Their top priority, Ian said, was to play music and to get the same kicks from it that they had as teenagers. In fact, they made it a point *not* to try for a recording deal. When people began to recognize them on the street, they decided things had gotten too big. Ian and several others headed back East, leaving the Burritos' name up for grabs.

But Gram was still a couple of bands and bumpy rides away from finding a use for that name. Right then, in 1966, he had a recording contract. A real one.

In 1972, he expressed regret over what it took to get to that point.

"I got an album together, but it took breaking the group up," he said. "The only way it got recorded was . . . I had to split and let all these guys down." He hinted that, like Ian, he'd been ready for a change before the move to California. "The time wasn't right; we got disappointed and we were broke and hungry," he said of the Sub Band's stay in the Bronx. "I came out here to California and had to hustle . . . had to get *Lee Hazlewood*"—Gram said the name as if he'd found it at the bottom of a barrel—"and say, 'Okay, just let me record an album, I won't take any money for it, unless it's a Top 10 album; just give me money to go into the studio.' And he said, 'Okay, but my old lady has to produce it.' I said, 'Yeah, great.'"

13

Safe at Home

With only John Nuese by his side, Gram called on his friend and neighbor, Bob Buchanan, to be part of the new International Submarine Band. But he still needed more help.

While Lee and Suzi Jane rounded up session musicians, Gram turned home in search of help. In June, he went to Winter Haven, looking up old Legends. He called on Jon Corneal, the drummer who'd gone off to Nashville, where he was making a good living, playing behind Grand Ole Opry acts and doing sessions. And he tried to lure another Legend, Jesse Chambers, westward. Jesse refused. He remembered Gram, in the old days in Florida, as prone to irrational actions and stranding people. He chose not to move across the country for him.

But Jon Corneal made the trip to Hollywood, and the sessions began, with Gram, John, and Jon as the nucleus, and with popular session player Joe Osborne on bass. John remembered going to a country club in Ontario, in Orange County, and finding a pedal steel player, J. D. Maness. "He had a DA haircut, skinny tie, and pointy shoes, and he was kinda leery of the hippie types, but we got him to come and do sessions." Veteran Nashville session man Earl

Safe at Home

"Les" Ball played piano. Suzi Jane and Glen Campbell, at that time a popular session guitarist, chipped in some harmony vocals.

The album was recorded in two sessions: one in July, which produced two songs—"Blue Eyes" and "Luxury Liner"—and one in November. For the second session, the bassist was Chris Ethridge, who'd worked with Judy Collins and heard about Gram through a chat with the guitarist Michael Bloomfield at a Monterey Jazz Festival.

To lend this long-haired group with the vaguely psychedelic name as much credibility as possible, Lee tapped various friends for the liner notes. Duane Eddy dropped all the right names: I hear that same George Jones, Buck Owens 'soul,' " he wrote. Don Everly, writing as if he'd just come from a conversation with Gram, chipped in: "I love R&B . . . but whatever happened to white soul? Whatever happened to music that is incredible *and* easy to believe? Some *youth* could get into it and really shake things up. Nashville needs to get some fresh air."

Gram called *Safe at Home* "the best country album I've done, because it had a lot of really quick-shuffle, brilliant-sounding country—" He was interrupted by his interviewer and never completed his point.

Others, however, did the job for him. In the *Los Angeles Times*, critic Pete Johnson gave the album a rave review. The songs, he wrote, were "done up purty authentic with a vitality not always found in traditional country performers." As for Gram: "His voice and pen seem meant for the medium, neither sounding artificial in the homey feel of good country music."

Hit Parader, which in 1968 had transformed itself from a fanzine with song lyrics into a solid, serious rock-and-roll magazine (with song lyrics), found the Sub Band of interest "for only one reason: The band is honestly dealing with country-western music. No gimmicks, no sound effects. Although the Buckaroos are much more exciting, the Submarine Band is at least exploring an area that most groups wouldn't touch with a ten-foot pole. . . . Get the album just to support the Submarine Band's bravery."

Although *Safe at Home* was traditional country, a rock-and-roll attitude was evident. Five songs were unadulterated country, including Merle Haggard's "I Must be Somebody Else You've Known"; Johnny Cash's "I Still Miss Someone" and "Folsom Prison Blues"; "A Satisfied Mind" by J. R. Hayes and J. Rhodes; and Jack Clement's "Miller's Cave." The last song was perfect for Gram, with its references to swamps and everglades, and the line, "I had a girl in Waycross, Georgia, but she had unfaithful ways." "Folsom Prison Blues" was coupled with Arthur Crudup's "That's All Right (Mama)," one of Elvis's first recordings. The other four songs were all Gram's: a rocking "Blue Eyes," the rolling "Luxury Liner," "Strong Boy," and the plaintive "Do You Know How It Feels to Be Lonesome?," which addressed the disorientation and distance the singer felt in a strange land:

> Did you ever try to smile at some people
> And all they ever seem to do is stare?

"Lonesome" echoed, ahead of its time, one of Gram's better and best-known songs, "Hickory Wind."

Safe at Home was, essentially, a solo album, a showcase for Gram and his music. He sang lead on every cut, showing off both the strengths and weaknesses of his crackly but emotional voice. As in his folkie days, he was willing to take chances on phrasings, like a Willie Nelson or a Frank Sinatra.

But the album's quick disappearance left Gram deflated. "We wanted to get something out of the ISB after all that time and effort, but it didn't happen," he complained.

With the album out, the next logical step for the Sub Band would have been to work it, to tour and promote the record.

They had a tour lined up. Gram, however, had other plans.

In his review published in mid-April of 1968, the *Los Angeles Times*'s Pete Johnson mentioned that Gram had appeared with the Byrds several times, "bolstering their incursions into country music." It was a liaison, Pete noted, that "could cause difficulties for the ISB."

He was right, just as Jesse Chambers, in declining to move from Florida to California for the Sub Band, had been right. Once Gram had met the Byrds and figured out two things—that the Byrds had a job opening and that *Safe at Home* wasn't going to be a hit—he lost all interest in the Sub Band.

Besides wanting to join an established band, Gram was having problems at home. Nancy was pregnant, and Gram was feeling tied down.

Marcia Katz, the Bronx teenager, followed Gram, Nancy, and the original Sub Band out to California. She lived on her own but was a frequent visitor to their apartment, and witnessed Gram and Nancy's ups and downs. For a long time, they loved each other. But once she became pregnant, things changed. As Marcia summarized the end of 1967: "Nancy was getting ready to have a baby; Gram was getting ready to be a star. Sadly, it separated them."

As uneasy as he was about being tied down, Gram continued to value what remained of his family ties.

Twice a year, he went home to Florida. True, he had to go to get the money from his trust fund. The amount ranged from about

Safe at Home

$30,000 to $100,000 a year depending on the status of the Snively family's various legal battles. Jim Carlton remembers watching Gram spilling about $15,000 in cash onto a bed at the Cypress Gardens Holiday Inn, and trying to put a dent into it by way of room service.

But also, Gram loved going home—especially to see his grandmothers, in Columbia, Tennessee, and in Winter Haven. In early 1968, he and Nancy, with Jim in tow, visited Haney at Cypress Gardens. She'd remarried and had a smaller house built just a short walk away from the big mansion, which John Jr. and May now occupied.

Jim remembered sitting and listening to Gram's grandmother talking about her childhood. "I could see the light in Gram's eyes come alive."

When the family wasn't around, Gram still managed to get lit up. Jim spent a weekend at the mansion with just Nancy and Gram. They dropped acid, and Gram spent an inordinate amount of time at the big Hammond B3 organ in the living room.

Aunt May, who thought her nephew was a member of the Rolling Stones, recalled jam sessions in the mansion, with Gram and local musicians blasting away on saxophones, drums, and her Hammond organ till two in the morning. Those, she said, "were the *fond* days."

One day, Gram and Jim went to a cafe on Cypress Gardens Road, and, after eating, Gram left behind the sunglasses he had gotten from Peter Fonda. Peter had worn them in *The Wild Angels*, the motorcycle movie he made in 1966 with Nancy Sinatra and Bruce Dern. The waitress ran out and brought them to Gram's car.

Gram took the glasses and fixed his sweetest smile on her. "Thank you very much," he said. "You're a *fine* country lady."

Nancy Parsons is talking about her life at 821¼ Sweetzer Avenue. They shared a one-bedroom apartment in a stately Tudor building that once belonged to Charlie Chaplin, and from their leaded windows they could look out to a Japanese garden and Charlie's old horse stables.

Inside, Nancy created a world that inspired novelist Eve Babitz to turn her and Gram into fiction. Eve, who had been photographing Gram since his arrival in Los Angeles, wrote in *Eve's Hollywood* about "Celeste" and "James Byrns" and their home.

> Instead of being furnished in LSD/Cowboys & Indians
> where the only place to sit was amps (or LSD/Victoriana

like San Francisco, where the only place to sit was chaises), this place was to stay in my personal history forever.

The floor was covered with a dark blue Persian rug, the walls hung with Chinese tapestries and the furniture was oak and polished; there was even a highboy with crystal glasses inside. And on top of all the surfaces were silver frames with flowers, roses, etched or embossed on them, and aged sepia faces smiling out from farther and farther away in the past until they seem to come equal with the very beginning of photography.

It was no wonder that Gram called Nancy "the Lady of the Manor."

★

Nancy, sitting at home in Santa Barbara, continues her story:

It was wonderful. It was everything I knew we were going to be. I purchased an antique set of scales to represent the light and the darkness, the yin and yang.

The house on Sweetzer really was beautiful. There was this little hobbit village . . . with panache. I found it, and we rented it.

Gram required of me vision. That I accompany him on his mission, that I be the female half of it.

Did Gram appreciate me? [Explodes] *I loved him and he loved me! Jesus Christ!*

But then with the baby . . . this other, powerful soul *blasted* in. Like, "I contracted to come through here, too, you guys! For all your big plans and all your stardom—just a minute—here I am!"

Larry Spector, who was a business manager, tried with all his might, which was considerable, to have my very own abortionist flown in. I ran to Susan Fonda, and Peter and Susan protected me from Gram, who was caught in between. A horrible place. This manager was telling him his career was at stake, and Peter Fonda turned on him and said, "And I thought you were an evolved . . . you're just a *punk*!" And Gram turned white. He wasn't convinced, no, but he didn't know which . . . all of a sudden, the great knowingness . . . the focus was totally, totally shattered.

One night, when Polly was four months old, it was about two in the morning. We'd just put her back down after a feeding. And I went to hold him in my arms, and he pulled away from me for the first time. It was like a *whoosh* . . . like you pulled two bars of light apart. And I went, "What's the matter? What's going on?" And he didn't do that silly song and dance. He said, "I know what I have to do."

Safe at Home

And I yelled: *"Don't leave me here alone!"*
And I saw in my mind's eye a long, winding road.
It was so painful . . . that he stopped feeling the way he had in the past.
Ever since that night, we didn't have that much time.

14

Sweetheart
of the Rodeo

Gram Parsons wasn't exactly
bursting with credentials when he came up for consideration as a
member of the Byrds after David Crosby was fired in 1968.

His first album was flopping; he wrote a song that Peter Fonda
recorded, and he had a few flickers of a bit part in *The Trip*.

He was just the kind of dilettante that a guy like Chris Hillman
should have snubbed.

Chris was the genuine article. He was from the San Diego area
and had gotten into folk music, as most young people had, through
Pete Seeger and the Weavers. But, while most college kids of the
early sixties, wary of juke-box pop, fell for the Sta-Prest folk music
of the Kingston Trio and the New Christy Minstrels, Chris made
another left turn—into the bluegrass music of Flatt and Scruggs
and the Gosdin Brothers.

Chris took up the mandolin, played local country music television shows, and got good enough at age sixteen to join the Golden
State Boys, a bluegrass institution in Southern California, where
he played alongside bassist-singer Rex Gosdin and guitarist-singer
Vern Gosdin. When the Gosdins made a shift toward folk music,
they renamed themselves the Hillmen. Their producer, Jim Dick-

son, moved on to co-manage a fledgling band called the Jet Set. When the Jet Set members found themselves in need of a bass player, Jim thought of Chris, even though he'd never played the instrument. Chris, who in 1964 was languishing, working for one of the folkie ensembles created by Christy Minstrels founder Randy Sparks, took the offer. Soon enough, the Jet Set became the Byrds.

Now, in March 1968, the band was a mess. Having lost original members Gene Clark and David Crosby, they were down to three. And, after completing their first post-Crosby album, *The Notorious Byrd Brothers*, they saw drummer Mike Clarke leave. The Byrds drafted Chris's cousin, Kevin Kelley. Now, with tour dates lined up, they were desperately looking for a new member when Chris remembered Gram Parsons.

They had met a few months earlier while waiting in line at their bank. "We had on the same kind of jeans and the same looks on our faces," Gram said in late 1972. Chris had heard of Gram; had heard some of the Submarine Band. And they had the same business manager: Larry Spector.

Chris brought Gram to a rehearsal studio, where Roger McGuinn, founder and leader of the Byrds, was thinking about hiring a piano player who could handle jazz as well as rock. He was still in an "Eight Miles High" mood, so he asked Gram if he could play some jazz. Gram, as he recalled, faked a blues figure of some sort, sang, played some guitar, and seemed like a nice guy who'd fit in with the band. Roger, in classic sixties, laissez-faire style, hired him on the spot. "I had no idea he was Hank Williams, Jr.," he said.

That remark was a trimmed-down, nineties version of the dilly of a comment Roger gave the rock magazine *Fusion* in the early seventies: "We just hired a piano player and he turned out to be Parsons, a monster in sheep's clothing. And he exploded out of this sheep's clothing. God! It's George Jones! In a sequin suit!"

Chris, thinking back, doesn't know how Gram got hired. The Byrds needed a tenor singer and an instrumentalist, preferably a keyboard player. Instead, they got a lead vocalist, a so-so-rhythm guitarist, and, once Gram and Chris found their common ground, yet another musical direction.

Country was hardly foreign to the Byrds. A year before Gram's arrival, and months before he was making the ISB album, the Byrds had Clarence White, the Kentucky Colonels' hot guitarist, playing on "Time Between" on their *Younger Than Yesterday* album. In 1965, the Byrds, at Chris's suggestion, recorded "Satisfied Mind," the Porter Wagoner hit of the mid-fifties.

Having gone from folk-rock to psychedelic music to electronic space sounds, McGuinn was thinking about a two-album set in which the Byrds would traverse nothing less than the history of twentieth-century music, beginning with traditional mountain music and ending, of course, electronically, state-of-the-future.

But his new Byrd put an end to that.

Gram, said Roger, had a "burning thing" for a contemporary take on country music—"to blend the Beatles and country; to really do something revolutionary. Gram thought we could win over the country audience. He figured, once they dig you, they never let go."

The Byrds' leader not only bought the pitch—lock, stock, and with both barrels blazing—he began listening to nothing but country radio stations. After Byrds shows, he said, the guys would go straight to the country music bars. Roger went to Nudie's and got properly outfitted. He even bought a Cadillac. "It was like an adventure."

Soon, the band decided to cut its next album in Nashville—Music City, U.S.A. And not only would they be the first long-haired folk-rock band from California to invade Nashville, they would crash the temple of all that was good and backward about country music: the Grand Ole Opry.

After rehearsals, the Byrds flew into Nashville for a week of sessions beginning on March 9 at the CBS Studios at Sixteenth and Hawkins Street (since renamed Music Square East and Music Circle South), a block away from the Country Music Hall of Fame. They were to work with producer Gary Usher, who'd steered them through the *Younger Than Yesterday* and *The Notorious Byrd Brothers* albums.

To help authenticate the Byrds' country efforts, Usher hired session players from Nashville, including steel guitarists J. D. Maness (who was on the ISB album) and Lloyd Green, and string bassist Roy M. Huskey (a veteran of sessions with, among many others, Lee Hazlewood). Clarence White, who'd been an uncredited sideman with the Byrds since Crosby's departure, signed on, as did John Hartford on fiddle and banjo, and Earl Ball (another ISB session player) on piano. Ex-Submarine Band drummer Jon Corneal also played.

At their first session, the Byrds recorded Bob Dylan's "You Ain't Goin' Nowhere" and a song Gram had written with Bob Buchanan, "Hickory Wind."

Meantime, Columbia had convinced the Grand Ole Opry's producers to let the Byrds on the show, on the very next night. At only twenty-one years old, Gram would be performing in country music's mecca. They would be guests in the half-hour slot hosted by Tompall Glaser and the Glaser Brothers. Years later, Tompall would emerge, along with Waylon Jennings, Willie Nelson, and Kris Kristofferson, as one of Nashville's "outlaw" country artists, singing and writing tough, rock-based music that rolled far away from the Music Row mainstream.

For now, the Byrds were in the mother church of country music, and they didn't need to be told to be on their best behavior. The Grand Ole Opry, started up in 1925, was the most powerful vehicle for country music from the forties through the sixties, with its 50,000-watt clear-channel signal reaching out from WSM, its flagship station in Nashville, to thirty states every Saturday night. It was a tightly run ship. When Hank Williams, who'd exploded onto the Ryman Auditorium stage with a debut that earned six encore calls, began missing shows, the Opry fired him.

It seems right that the Opry, since 1943, had been produced out of the Ryman, which was built as a tabernacle in 1912, and which still offered seating in long, curved, wooden pews and no air conditioning. On summer evenings, the Opry handed out paper fans.

On the evening of March 10, 1968, things were decidedly cool. Tompall Glaser gave the Byrds a big buildup, making sure to say that the boys were on Columbia Records and that they were singing a real country tune, Merle Haggard's "Sing Me Back Home," with Tennessee's own Gram Parsons on lead vocals.

Homegrown or not, Gram and the Byrds looked like spacemen to the audience. But, good Southerners most of them, they offered a polite hand. Some hooted at the band. Chris heard shouts of "Tweet-tweet!" and "Cut your hair!" But the audience warmed up when they found that these weirdos from out West could actually play.

After the first song, Tompall strode out, leading the applause. The Byrds had told the Opry that their second number would be "Life in Prison," so Glaser cued them: "Well, now you're going to do another Merle Haggard song, aren't you?"

Gram took the microphone. "We're not going to do that tonight," he said, taking everyone on stage and behind the scenes by surprise. "We're going to do a song for my grandmother, who used to listen to the 'Grand Ole Opry' with me when I was little. It's a song I wrote, called 'Hickory Wind.'"

The other Byrds looked at each other. They had gotten stoned backstage, and they weren't ready for a plot twist like this. They just managed to catch up with Gram, and the song proceeded smoothly.

Even as he sang, Gram could see, off to the side of the stage, the Opry's reaction. "The Glaser brothers just flipped out," he said. "They were yelling at us from off stage and stomping up and down. Roy Acuff [the 'King of the Cowboys,' who joined the Opry in 1938] was having fits."

After the two-song set, the Byrds strode by a crew of hostile Opry producers and staffers. Tompall Glaser collared Chris and yelled: "You made me look like a fool on the radio." Meanwhile, Skeeter Davis, who'd had her own skirmishes with Opry officials, ran over to the Byrds and greeted them with kisses. Said Gram: "She was so happy that somebody had finally blown those guys off."

In the audience, few knew that anything untoward had happened. But, as Roger McGuinn reminded me, the Opry was a controlled broadcast environment, complete with applause signs. Light them up and they'd clap. Shut them off and they'd shut up.

Gram's aunt Pauline, who was there with her mother and several other family members and friends, was unaware that anything was wrong. From where she sat, everybody loved the Byrds. As for Gram breaking format and upsetting the Opry, she responded with a rhetorical question. "Don't you think that was rather typical of him? He did what you didn't expect."

Chris figured that all Gram did was make his dream come true. "He took the reins. He was right smack into that—'Here I am on the Opry. I'm Hank Williams!'—so he went with it. He played the whole role out."

Returning to the CBS studio, the Byrds cut Woody Guthrie's "Pretty Boy Floyd" on Monday, the traditional "I Am a Pilgrim" the next day, and wrapped up their week with another Dylan song, "Nothing Was Delivered." Gram invited Grandma Nancy and Aunt Pauline and her kids to one session, proudly introducing them to the Byrds and some of the side musicians. Gram and several Byrds also visited her house for a late supper.

Gram clearly enjoyed being home. The South had not been kind to him, but in the song he'd dedicated to his grandmother, Gram addressed its tug-and-pull:

> It's a hard way to find out
> That trouble is real
> In a faraway city, with a faraway feel
> But it makes me feel better
> Each time it begins
> Callin' me home, hickory wind

"Hickory Wind," simply structured as it was—three verses, no chorus—was one of Gram's finest moments as a songwriter. He wrote the song on a train, on his way back to Los Angeles from Florida in early 1968. In Coconut Grove, where he'd gone to see Fred Neil, he'd run into Bob Buchanan, the former Christy Minstrels member whom he'd met in L.A., who was also visiting Fred.

Bob and Gram decided to ride back to L.A. together. On the Santa Fe Super Chief, the two men stayed mostly to themselves—Gram was having problems with Nancy, and Bob was having problems with drugs—until Gram pulled out a guitar and asked Bob to help out with a song he was writing.

Gram had the first verse down, recalling oak trees in South Carolina that he used to climb and establishing the hickory wind as a nostalgic symbol of his youth in the South.

But he needed a second verse. Bob drew on their common experiences in the music business in L.A. and came up with a second verse based on their experiences there, and the hollowness even its promised riches and pleasures could bring.

They worked together on the final verse, about a distant city with a distant feel. That, to Bob, was the key. "That's the theme of the song: it's pretty damned rough trying to make it in the city, with all the business and bullshit."

What made the song so universal was its recognition of one of life's big questions—Is that all there is?—combined with pleasant evocations of youth and the safety a kid felt being at home among the pines, the oak, and the brush. All recalled by the gentle sound, even if it's only in one's mind, of a hickory wind.

★

After wrapping up the sessions in Music City, the Byrds took off for a tour of East Coast colleges. Buoyed by a standing ovation at MIT, the band returned to Los Angeles in early April for their West Coast debut, in the form of a farewell party for their former publicist, Derek Taylor, whose clients included the Monterey Pop Festival, A&M Records, and the Beatles. For the farewell, the Byrds chose to play the Hollywood club in which they'd made their debut three years before: Ciro's.

Rolling Stone magazine's L.A. correspondent, Jerry Hopkins, was there, and filed a report giving Gram his first ink in what was emerging as the rock world's most important journal.

In the story, Gram was referred to as "Graham Parsons," but he got an endorsement from McGuinn: "Graham's bag is country and we're going to let him do his thing, and support him and work together on things." Gram also got a good review: "They appear secure in the country milieu," Hopkins wrote about their set at Ciro's. "Graham sings often and he sings well, sharing 'lead voice' with Roger."

In Los Angeles, the Byrds completed the *Sweetheart of the Rodeo* sessions with a Tim Hardin song, "Reputation"; the traditional British ballad "Pretty Polly"; the two Haggard songs "Life in

Prison" and "Sing Me Back Home"; another country standard, "You're Still On My Mind"; two songs suggested by Gram, "You Don't Miss Your Water" and the Louvin Brothers' "The Christian Life"; and two more songs written by Gram, "One Hundred Years from Now" and "Lazy Days" (the song that had been rejected for *The Trip*).

In early May, the Byrds took off to Europe, where they played two concerts at the site of the former underground mecca, Middle Earth, in Covent Garden. Gram was on electric piano and rhythm guitar; to underline the country sound, Doug Dillard played banjo. Among the audience were Mick Jagger and his girlfriend, the singer Marianne Faithfull.

The Byrds had shared concert bills with the Stones, and in London, Mick and Keith had played host to the Byrds. Keith was unaware of any personnel changes. "I went to see McGuinn," he said.

Roger remembered going out to Stonehenge with the other Byrds and Mick and Keith. It was a wet, blustery night, and the musicians passed a bottle of Johnny Walker Red around to fight the cold during the long trek out to the monument. The Byrds got so soaked that night that, while they were having breakfast, Mick sent a driver out to buy them socks.

Sometime during the visit to the monument, Roger told the Stones about the Byrds' plans to play in South Africa after another London engagement in July.

Miriam Makeba, the South African folk singer, had suggested that Roger go to her native country and witness apartheid—the governmental policy keeping blacks separated from whites—for himself.

Roger was a seeker. He wanted to know about things firsthand. He knew that fellow entertainers had boycotted the country, but after making inquiries, he received assurances that the Byrds would be playing to both black and white people. He naively interpreted that to mean mixed audiences, and he thought that he'd be striking a blow against apartheid.

The Stones didn't argue with Roger about his plans, but he remembered them getting onto Gram about it. Gram, at twenty-one, was already listening hard to the more worldly, twenty-four-year-old Keith Richards.

Between the two Middle Earth concerts, the Byrds flew to Rome and played the Piper Club. The shows were a knockout, but as they flew back to Los Angeles, they were headed for trouble. And, having met the Rolling Stones, Gram had more than a little stardust in his eyes.

15

You Ain't Goin' Nowhere

Lee Hazlewood had worked hard to establish his first record company, and he didn't like watching the Submarine Band falling apart just as its first album was being issued. Nor did he appreciate the leader of that band wandering off to another group. He decided to get hard-nosed.

He contacted CBS Records to inform the company that LHI Productions still owned the rights to Gram's vocal performances, if not to his compositions or to his work as an instrumentalist.

On the album *Sweetheart of the Rodeo*, Gram had sung lead vocals on "The Christian Life," "You Don't Miss Your Water," "Hickory Wind," and several others. After Lee's call, Columbia ordered Gram's voice stripped off the album and replaced by Roger's and Chris's. Roger got to work putting his own voice—with a brand-new southern accent—where Gram's had been.

Gram, who admitted that his release from LHI was "kind of shaky"—that is, he marched into LHI's offices one day and simply announced that he was going with the Byrds—was upset with the results. On at least one track, "The Christian Life," his voice was left on, he said, but "way in the background, as a guide to go by; it didn't work."

Hickory Wind

As Emmylou Harris told writer Alanna Nash, in her book, *Behind Closed Doors:* "If you listen real close in the headset, you can hear him, because his phrasing is so different from Roger McGuinn's. It's like hearing a ghost, because his phrasing is the real traditional, Louvin Brothers phrasing, and Roger McGuinn sang it like, you know, Roger McGuinn. And there's such an overlapping that you can hear him in the spaces where Roger doesn't sing, because Gram elongates his phrasing."

Gram thought the strange mix "gave it too much of the old Byrds sound, which we were fighting against—not because it wasn't any good, but because there was all this other stuff to work with, and we didn't need to look back, as Bob Dylan once sort of said."

Producer Gary Usher also dropped three cuts: "Pretty Polly," which Gram had picked for his daughter Polly, and on which Roger sang lead; "Reputation," with Gram on lead vocals; and Gram's "Lazy Days," again with Gram up front. Although CBS and LHI resolved the legal matter, those tracks stayed off the album. "We were just about to scratch 'Hickory Wind' when somebody ran in with a piece of paper," said Gram. "That's the last one they had saved."

On another occasion, Gram said that the sessions went well—until the threat from LHI. "They had to pull a few things out of the can that weren't supposed to be used, things like 'Life in Prison' and '(An Empty Bottle, a Broken Heart, and) You're Still on My Mind.' We just did them as warm-up numbers. We could've done them a lot better. . . . They just chopped up the album however they wanted to."

Gram blamed Roger: "He erased it and did the vocals himself and fucked it up," he told Cameron Crowe in early 1973. In another interview, he blamed Gary Usher. "The producer decided it should go Hollywood freaky, and it wasn't the time for that. I thought it was the time for a *Nashville Skyline* or something like the album as I remember it, a serious country album. It was a great album that might as well have never been recorded. So there's another *Sweetheart of the Rodeo*, and, uh, I dig it."

Gary, who died of cancer in 1990, claimed that the threat of a lawsuit had no bearing on the album. Speaking in 1988 with *The Cosmic American Music News*, the magazine of the Gram Parsons Memorial Foundation, the producer said Roger did overdub some songs because of legal problems, but that the differences were resolved while the group was in Nashville, "so whoever sang leads on the songs . . . were there because that's how we wanted to slice the album up." Roger, he said, was wary "that Parsons was getting a little bit too much out of this thing. . . . He didn't want the album to turn into a Gram Parsons album."

You Ain't Goin' Nowhere

Terry Melcher, the early Byrds producer who later worked with Gram, said Gram deeply resented Roger for what happened with *Sweetheart* and bore a grudge for years.

Both Roger and Chris disputed Gary Usher's version of events. Roger insisted that there was a legal problem, that all of Gram's lead vocals had to be erased, and that when the problem was resolved, Gram restored his vocals. Roger's was left on some tracks, but, he pointed out, he'd redone "Hickory Wind," and Gram wound up with the lead vocal on it.

With the album finally completed, the Byrds returned to London in July for "Sounds '68," a charity concert at Albert Hall, headlined by the Move and including the Easybeats, Bonzo Dog Doo Da Band, and a young white soul singer named Joe Cocker. But it was the Byrds, who kicked their set off with a searing "So You Want to Be a Rock 'n' Roll Star," who stole the show. *The New Musical Express* added "Grahm" Parsons to the growing list of misspellings, but reporter Nick Logan reported: "A good section of the 4,000 audience was there to see them alone, and they let them know it."

With their popularity in Europe happily reconfirmed, the Byrds prepared to leave for their next engagements—all in South Africa—when Gram announced that he would not be going.

In a statement to *Melody Maker*, the British pop newspaper, Gram said he'd been thinking about the issue of South Africa's policy of apartheid for some time. "I first heard about the South African tour two months ago," he said. "I knew right off when I heard about it that I didn't want to go. I stood firmly on my conviction."

"It was total garbage," said Chris, who flew into a rage when Gram deserted the band. "I really wanted to murder him," he said. He was certain that Gram simply wanted to hang out with Mick and Keith. "They were filling his head, I'm sure, with stories about South Africa."

They were. Almost from the moment they met, said Keith, Gram was confiding in him.

"I've got something I want to talk to you about," Gram began. "Maybe you can help me." He told Keith about the Byrds' plans and added, "I have a funny feeling about it and I don't know much about it. What's the deal with South Africa?"

"Well," Keith remembered telling Gram, "it's like when you were growing up down South, if you were the wrong color. It's exactly the same."

Later—possibly at Stonehenge, or at Mick's flat on Chester Square afterward—Gram asked Mick and Keith point-blank whether he should drop out of the trip to South Africa. Keith said: "Well, let me put it this way: *We* wouldn't go." And that settled it.

"I was instrumental in his leaving the Byrds," said Keith, "because I said, 'Nobody goes to play South Africa.' "

Gram later said that his hatred of racial segregation dated much further back than his last cup of tea with the Stones.

"Something a lot of people don't know about me is that I was brought up with a Negro for a brother," he said. "Like all Southern families, we had maids and servants, a whole family called the Dixons that took care of us. Sammy Dixon was a little older than me, and he lived with and grew up with me, so I learned at a real close level that segregation was just not it."

Aside from the slight overstatement about all Southern families having servants, Gram was reaching a bit when he recalled his occasional baby-sitter as a "brother;" none of his childhood playmates recalled Sammy being around.

However sincere Gram might have been, few who knew him believed him. Besides his attachment to the Stones, theories on why he pulled out ranged from his anger at Roger over *Sweetheart of the Rodeo* to an increasing fear of flying—the trip to Johannesburg required a stopover in the Canary Islands, off the coast of Morocco, for refueling—to one advanced by Carlos Bernal, a Byrds roadie who was pressed into service as a guitarist.

Gram dropped out, he said, "because he couldn't have things just exactly how he wanted them. . . . He wanted a steel guitar to do a lot of his tunes. He wanted things that the band wasn't prepared to jump into overnight. So Gram didn't make it to the airport."

The South African tour was a disaster physically, mentally, musically, and politically. The tour, Chris conceded, "was a stupid farce and he [Gram] was right. We shouldn't have gone. But he shouldn't have let us down by copping out at the end."

On their return, and after recovering from his exhaustion, Roger announced a replacement for Gram: Clarence White. It was August, and Gram Parsons had been a Byrd for just over four months.

At the end of the month, CBS released *Sweetheart of the Rodeo* with an ad showing the band—Gram included—behind a half-height brick wall on which was scrawled a too-neat graffito: THIS COUNTRY'S FOR THE BYRDS.

Rolling Stone gave *Sweetheart* a lukewarm review in its September 14 issue. Critic Barry Gifford suggested that no purist country fans listen to the "affectedly-straight C&W" effort. He left Gram unmentioned and judged the band's overall performance "simple, relaxed and folky." His final line: "It ought to make the 'Easy Listening' charts. 'Bringing it all back home' has never been an easy thing to do."

The review drove Jon Landau, *Rolling Stone*'s chief music essayist, to his typewriter. He singled out the Byrds as the most consistently appreciative of country music among various rock bands dipping into the music.

Compared to Buffalo Springfield, Jon wrote, "the Byrds have approached country music as an entity in itself and have aimed for a greater degree of fidelity to the rules of the style." He praised Gram Parsons and various Nashville session players, and he concluded, as if in response to Barry: "The Byrds, in doing country as country, show just how powerful and relevant unadorned country music is to the music of today. And they leave just enough rock in the drums to let you know that they can still play rock and roll. That's what I call bringing it all back home."

Musically, *Sweetheart* was on solid ground. "The Byrds have always jumped around in different forms," Jon noted. "Every Byrds album is like an audio magazine containing the things that interest us at the moment."

But rock fans rejected the album. *Sweetheart* sold less than 50,000 and was the Byrds' poorest-selling album to date.

In 1968, the most uproarious year of the sixties, with 10,000 dead in Vietnam, campus revolts, King and Kennedy assassinated, the riots in Watts and Chicago, and the continuing wars against wars, young people were ripping and burning symbols of the Establishment everywhere. If any music form represented the straight world, it was country—even if it was being played by dope smokers.

Forget educated arguments about the purity of the music. Forget its embrace by the Spoonful, the Springfield, and Bob Dylan. Forget that Jann Wenner, editor of *Rolling Stone*, in a persuasive essay in 1968, stated, "There is no question that rock and roll is connected with much of the country and western tradition"—and went further: "The soul music tradition has been deeply involved with country sounds; they are both from the South, and the marriage of the two is what was called rock and roll. In many ways it is the music of reconciliation, of people who have been wronged or wronged others, but who, in the end, found out that that's the way it is."

But in 1968, country music, to most left-thinking hipsters, was backwood, hillbilly, rednecks—in short, square. Kind of like Ralph Emery, the Nashville deejay who slapped at the Byrds when they were in town, and whom the Byrds slapped back, by way of a Gram Parsons composition, in "Drug Store Truck Driving Man."

The Byrds, however, felt the longest sting. Going country, Roger concluded, was a bad move. The band never attracted the country audience it hoped to gain, and it lost a good part of its rock following.

What Roger forgot was the album itself. Flawed as it was,

Sweetheart of the Rodeo was a musical landmark, a statement that few others could make. For their daring as well as for their music, the Byrds have been rewarded with induction into the Rock and Roll Hall of Fame, and Columbia issued a four-CD retrospective of the Byrds in 1990, including several of the lost *Sweetheart* tracks featuring Gram Parsons on lead vocals.

On its own, the *Sweetheart* album has worn well through the years, and even inspired a young female country act to name itself Sweethearts of the Rodeo.

Roger admits that, in recent years, *Sweetheart* has become a classic. "It was picked by *Rolling Stone* as one of the top 200 albums of the last twenty-five years," he noted.

But back when it counted, *Sweetheart* was ignored. The album stalled at number seventy-seven on the *Billboard* album charts. The Byrds' previous album, *The Notorious Byrd Brothers*, peaked at number forty-seven. Before that, *Fifth Dimension* and its follow-up, *Younger than Yesterday*, had hit number twenty-four.

In the summer of 1968, all Gram Parsons meant to Roger was trouble. In South Africa, Roger had barely survived a near nervous breakdown.

Meanwhile, Gram went with Keith and his common-law wife, actress Anita Pallenberg, to Redlands, Keith's country house in West Wittering, a resort village ninety minutes southwest of London on the coast of the English Channel.

Here the Okefenokee Kid and the Dartford Devil traded licks and forged a friendship. And when Gram returned to Los Angeles in August, he was accompanied by Keith and Anita. At the airport, they were met in style by a car and driver.

The driver was Phil Kaufman.

16

Flying Again

Even while the presses were rolling with the story of his departure from the Byrds, and while he was getting to know Keith Richards, Gram was putting his next band together. From Redlands, he was on the phone to Chris Ethridge in Los Angeles.

Chris, remember, had worked on the International Submarine Band album. When the Sub Band never surfaced again, he joined the crowd that got involved with the first Flying Burrito Brothers.

Gram had also thought back to conversations he'd had with Chris Hillman about someday putting together a country band outside the confines of the Byrds, as relaxed as those were. It'd be a traditional country band, only with young hipsters playing the music.

In August, the Byrds were going through the hell that was their South African visit, and Chris was not in the mood to talk to Gram about anything.

That, of course, didn't deter Gram from telling the London press that he had a new band together. He told *Melody Maker:* "The group's already formed, although I can't say too much about it. . . . It's basically a southern soul group playing country and gospel-oriented music with a steel guitar."

Hickory Wind

While Gram and Chris Hillman were with the Byrds, they sat in on a session or two with Clarence White, longtime country drummer Gene Parsons (no relation), and fiddler-singer Gib Gilbeau. Gene and Gib had worked together since 1963, and with Clarence since 1966. Gene saw the hookup with Gram and Chris as "prototype Burritos," but before anything could happen, Gram left the Byrds, Chris Hillman recruited Clarence to replace him, and Clarence, in turn, lobbied successfully to get Gene into the band.

Returning to Los Angeles from London, Gram ran into Richie Furay, whom he'd met years before in New York. Furay had gone on to form Buffalo Springfield with Stephen Stills. Now, Richie, along with guitarist Jim Messina, was putting a new band together, to be known as Pogo.

For a time, Richie and Gram talked about working together. But Richie, who'd blended rock with country in the past by way of Rusty Young's steel guitar on countrified songs like "Kind Woman," was leaning toward a rock sound. Gram maintained his country vision. When it became clear that they couldn't agree on a lineup for their band, each decided to form his own group.

Meanwhile, Chris Hillman quit the Byrds. In addition to the South Africa debacle and the personnel changes, there were financial problems. Chris was a partner with Roger in the Byrds (other musicians were considered hired hands) but had given Larry Spector power of attorney and access to their bank accounts. When the accounts dwindled from $100,000 to $20,000—due to expenses, Larry explained—Chris exploded and quit.

Using music and marijuana to help mend fences, he and Gram got together, played a few country tunes, and, with Chris Ethridge all set to play bass, began looking for a pedal steel player. "We found Sneeky Pete," Gram told Bud Scoppa a few years later, "and it was just like that, one thing right after another. All of a sudden we had a band."

Well, not exactly. It was only after they'd failed to lure two Nashville veterans that the Burritos called on "Sneeky" Pete Kleinow, a native of Michigan, an animator whose credits included the Gumby cartoon character. Pete was a regular around L.A.'s country music club scene and had sat in with the Byrds on occasion after *Sweetheart*.

Gram tried to get Clarence White to leave the Byrds. According to fiddler Byron Berline, Clarence was up for a job with the Byrds when Gram got the position. Now that he'd finally become a Byrd, he wasn't about to give it up. Gene Parsons also got an offer to join Gram and Chris's new band. He chose to honor his commitment to Roger, and he wanted the chance, along with Clarence, to help revamp the Byrds' historically erratic live performances.

Flying Again

That left Gram and company without an official drummer. But they had the core of a band and a dandy name. It was the one left behind by Ian Dunlop: The Flying Burrito Brothers lived again.

While the Burritos jelled, Gram and various musician buddies became regulars at the country music clubs, running into a floating jam party led by a pair of musical magnets named Delaney and Bonnie Bramlett.

Delaney was a guitarist from Randolph, Mississippi, whose love of country music led to a gig in a bowling alley near the L.A. airport. There he met Bonnie Lynn, a singer from Granite City, Illinois. She loved the blues and R&B—she even worked once as a temp Ikette—and together they made the rounds of small clubs around Los Angeles—clubs like the Prelude and Snoopy's Opera House—the same ones Gram had hit. They used not so much a set band as a group of "friends," usually anyone who'd be willing to make the trips out to tiny country joints in the San Fernando Valley, and beyond, and work for nothing.

They gathered plenty of musicians who found the Bramletts' stew of country, gospel, R&B, and rock and roll too delicious to pass up. Songs like Bonnie and Carl Radle's "Get Ourselves Together" were put on earth for this endless layering of countless jam-happy players, including Leon Russell and several musicians who'd go on to work with the Rolling Stones: drummer Jim Keltner, keyboardist Bobby Whitlock, and horn players Bobby Keyes and Jim Price.

In the audience, Gram listened intently. "That's where the idea for big-time country music started hitting me," he said. Watching Delaney and Bonnie, "I realized that I could do it, too, and that people were not so hung up on sick music as I thought. There was a little bit of room for funk, and I got that crazy idea again."

Gram lent the couple a hand by introducing them to Alan Pariser, a rock manager who helped get them onto Elektra Records. As a sign of gratitude, Delaney and Bonnie presented Gram with a plaque inscribed "to Graham Parsons." Gram went nuts over the typo—"Why can't they *ever* get it right?" he complained to Nancy—but he cherished the token of their friendship.

Delaney and Bonnie were always pulling him aside, Gram liked to remember. "They were saying how much country music meant, and it was important that somebody did it. 'Listen, pal, you've got to keep doing this.' And we kept doing it."

Gram's only problem was figuring out what "it" was.

The Delaney and Bonnie jams rekindled his interest in an eclectic, anything-goes approach. But he still wanted to make music based on traditional country. One minute, he'd downgrade the band's chances for success: "We were like punks. I mean, how could we ever be commercial with a name like 'Flying Burrito Brothers'?" The next, he'd talk about wanting to become a "hot country group that could provide material that would become classic songs everyone would record."

Consistent with his vision of country being performed by long-haired guys with a rock-and-roll consciousness, he wanted songs that would eschew the Nashville staples of drunken cowpokes pining away for lost love and decrying their cheatin' ways. The Burritos would be more contemporary in their song subjects and outlook. However, Gram said, to stay true to country, the music would be simple. "We are playing roots music. . . . It's a form of love music, a binding type of music between people. Our music is emotional because all our music takes all our emotions. . . . The Burritos exist solely through music, which is just a shade different from what most other people do in this area. It's entirely us. . . . We're playing with white soul, and soul is universal. And the universality of roots music has stood the test of time."

The Burritos had no problem scoring a record deal. It didn't hurt that they were fronted by two former Byrds. "We had more Byrds than the Byrds did," said Chris Ethridge. Mo Ostin, president of Reprise, one of Warner Bros. Records' two major labels, had heard Joan Baez singing "Hickory Wind," and he was impressed enough to make an offer. (Mo was also impressed when Gram told him that his friend, Keith Richards, might produce the album.)

But before he could work out a deal, Tom Wilkes, the art director at A&M Records and a neighbor of Chris Hillman's, got the word on the Burritos to A&M Records. Gram and Chris paid a visit to Jerry Moss, cochairman of A&M.

A&M stood for the last names of its founders: trumpet player, singer, and record producer Herb Alpert and executive Jerry Moss. Alpert and his band, the Tijuana Brass, gave the label its first hit in 1962 with "The Lonely Bull," and in the mid-sixties had established itself with a contemporary take on what was being called middle-of-the-road music—youthful but decidedly easy-listening by such artists as the Baja Marimba Band, Claudine Longet, and the Sandpipers.

Now A&M wanted to rock. Through a distribution deal, it had hooked up with several British acts, including Procol Harum and Joe Cocker. It had signed a few California bands, including the Merry-Go-Round and We Five ("You Were Always On My Mind").

Along came the Burrito Brothers, and A&M snapped to. "They showed us some *toys* or something," said Gram. "They were fast talkers. Jerry and Herb came in real fast and said, 'Oh, well, gee, you can start right away here, and we'll give you the equipment and stuff.' "

Flying Again

Later on, Gram would complain that the Burritos' advance was minuscule. Chris Hillman thought each member got no more than a $1,500 advance. But the company would spend a handsome sum on the group, for little return.

The shopping spree began when Gram led his band into his favorite clothing store, Nudie's Rodeo Tailors on Lankershim. By now, Nudie Cohen had turned over the tailoring to an assistant named Manuel, but the flash had dimmed not one watt. Before long, the Burritos were the owners of some of the most outrageous outfits to come out of that shop. Chris Ethridge got a white jacket festooned with red and yellow roses, and matching slacks with roses running down the sides. Chris Hillman's suit was blue, with satin lapels and double-breasted peacocks, their feathers flowing over onto the sleeves. The back was taken up with a golden sunburst. Sneeky Pete, up to now a straight family man, found himself in a black jumpsuit decorated with a flying golden pterodactyl, a favored reptile from his days as an animator. For the drummer, yet to be chosen, Gram ordered a blazing red jacket decorated with glittering submarines, a nostalgic nod to one of his previous bands.

And for himself, Gram designed an outfit: a short-waisted white jacket and pants, the jacket festooned with cannabis sativa leaves and flowers. More flowers ringed the upper portion of the tight white slacks, so that each cheek was adorned with a pink rose. The back of the jacket was dominated by a red cross sending off showers of sequins and glitter. And on the lapel, Manuel embroidered a pair of girls taking the name Nudie to heart.

As Gram reasoned: *"Somebody* had to make a show out of it."

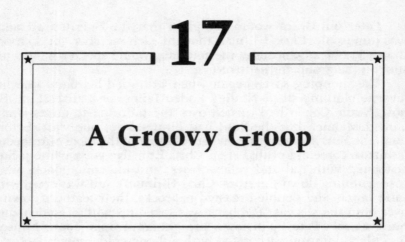

17

A Groovy Groop

There were some who thought that Gram was too much surface and not enough substance, that he was more interested in the deal—and what it would bring in money, limos, and Nudie suits—than in the music.

But surface rarely hurt pop phenomena. Sometimes, a little surface was just what was needed to give the substance a chance. The Burritos had more than a bit of each. On the surface side, they got into such publications as a teen fanzine's quickie paperback, Flip's *Groovy Guide to the Groops!* At the end of a straightforward description of the band's members and their *raison d'être* ("It's an effort to make country music the music of the young"), the entry concluded: "Their only message to the world is, 'Find a way to love, and get out of your rut.'"

Among the Burritos' most adoring followers were two members of Frank Zappa's all-girl group, the GTOs (Girls Together Outrageously). They were Mercy Peters ("Miss Mercy") and Pamela DesBarres ("Miss Pamela," author of the book *I'm With the Band: Confessions of a Groupie*).

Pamela, who described Gram in her book as "totally countrified in a slinky bedroom-eyed way," saw the Burritos 200 times.

A Groovy Groop

She admitted having a crush on Gram, even though her main target was Chris Hillman.

Miss Mercy once won a writing contest sponsored by *L.A. Weekly* with an engaging, if awe-struck paean to Gram. She had seen him at the Hollywood premiere of the Beatles' movie *Yellow Submarine* in the winter of 1968.

"I went comatose and I was captured and spellbound from here to eternity because he was so unreal," she wrote.

"Miss Pamela had grabbed my arm and pointed my eyes to the left aisle. The lights dimmed and a tall lean cat in a sparkling Nudie suit drifted by. He was true glitter, true glamour rock. The suit sparkled like diamonds; it had submarines all over it outlined in rhinestones and the color was scarlet red. . . .

"Pamela always raved on about Gram, too. She always was in contact with the special earth angels on this planet, so during a recording session for *Permanent Damage* she called Gram and we got an invitation to visit him. . . . Off we went to the outskirts of town into the San Fernando Valley. We drove to a modern cowboy ranch with wagon wheels paving the driveway. . . . We entered the house and shy Chris Hillman and the cat in the Nudie suit greeted us with a grocery bag full of grass, and Gram was so down-home dazzling with sensuous southern hospitality, it just slayed me.

"These are the first words I recall him speaking to me: As he leaned over his pile of records, and put on an old George Jones album, a tear fell from his eye, and he spoke. 'This is George Jones, the king of broken hearts.' "

Women gave Gram—who'd left Nancy—and Chris—who was going through a separation—plenty of material.

The two had moved into a house on DeSoto up in the northwest corner of the San Fernando Valley, north of Hollywood. They were suddenly a pair of bachelors with a project—the first Burritos album—and they dove into one of the most productive periods of their lives.

No one could stop Chris and Gram from going out at night, but in the daytime, they'd be at the house with their guitars, working on new songs.

One afternoon, Gram, still brushing sleep out of his eyes, stumbled into the living room to find Chris working on a tune about a town occupied by insanity, Satan, and sharks in mohair suits. It was "Sin City," and although it was heard as a dire warning about the trials of a big city, for Chris, it was a personal matter.

"I was just going through this horrible divorce at the time, where the wife had been going out with the road manager, and it was just a nightmare and it was making me crazy. Our manager had robbed us and I had quit the Byrds and there went my life." Chris shrugged and smiled. "And this whole town is filled with sin."

Gram and Chris wrote about their common love for motorcycles ("Wheels") and about their common disdain for military service. Gram had his 4-F deferment, but one day, he got a piece of mail from the Selective Service asking for a confirmation of his medical records. The letter was close enough to a draft notice so that he and Chris wrote "My Uncle," about a country boy who's gained just enough social awareness—or who's developed just enough of a defense mechanism—not to want to join Uncle Sam's Army. In the studio, the Burritos made it a perfect mesh of rock and country flavors.

"Hippie Boy" was a spoken-word number, a takeoff on old Baptist singalongs, à la Red Foley's "Peace in the Valley." The story was about a man's encounter with a smelly, stoned hippie and how they found a common ground. Although the words were mostly Chris's, the song reflected a stated goal of Gram's. In 1969, he said: "We want the rock fans at the Whisky and the truck drivers at the Palomino to get together and talk to each other and understand each other."

Women inspired the songs "Juanita" (named for a girl Chris met at the Troubadour one night) and "Christine's Tune," about a devoted fan who caused some problems with some of the Byrds' spouses at the time. When she died several years later, the Burritos moved to shield her identity by renaming the song "Devil in Disguise."

Gram and Chris were still short of an album's worth of songs by the time recording sessions began.

One day after a rehearsal, Chris Ethridge approached Gram with a couple of melodies he'd been carrying with him since childhood. They were what he called "go songs." That is, when he was a kid in Mississippi and wanted to go out to play with friends, and his parents wouldn't let him, he'd march to the family piano and bang out one of his tunes until his folks relented. "Go, go," they'd say. "Get out of here!"

Now he offered those shards of songs to Gram, who grabbed a pencil, a notepad, and a handful of uppers. He dispensed two to Ethridge, took two himself, and propped his notebook up while Ethridge sat at the piano, picking out one of his songs. They tossed lines at each other, and within a couple of hours, they nailed two songs, which they lazily titled "Hot Burrito #1" and "Hot Burrito #2."

Both were reflective songs about love gone sad, and "#1" was especially poignant, as a man in conflict pled his case to his woman.

A Groovy Groop

You may be sweet and nice
  but that won't keep you warm at night
I'm the one who showed you how
  to do the things you're doing now

Before recording "Hot Burrito #1," Gram sang it for Miss Pamela and her roommate, Andee Cohen, a photographer. Several of the GTOs were in the studio to help out on the ragtag chorus of "Hippie Boy." In fact, whenever Nancy was in town with Polly, Pamela offered herself as baby-sitter. Nancy was still so in love with Gram, said Pamela, "that I could smell it on her skin. She called him her 'old boy,' and I was a little in awe of her."

In a side room at Wally Heider's recording studio, Gram sang his song, and when his voice cracked on the line, "I'm your toy, I'm your old boy, but I don't want no one but you to love me," Pamela knew it was about Nancy.

That evening the Burritos recorded both tunes, with Gram and Chris Ethridge sharing keyboards, with Gram playing the high parts. Gram never sang better, said Chris Hillman. Of the thirty or so songs that Gram recorded, "Those were the only two that had the power and depth of the artist he could have been. Very soulful readings."

After lifting a couple of country and R&B classics—"Do Right Woman—Do Right Man" and "Dark End of the Street"—and grabbing one of Gram's Sub Band songs, "Do You Know How It Feels," the Burritos had a full album. Now all they needed was a drummer.

Crack session player Eddie Hoh was the first Burritos drummer, but he dropped out during the making of the first album. Gram next had Maurice Tarp, a former Jerry Lee Lewis drummer, in mind, but that didn't work out. Before the sessions were finished, the band called on Sam Goldstein, a friend of Sneeky Pete's, for a couple of tracks; Popeye Phillips, a friend of Ethridge's, for several; and Jon Corneal, who worked on five songs but wasn't hired permanently. Gram, said Chris, looked down on Jon. "Here they were, both from Florida, but Jon was from the other side of the tracks; somebody who should be in the orange groves picking oranges: 'How dare you play in a band with me!'"

From Jon's point of view, the other side of the tracks—at least in Hollywood—was just too strange. "The scene was getting a little heavy for me," he said. "It's just a different world, the whole excessiveness thing. In L.A. wherever you turned the corner, there was a scene somewhere. You'd go to somebody's house and there was a party. It was like everybody was in the same route. To me, it was Greek."

★

★ **107** ★

Hickory Wind

"Gram was infatuated with the desert. We went out to the
Joshua Tree motel a couple of times just to hang out. It's
pretty . . . eerie."

—Chris Hillman

Gram, the kid from the Swamps and the town of a hundred lakes,
first encountered truly dry land in the Mojave Desert in 1969.

At first it wasn't Joshua Tree but an area known as Pearl
Blossom, sixty miles north of Los Angeles and not at all far from
the clubs he'd been hitting at night.

By day the Mojave was mostly dry heat, 15,000 square miles of
desert wilderness dotted by Joshua trees, the sturdy yucca plants
with spindly, up-reaching limbs. Mormons traveling through the
desert named the trees after the Old Testament prophet Joshua,
because they reminded them of the way he raised his arms to God.
The trees seemed to beckon them forward, on to the promised land.

Joshua Tree National Monument marks the transition from
high desert to low, from the Mojave to the Colorado Desert. It is a
vast and timeless land, awesome in both beauty and danger; in its
views and its unrelenting heat from spring through fall. The Mojave is the only home in the world to the Joshua trees, an unreal
(and, to some, grotesque) desert plant. They have come to be
recognized as the essence of life force, providing nourishment to
squirrels and deer, and nesting places for birds that can perch on
them safely, as high as forty feet off the ground.

Through Nancy, Gram had dabbled in metaphysics, and in
Joshua Tree, Gram found a place to sit and meditate, or just to get
high.

But Joshua Tree was still in his future.

To get photographs for the cover of their first album, *Gilded
Palace of Sin*, A&M art director Tom Wilkes took the Burritos to
Pearl Blossom. To back up Mother Nature, Tom and photographer
Barry Feinstein also hired two models, dressed and made up to
look like hookers.

The models, a miniskirted brunette and a blonde in a knit cap
and wine-colored pantsuit, posed like the mannequins they were
hired to be; they allowed themselves to be embraced and held aloft
by various Burritos.

It didn't work. The Burritos looked stiff in their Nudies. They
looked, in short, exactly like what they were—a bunch of guys in
costumes mainly because one of them wanted to be.

Gram was disappointed by the cover. He said he preferred
some of the pictures that were rejected. He especially liked one of
the Burritos grouped in front of a Joshua tree.

★

A Groovy Groop

The summer winds of America had blown hot and fiery. 1968 had become the year of darkness. By Thanksgiving, the United States had dropped more bombs on Vietnam than it had on all the enemies of World War II, and hadn't moved an inch closer to any kind of victory. Martin Luther King, Jr., was killed, and ghettos across the country erupted in flames. Bobby Kennedy was assassinated, and Chicago, site of the Democratic National Convention, became a battlefield.

The Beatles issued calming music—"Hey, Jude, don't be afraid." Bob Dylan's backup band, called the Band, combined backwoods roots with gritty rock in hits like "Wheels of Fire." The Stones sang about revolution in "Street Fighting Man," and the group that the Sub Band used to open for, the Rascals, hit number one with "People Got to Be Free."

Gram let that parade pass by. He may have helped write songs about ducking the draft and about hippies mixing with straights, but he had no interest in protest songs. As he told Bud Scoppa in 1970: "I don't like the 'I ain't marchin' anymore' attitude." He would attempt social comment, he said, "only if it's positive and not deeply philosophical, any more than I can avoid."

Besides, in his own quiet way, he'd tried building bridges, by way of music, between rock and traditional country—two worlds separated by age, politics, life-style, and musical tastes.

Back home in Waycross, two elections were being watched carefully. In Ware County, Richard Nixon was a cinch to trash Hubert Humphrey; the deep South was wired Republican. But what about Sheriff Robert E. Lee? He was up for his fourth consecutive four-year term as sheriff of Ware County. He was a Democrat; a backer, in fact, of Robert Kennedy. Lee was a popular man— many said that he was adept at doing favors, and some said he was corrupt—but he was a Democrat who'd attended the California state primary for Robert F. Kennedy.

In 1960 Sheriff Lee and his wife, Marie, moved into the house left behind by the Connor family after Coon Dog's suicide. Eight years later, on the eve of elections, the house blew up.

Most Waycrossians thought the house had been burned to the ground. Actually, it was an explosion inside the house that popped bricks off the exterior walls. Marie Lee was certain that it was political sabotage of some sort.

But if Waycross could vote on the issue of what happened, the town might have named none other than Sheriff Lee himself as the bomber. "It's been said he blew up the house to get sympathy to win the sheriff's race," said Billy Ray Herrin. "He won." The timing, he said, was considered too coincidental for the explosion to be an accident.

The sheriff may have thought he needed the boost, said Billy

Ray, because "Robert E. Lee was a real crook; everybody knew it and was scared to death of him."

Jack Williams, the managing editor of the town paper, said that the sheriff was rumored to have had an interest in a local gambling club. It was said that he was involved in the sale of pills and that he sold protection for moonshiners in Ware County. But these, he emphasized, were only allegations.

Marie heard some of the talk. "Ridiculous things—that he was delivering moonshine on milk trucks." When it came to political enemies, Richard Nixon sure didn't have the whole franchise.

Avis Snively on her wedding day, March 22, 1945.

Gram Connor and baby sister Avis visit with grandfather John Snively in Winter Haven.

In 1957, at age 11, Gram goes hunting with *(left to right)* Uncle Tom, Coon Dog, and grandfather Ingram Cecil Connor.

Gram's first band, the Pacers *(left to right):* Marvin Clevenger, Skip "Flat Top" Rosser, Jimmy Allen, and Gram.

Marvin C. Clevenger

Gram, at right, with one version of the Legends *(left to right):* **Jim Stafford, Bill Waldrup, and Lamar Braxton.**

The Shilos were *(left to right):* **George Wrigley, Joe Kelly, Paul Surratt, and Gram.**

Gram on his bittersweet graduation day from the Bolles School *(left to right):* grandfather Ingram Connor, an unidentified friend, Gram, sister Avis, and grandmother Nancy.

The first International Submarine Band *(left to right):* John Nuese, Gram, Ian Dunlop, and Mickey Gauvin.

Gram with expectant
Nancy at Capitol
Records studios.
Nancy said Gram was
admonishing her
"not to expose our
baby to loud music."

Bob Buchanan

"I loved Gram
because he was the
first to lead me to
freak cowboys and
drive-ins with huge
doughnuts in the
sky," said
Andee Cohen.

Andee Cohen

A short flight with the Byrds *(left to right):* Kevin Kelley, Gram, Roger McGuinn, and Chris Hillman.

The Flying Burrito Brothers *(left to right):* Chris Ethridge, Gram, Chris Hillman, "Sneeky" Pete Kleinow, and Michael Clarke.

Jim McCrary

Gram, Emmylou, and the Fallen Angels rehearse in early 1973.

An early edition of the Fallen Angels at Philip Kaufman's house *(left to right):* Kyle Tullis, Emmylou Harris, Jon Corneal, N. D. Smart, Gram, and "road mangler" Philip Clark Kaufman.

On tour, Gretchen stayed near Gram backstage.

Gram with Margaret
Fisher at the Joshua
Tree Inn.

Polly Parsons poses
with her father's
Nudie jacket at the
Nashville tribute,
1988.

18

The Train Song

Gilded Palace of Sin was greeted like a champion. In *Rolling Stone,* Stanley Booth reviewed it like a Gram Parsons solo album. After kicking off the review with a lengthy treatise on Waycross and on Gram's musical history, he called the Burritos album "the best, most personal Gram has yet done."

Years later, Robert Hilburn, the *Los Angeles Times*'s pop music critic and a great fan of country music, described *Gilded Palace* in terms that might have been dictated by Gram and Chris Hillman. "The album," he wrote, "mixed the country music emotion/feel and the rock music themes/attitudes. 'Sin City,' a Parsons-Hillman song that remains a classic in the development of the Parsons/ country rock tradition, deals with the ills/temptations of urban life." That song, he said, obviously stuck with other musicians. "The Eagles' 'Lyin' Eyes' is . . . very much in the warning-against-urban temptation tradition of 'Sin City.' "

Bob Hilburn also praised Gram's fragile vocals, which came "straight from the sentimental, George Jones heart of country music" and "could be as emotionally persuasive as anyone who has ever dealt in the country fringes of pop."

Hickory Wind

Gram could take a sad song and make it sadder. In front of a microphone, Gram kept no secrets.

In choosing Nudie's outfits, and in fashioning himself after Hank Williams and Elvis, he was being true to himself. He was confident to the point of being brazen. Beneath the glitter and rhinestones, he was naked. And he didn't mind being that way.

As Andee Cohen, Pamela DesBarres's one-time roommate, told me, "his sadness was like his image, like an imprint you have of yourself. He should have played the blues."

It was a $1,000 wedding supposed to be
   held the other day and
With all the invitations sent,
   the young bride went away . . .

It was the morning after a big storm. Having vacated the Sweetzer Avenue house, Nancy and baby Polly had moved to Santa Barbara. On a trip to Los Angeles in mid-January, they stayed at Susan and Brandon deWilde's house in Topanga, which had become a commune of sorts, with Barry Tashian, Mickey Gauvin, Billy Briggs, and Ian Dunlop either living or hanging out there. They had all been frightened by the storm and the landslides, and several of them spent the morning helping sandbag nearby properties.

Then Gram showed up and found Nancy and Polly in Susan's dressing room. He had a surprise for her. Putting on his softest southern accent, he said: "I'd like to ask you to be my wife."

Nancy, for whom nothing was much of a surprise anymore, faced Gram. She didn't think he was serious. By his actions at Sweetzer; by his having wasted no time seeing other women; by his obvious priorities, she knew they had no future.

"Yes, thank you, Gram, I'd like to," she said.

"You've made me the happiest man alive," said Gram, with a slight bow.

A moment later, everything changed again. Gram spotted Mickey, grabbed him, hustled him out of the house and down the driveway, where they had what appeared to be an emotionally charged conversation. When Mickey got back inside, Nancy asked what was going on.

"He thinks I slept with you," Mickey said.

The real problem between them, said Nancy, was that *Gram* no longer wanted to sleep with her.

"He couldn't relate to me anymore, as a mother. It was the madonna/whore thing. Once you became a mother, you were elevated beyond the carnal, lustful interaction of mere mortals and you weren't to be touched."

The Train Song

Soon after Gram's theatrical proposal, Nancy went back to Santa Barbara, where she awaited the next word from her intended.

Gram decided that if he was going to get married he'd do it in grand style. He'd make it an Event. He was, after all, a Byrd, a Burrito Brother, a friend of the Stones and of rock and movie stars everywhere. He'd invite them all. He'd get married—Jet Thomas would be the perfect minister—and then all the stars could jam. *That's it!* Not just a wedding but a concert! And, and . . . it could be *televised!*

This wouldn't be only a wedding; it'd be a career move.

None of this, of course, was original. All Gram was doing was evoking, once more, the crazed spirit of Hank Williams. In the fall of 1952, Hank came up with the idea of making his second marriage, to one Billie Jean Jones, into a concert—*two* concerts, in fact, the better to accommodate all his fans. Invitations told guests that, at both the 3:00 P.M. and 7:00 P.M. weddings, ceremonies would take place "immediately following the gala performance at which public officials and stars of stage, screen, and radio will be in attendance."

Hank's scheme worked. Some 14,000 fans paid between 75 cents and $1.50 to be part of his wedding(s).

Hank came up with the idea for two reasons: One was to make some money. But most of all, he wanted to go public—and beyond—to spite his first wife, Audrey. He barely even knew Billie Jean, and wouldn't get to. Less than three months later, Hank Williams was dead.

Whatever Gram's motives, he kept them to himself. All he told Nancy was that she ought to get herself over to Nudie—one of Hank's old friends—and get a wedding dress together. Nancy protested Gram's grandiose plans. "I just want to get married," she said.

Gram wouldn't budge. He kept talking up the big wedding, but he remained vague about just enough details—such as a date, a place, and a guest list—to drive Nancy nuts. With Nudie Cohen's help, she'd come up with a beautiful dress made of the same linen twill that Nudie and Mañuel had used for Gram's Burritos outfit. It was a cowboy shirt gone full-length, embroidered with roses and rhinestones.

Bob Buchanan took Nancy to Nudie's for a visit, and Nancy became hysterical looking at the lovely wedding dress that, deep down inside, she wasn't sure she wanted to wear. "This isn't right," she told Bob and Nudie. "Gram's flipped out!"

Nudie looked at her with compassion. He'd known a few crazies in his time. "Honey," he said, "I don't know what the boy's doing, but this isn't like him."

In the end, Gram pulled back. He never paid Nudie, so the $1,000 wedding dress stayed in Nudie's shop. And, if only for the sake of Polly, Nancy and Gram continued to see each other.

In her pocketbook diary, Lee Marthai, Nancy's mother, drew a sad face next to the square for January 31, 1969, and wrote: "Nancy No Marry."

And where are the flowers for the girl?
She only knew she loved the world.
And why ain't there one lonely horn
And one sad note to play?
Supposed to be a funeral.
It's been a bad, bad day.

★

In January, with their first album about to be released, the Burritos called on Michael Clarke, the former Byrds drummer, to try out for the group. At a rehearsal hall, Michael played along on some of the album tracks and knew he was in when Gram swept by and shouted, "Hey, drummer, let's have some fun." After a couple of warm-ups at small local clubs, the Burritos declared themselves ready to tour.

Aside from Chris Hillman, none of the Burritos was much into so mundane an activity as *practicing*. Not even Michael, who had a whole set of songs to learn. But he had a theory about music, and he didn't learn it at the Berkelee College: "What the hell," he said. "It's just music, right? You feel it; you do it."

When the Burritos first did it—at a media showcase at A&M Records' soundstage—they were a mess.

A&M's promotion department had set up the showcase as a barn dance and sent out packages of hay to the media to hype its excursion into country. Not the greatest move, if they were trying to equate country with hip—until the U.S. Postal Service got into the act. The post office stopped the mailing, saying it had to certify that the packets weren't stuffed with some kind of herb that might lead recipients to walk out windows. Suddenly the Burritos were the talk of the town, and 300 scene makers crowded into the soundstage.

But while the post office ultimately delivered, the boys didn't. The show, Michael conceded, was "a bit strange."

Bernie Leadon, a guitar, banjo and mandolin player seasoned through stints with the Scottsville Squirrel Barkers (with Chris Hillman), Hearts and Flowers, Linda Ronstadt, Dillard and Clark (bluegrass veteran Doug Dillard and ex-Byrd Gene Clark), and the Nitty Gritty Dirt Band, saw the Burritos at a hoot night at West

The Train Song

Hollywood's prime folk and rock club of the late sixties, the Troubadour.

He couldn't believe what he was hearing. The Burritos sang out of tune and played worse. He thought to himself, "Yeah, they got the look; yeah, they got the attitude; they got the record deal; they got everything. But they forgot something fundamental here: They just can't play or sing."

★

The idea of the Burritos traveling across America's fruited plains by train to bring their new blend of music to the masses seemed downright romantic.

Fact is, the Flying Burrito Brothers were riding the rails because of Gram's fear of flying. And so it was that the Burritos gathered at the train station in early February.

Pamela DesBarres, who'd gone to the train depot along with Brandon deWilde and other friends to see the Burritos off, wrote in her diary: "Gram was practically stuffing it up people's noses on the train last night. Big globs of it. Oh, GP, stay safe, my dear friend."

Michael Vosse worked for A&M as assistant to Vice-President Gil Friesen and saw himself as the "company hippie." On the train, he carried two valuable items: a movie camera and a corporate credit card. He remembered the send-off party bringing platefuls of sixties sustenance, including cookies laced with marijuana. By about eight o'clock, the group had digested the cookies and conducted a baggage check, mainly to make sure the drugs were on board. With a day and a half before their first stop in Chicago, the priorities had little to do with music and a lot to do with playing poker and taking drugs. Michael remembered the private discoveries: "Oh, here's the big bag of cocaine. . . . There's the bag of mescaline."

Between poker games, the Burritos dipped into their various goodies. The first morning, the group decided on a psychedelic breakfast and ate assorted mescaline and psilocybin capsules.

With Michael's camera running, and Gram or Chris Hillman sometimes doing the camera work, the Burritos decided to make a movie and proceeded to do a version of *A Hard Day's Night* along the train, hanging on the runners between cars until porters shooed them away.

By lunchtime, the Super Chief's crew had figured out that these Burrito fellows were on their own trip, destination unknown, and told their two managers—Steve Aldsberg, who'd helped Gram connect with Lee Hazlewood, and another young man, named Rick Sutherland—that they were being given their very own dining car—for their convenience, of course, so that their many fans wouldn't bother them.

The chief caretaker of the Burritos was neither of their two young managers. It was Phil Kaufman.

Little is known about Phil's early career. He refused to talk to me, after a brief first conversation, unless he was paid.

But because of frequent run-ins with the law, and because his style was distinctly high profile, his escapades since the mid-sixties have become the stuff of legend, as well as of police records.

In Hollywood, Phil dabbled in the film industry—he was said to have had a bit part in *Spartacus*—when he got popped into prison on federal drug charges. He was at Terminal Island Federal Correctional Institute in San Pedro, California, just outside Long Beach, when he took notice of a fellow inmate with an interest in show business. It was Charlie Manson, a dark, diminutive man who'd been in trouble since 1954, when he was twenty-one. Manson was at Terminal Island for parole violation following various convictions and dismissals on charges of forgery, credit card theft, and pimping.

In the book *Mindfuckers*, Phil reminisced about Manson. "There was this guy playing guitar in the yard one day at Terminal Island. And it was Charlie, singing his ass off. He had an old guitar with all kinds of writing on it, all kinds of songs. And the guards kept taking it away from him, saying, 'If you play it in this place at this time, you are violating this rule.' They had these rules so you'd continually know that you were captive."

After doing more than seven years of a ten-year sentence, Manson was released, and Phil, from prison, connected him to people he knew in the music business. Manson was able to make recordings of some of his songs. When Phil got out in 1968, he lived with Manson and the beginnings of his following for a couple of months before deciding that his former prisonmate was too "overbearing." But, he said, he remained a "sympathetic cousin." Manson never got a record deal, but, after the Tate–La Bianca murders, Phil issued an album of tapes of his songs, called *LIE*.

Phil Kaufman got back into the flow of show biz through rock and roll. He was a close friend of publicist Gary Stromberg; one of Gary's clients, when he was a partner in the Gibson and Stromberg agency, was the Rolling Stones.

Phil became an "executive nanny" to the stars. He was the road manager par excellence, taking care of anything anyone needed, from arranging housing and transportation to personal baby-sitting. A beer-bellied man with a high, pinched voice, Phil parlayed a storied background, a penchant for self-promotion, and a robust sense of humor into a string of jobs that connected him to some of the biggest names in rock and roll. Just months out of

The Train Song

prison, Phil hooked up with the Stones when they were in Los Angeles in the summer of 1968 to mix their *Beggar's Banquet* album.

By the time Phil met Gram in August, the Stones had begun to employ his "nanny" services. Gram was forming his next band, and Phil put himself first in line to be the road manager—and more—to this intriguing young friend of the Rolling Stones.

The Santa Fe Super Chief took the Flying Burritos to Chicago, and from there, the Burritos drove to Detroit for their first concert, doubled back to Chicago, then proceeded to Boston, New York, and Philadelphia.

Michael thought the band improved show by show, and that he and Ethridge became a pretty tight little rhythm section. Gram, on stage, was sounding strong. But, by his telling, the band spent as much time playing poker as they did music.

Around the table, said Michael, Gram was the best player because he had the best poker face. And he had that because he could afford it. "He could sit there with shit and you've got a full boat and he'd raise you $500."

Arriving in Chicago, the Burritos checked into the posh Astor Towers, situated—bad news for A&M—just above Maxim's restaurant. They played poker all night long, and when morning came, they ordered up a $300 breakfast for four, including such get-up-and-go nourishment as lemon soufflés. The band was living it up, and the poker was going strong, with the exceptions, maybe, of Chris Ethridge, who'd folded, and Michael, who was down to his last couple of dollars and set to fold.

He'd even torn up one of his few remaining dollar bills in disgust. As the currency fluttered to the floor, Chris materialized at his side and handed him a beaded Indian purse. Michael opened it. It was empty. "What the hell's this gonna do for me?" Michael whined. "It's a lucky purse," Chris replied.

Within two hours, Michael had turned the tables on Gram, winning nearly $3,000. Gram slammed the table but didn't quit.

Nothing could stop a game. Gram drove from Chicago to Detroit in a rental car; the party included Michael, Chris Hillman, and Sneeky Pete. As they rode, Chris dealt a game of seven-card showdown from the backseat, using his briefcase, propped between Gram and Michael, for a table. Sneeky Pete, who didn't play cards, sat with Chris in the back. With three cards showing, Chris suddenly shouted: "There's the Detroit exit!"

Gram took just enough of a microsecond too long to react, and the car jumped a highway median and leaped into the air. Despite his fear of flight, Gram managed to steer the car in the right direction, and when it landed, it was on the off ramp to Motor City. Through the panic, all three Burritos held onto their cards. "We all had relatively good hands," said Michael, who thinks Chris won the game. "He had four queens, and I always wonder if he cheated. Anybody who plays mandolin's got to have fast hands."

In Chicago, Gram and Chris Ethridge found time to visit with radio interviewer Studs Terkel and, incidentally, perform a concert. Their first highlight came at the next stop, Boston, where they were co-billed for a four-night run with the Byrds at the popular, 1,000-capacity club, the Boston Tea Party.

Jon Landau of *Rolling Stone* was there, and he reported that, on the closing night, the Byrds—now composed of Roger McGuinn, guitarist Clarence White, drummer Gene Parsons, and bassist John York—jammed with the Burritos—most of them former Byrds, anyway.

The night before, Roger had invited Gram to sing his song "Hickory Wind" with the Byrds.

Jon Landau described Gram's moment in *Rolling Stone*:

"Eyes closed, Gram seemed to be entranced and in touch with his music in a way that he is not with the Burritos. That group is a competent, straightforward country band which lacks imagination. Each individual is an excellent musician but the collective sound is seldom satisfying. They generally lack McGuinn's ability to transcend the parochial in country without cheapening the style. But Gram Parsons with the Byrds was beautiful on *Sweetheart of the Rodeo* and was beautiful that night.

"Like everyone else on the stage, he was playing for himself."

On closing night, Jon wrote, the two bands flowed into each other, and he especially enjoyed Gram's singing of "You Don't Miss Your Water," which, the critic noted, was sung on the *Sweetheart* album "for some reason" by Roger, "even though it was Gram Parsons who had taught it to the group. Now Gram sang lead and the harmony between him and Roger was gorgeous in its flowing tranquility."

For all the nice moments on stage, however, the Burritos were already beginning to fragment.

One of the big problems, said Michael Vosse, was cocaine. "Things were more difficult than anticipated. Shows weren't all that steady, and here we were, just halfway through this thing, and it was cold. And people started to snap. There were a lot of speaking through gritted teeth and screaming."

The main antagonists were Hillman and the Burritos' two young managers. Hillman accused the managers of not taking care of business, while the managers complained that the Burritos were doing little more than getting high all the time.

Even when they visited Gram's friend from his days at Harvard, the Rev. Jet Thomas, they smoked marijuana in the minister's apartment.

The Train Song

The visit with Jet was but a momentary respite from the wintry weather of New England. The Burritos, headed next for a series of shows at The Scene in New York, found themselves snowbound in Boston, and, instead of hopping on a commuter jet, had to employ a variety of vehicles to get there. Several of the band's members showed up too late to perform, spoiling an opening night packed with record company people, Manhattan media, and a few stars, including Janis Joplin. They were all left with no show.

And when Gram made it to the band's designated hotel, he learned at the front desk that the management required proper jackets for the dining room. He stopped everyone from checking in and marched the band and crew—a party of twelve altogether—several blocks to the Gramercy Park, a hotel he knew was friendlier to rock bands and which was, incidentally, priced higher than the original hotel.

"It changed the budget considerably," said Michael Vosse, "and [Jerry] Moss was really pissed."

As if the Burritos weren't spending enough money on the road, they had Michael call Jerry Moss with a little request: Could A&M stop promoting the album and whatever they were thinking of as a first single? On the tour, Gram and Chris Hillman had come up with a tune called "The Train Song," and it was getting enthusiastic responses from their audiences. The Burritos wanted to get into the studios as soon as they got home and cut "The Train Song" for rush release.

Jerry refused. But at least he got a sense that the boys were actually creating music while on the road.

Even if they were, the work was a distant second to play. Gram's insistent vision, conjured in those country music clubs in and beyond the Valley, was getting lost in the constant partying. "We were still trying to do my deluxe number," Gram said later, "a dream of soul-country-cosmic, what I called in my earlier days, 'cosmic American music.' I would do numbers, buy bottles of tequila, five turbans, and I always insisted on having an organ around so I could do Jerry Lee Lewis numbers and try to get a big sound."

Everyone remembered the five turbans. The Burritos were in Philadelphia, opening a concert for Three Dog Night, when Gram decided to top off their Nudie suits with a touch of R&B. In Philadelphia, Gram found a shop that sold bejeweled turbans, and they reminded him of some of the R&B artists and groups of the Fifties who wore turbans so that they would look more East Indian than black. Gram got a different jewel for each Burrito, and, for an extra bit of show, ended the set by falling off the organ stool.

The pop crowd that had shown up to hear "Joy to the World" never knew what hit them.

Hickory Wind

In Philadelphia, the Burritos got onto a dance-party show on a UHF station, along with Three Dog Night. Captured on videotape, the Burritos were clearly dominated, at least on showbiz levels, by Gram.

The song they performed, "Devil in Disguise," featured Chris Hillman and Gram on vocals and two breaks by Sneeky Pete. Chris Ethridge, pale, bearded and thin, and Michael Clarke, all blond hair and red outfit, were backdrop.

Chris Hillman, who took the first lead vocal, was a perfect sideman. A fine singer and an even better player, he was stiffened by self-consciousness. Trying to look casual with a tight-lipped smile after one line, he flubbed his lip sync of the following one.

Next to him, Gram was all motion and fun, his feet tapping and his eyes dancing. With his Nudie outfit topped off by a wide-brimmed black hat ringed with a band of white silk, he was a natural performer and show-off, pointing—extravagantly and quite unnecessarily—to Chris and to Sneeky Pete as they took their solos. When it came his turn to sing, he made immediate eye contact with the camera; he shook his head and raised his brows to accentuate the story he was singing. Working behind Chris, he snuck in a tribute to Elvis, spreading his legs and pulsing his chest and hips, as if rock and roll had taken control of his body. When, at song's end, it came time for the two leads to toss the phrase "in disguise" at each other, Gram leaned into Chris and sang into his ear; Chris looked back at Gram, but he had no idea what to do with this precocious guy prancing next to him.

Shortly after the Burritos returned to Los Angeles in March, they were off to San Francisco to play a benefit concert for a struggling rock dance hall, the Avalon Ballroom. The Burritos shared the bill with Moby Grape and Quicksilver Messenger Service, and their show was broadcast locally.

A tape of their set still makes the rounds of GP fans and, like the videotape from Philadelphia, it's a revealing document of what the Burritos were trying to do.

They could sound as bad as Bernie Leadon's worst nightmare. On "Dark End of the Street," Gram's voice, aching to reach high notes, broke, to no particular effect; a vocal harmony never took hold; a lead guitar line ran ragged; the drumming was indifferent. There was no point to the song. Likewise, "We've Got to Get Our-selves Together," a soul-sweet jam of gospel proportions in the hands of Delaney and Bonnie and Friends, lost its spirit in the relatively rigid structure of the Burrito Brothers. It didn't help any that they messed up several lines.

But the band shone on a country medley of "If You Can't Undo the Wrong, Undo the Right" and "Somebody's Back in Town"; on

The Train Song

"Sin City," featuring Hillman's sweet, Everly Brothers–like harmonies; and on a surprisingly metallic, hard-rocking "Sweet Mental Revenge" that got the Winterland crowd riled up. Gram also kicked things up when he returned to his days as a Pacer and a Legend with the Little Richard song "Lucille."

Gram didn't usually say much between songs, but at the Avalon, he spoke to the crowd. Affecting a honeyed twang, he was Mr. Sincere. "It's really great the way everybody here sits around and listens, and, um, that's what this is all for. Maybe the two things are gonna get together, a lot." Then, to introduce, "Town Without Memories," he said, "This is where it all comes from: nostalgia and slow country."

And this was where Gram wanted to go, to loping, waltz-time songs with lovely melodies from various worlds of music: "Do Right Woman—Do Right Man," "You Win Again," and his own beauty, "Hot Burrito #1." But in the end, his voice and range were overmatched, and he couldn't sustain an entire show singing lead on every song.

And yet, just when it seemed he could be written off, he'd bounce back with a jewel of a performance, and all was forgiven.

The erratic nature of the Burritos on stage drew predictably mixed notices not only from rock critics but from fellow musicians as well. The band members responded in various ways. Sneeky Pete said the Burritos *meant* to play rough because they were musical rebels. The Burritos, he said proudly, were outlaws.

Gram agreed. "We're treated great in one way and, on the other hand, we're completely misunderstood," he said. "Rock critics and country critics completely misunderstand; it would be the same with R&B critics if they had the opportunity."

Maybe; maybe not. Chris Hillman, whose career depended on his being objective about his work, summarized the Burritos' tour: "We weren't very good on stage. We spent a fortune and didn't accomplish anything. It was a stupid tour, really."

Back in Los Angeles, Gram saw Nancy and Polly, but it was not a pleasant visit. It ended with Gram taking the car Nancy had driven in from Santa Barbara. Marcia Katz had to drive Nancy and Polly home. Gram, apparently, was still obsessed with Mickey Gauvin, ISB's original drummer and Nancy's friend, whom he suspected was having an affair with her.

One day, Miss Mercy Peters was sitting in front of the Country Store, Laurel Canyon's homey grocery store, when she saw Gram. He was angry. "I'm going down to Santa Barbara and I'm going to kill Mickey," he shouted. The next moment, he spotted a beautiful aspiring actress named Johanna. He got her name and number, and when he returned from out of town (without killing Mickey), he announced to Mercy: "I want Johanna." He soon had her, and was so taken with her that he outfitted her in a Nudie jacket that matched one of his own.

With the Burritos album stalling at the record stores, Gram pressed his idea of rush-recording and releasing "The Train Song" as a single. As angry as he might have been about the Burritos' overspending, Jerry Moss relented. Gram than came up with the idea of having the record produced by Larry Williams, who came to fame in the fifties with "Short Fat Fannie" and "Bony Moronie." (He also wrote "Dizzy Miss Lizzy," made famous by the Beatles when they included it in their *Beatles VI* album in 1965.) In 1967, Larry had scored a couple of R&B hits with Johnny "Guitar" Watson, including "A Quitter Never Wins" and "Mercy, Mercy, Mercy."

Gram called Larry and told him about the Flying Burrito Brothers.

"The Flying *what?*" said Larry.

He and Johnny soon learned all about the Burritos when they visited the band at one of their homes in Laurel Canyon. When the supply of marijuana evaporated, Johnny proved to be a Mr. Manners. He pulled up his pants leg and whipped a joint out of his sock. "Allow me, gentlemen," he said. "I call this butter. It'll make you feel like you're wearing a crown!"

To support the Burritos, Leon Russell and Clarence White sat in on the session. Leon, a master pianist, marveled at Johnny when he took over the keyboards at one point. "Damn, man, they oughta call him Johnny 'Piano' Watson," he said.

The session produced "The Train Song," but Chris Hillman remembered more laughs than music. "Gram kept giving them blow, and it was hilarious. Larry would go, 'Watson, what'd you think about that there take?' And Watson would respond, 'Oh, I think it's great, man. Give me another toot.'"

Chris laughed. As he admitted, "It was a horrible song—and I wrote half of it!"

"The Train Song," released in July, was a stiff, as it should have been. Gram had executed another of his mismatches, and it cost the Burritos. By now, A&M had learned that Mike Vosse's gold card had piled up some $80,000 in charges. And that didn't include the costs of recording the first album and "The Train Song." With so much money down the drain, A&M pulled back on promotion and the kind of unspoken general support artists need.

"A&M always hated us," said Michael Clarke.

19

Flying Burritos and Saucers

Gram kept moving around. After Sweetzer Avenue, he'd moved into Chris's house in the Valley for the productive, songwriting period. After the train tour, Chris found a house on LaCastana in Nichols Canyon. In the summer of 1969 Chris, by now a bachelor in overdrive, established the rowdiest of all the Burrito manors in a house on Beverly Glen Drive, in the canyons north of Bel Air.

Here the Burritos may have made more money than they ever did as musicians. But what they were playing was poker.

The games, said Michael Clarke, made up the Burritos' social life. "We'd have private poker games and we'd call all the people we knew who had money and get them over there and take it all." One night the victim was a friend of one of the Burritos' wives, and by the time Gram, Chris Hillman, and horn player Junior Markham were finished with him, he had to borrow money from the Burritos for a cab ride home.

The Beverly Glen house was also the home of what Chris called "the physical abuse program. Strange women coming in and out, a lot of powder, liquor. Gram was drunk and stupid a lot.

Hickory Wind

After a couple of months in Beverly Glen, Gram began to split his time between the Burritos' hangout and a mini-manor of his own, paid for with money from his seemingly endless Snively trust fund, inside one of Hollywood's most star-dusted hotels.

Perched on a hillside just off the Sunset Strip, the Chateau Marmont was, for rock stars, the flip side of the Continental Hyatt House just down the street. The Hyatt—better known as "The Riot House" in the pop music industry—was one big crackerbox building, a dorm with room service. No wonder rock artists took to heaving television sets out of hotel room windows.

Up the road, it was a different world. The Chateau resembled a French Norman castle; like the Beverly Hills Hotel, it offered separate one- and two-bedroom bungalows, approached through woodsy paths. The Chateau's guests (many of whom stayed for months at a time) included Warren Beatty, Faye Dunaway, Diane Keaton, and, while Gram was there, such rock musicians as Janis Joplin, Rod Stewart, and Rick Grech. Rick had quit as bassist of Family, the English progressive-rock band, on the eve of its first U.S. tour to jump to Blind Faith, one of the supergroups of the time. He seemed a perfect match for Gram.

Eve Babitz, Gram's photographer friend, who knew the lay of the land as well as anyone, figured that he chose to live at the Chateau for convenience. It was steps away, for example, from a Japanese restaurant with a full bar. The Chateau had maid service. And it housed stars.

Gram began his stay by sharing a suite with filmmaker Tony Foutz, whom friends of Gram's remembered as a scene maker who was rarely without a movie camera, and who Gram described as "a loony character." Tony had created special effects for the film *2001*, and he was planning to direct a flying-saucers movie in the Joshua Tree desert. He was another perfect buddy for Gram.

By fall, Gram had moved from Johanna to another girlfriend, a twenty-two-year-old Briton named Linda Lawrence. Linda had been involved with Brian Jones of the Rolling Stones for two years, and was the mother of their son, Julian. After breaking up with Brian and moving to New York in 1965, Linda worked as a nanny for Mary Travers of Peter, Paul, and Mary. Then she moved to Los Angeles, and in mid-1969, when she and Julian found themselves homeless, she met Gram. They moved in with him at the Chateau.

"I began to think that I was going to fall in love again," she said.

In the fall of 1969, paranoia struck deep in Los Angeles. In August the Manson Family had gone on its murderous rampage and sent shock waves throughout the city, but especially in the surrounding neighborhoods and among people in show business who feared that they might for some unknown reason be on the same list as the actress Sharon Tate.

Chris Hillman closed down the Burrito Manor on Beverly Glen and moved to Malibu Beach, where he was occasionally joined by Gram, Linda, and her son, Julian.

Tony Foutz, meanwhile, began production on his UFO film, *Saturation 70*, and he made Gram one of the main characters. Gram had become a regular at Joshua Tree, taking Linda and various friends to the desert to take psychedelic mushrooms and talk to the stars. Tony cast several other first-time actors: Michelle Phillips of the Mamas and the Papas; Andee Cohen; and Prince Stanislau ("Stash") Klossowski, a friend of the Rolling Stones.

Few participants could recall a plot line, if, in fact, there was one. Ann Marshall, a friend of Michelle's, thought Tony's film was based on his knowledge of George Van Tassel, author of *I Rode a Flying Saucer* and proprietor of the College of Universal Wisdom, better known as the Giant Rock Airport, in the Mojave Desert. Van Tassel had built a domed structure he called the "Integratron," which he described as a "generator of bioelectrical energies" that had rejuvenative powers and made its operator capable of time travel. It looked like a Hollywood prop from *Flash Gordon*, and it worked about as well. As Tom Wilkes, the A&M Records art director who was with the crew to shoot still photos, pointed out, "It was supposed to rejuvenate people, but it didn't work for George; he died of old age."

Ann Marshall immediately saw the connection between Joshua Tree and flying saucers. "The sky is very clear, very high in the desert, and there is no light pollution. You can see more of the sky than you can see from the cities. These people with Airstream trailers and other recreational vehicles met every year at Joshua Tree because they felt they had definitely seen unidentified flying objects. They were very normal people, not hippies at all. Family people who would just take their vacations going into the wilderness."

Andee Cohen thought Tony's idea was to use one of George's annual UFO Sighters Conventions in Joshua Tree as a real-life backdrop for a story about "four cosmic kittens who were banished in outer space and came here to clean up the planet."

All Michelle Phillips knew was that she was asked to make a little movie. She piled into a Winnebago with Gram and several others and took off to Joshua Tree. The cast and crew stayed at a simple roadside motel that Gram had come to know: the Joshua Tree Inn.

In the desert, Michelle remembered Tony giving such directions as: "Now you're going to be creeping along the side here."

Tony was so casual that when he spotted Linda's son, Julian, cavorting on the set, he not only cast the five-year-old in the film as an alien but ultimately made Julian the central character.

It was all for naught. After a long weekend of shooting in October, including some scenes shot in Los Angeles, Tony and the producer had a falling out. Tony wanted the budget increased; the producer didn't like what had been shot and backed out. Linda said he was offended by a scene in a supermarket involving a dead Vietnamese man at the meat counter. The producer, she said, decided the film had become too political.

While Gram cavorted in the high desert and gigged with the Burritos wherever a job came up—usually at a small club in L.A.— many of the biggest names in rock were gathering, along with about 400,000 fans, at the Woodstock festival in upstate New York. Joan Baez, who helped to open the three-day concert, sang "Drug Store Truck Driving Man," the song Gram and Roger McGuinn wrote, and which appeared in the Byrds' first album after Gram's departure. Later, on the soundtrack album of the Woodstock movie, the song would be credited to James Roger McGuinn and Graham Parsons.

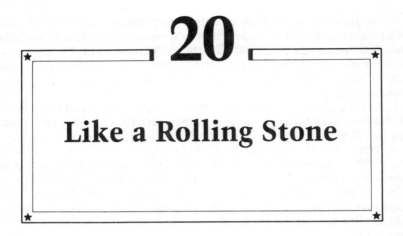

20

Like a Rolling Stone

On October 17 the greatest rock-and-roll band in the world arrived in Los Angeles to complete their album, *Let It Bleed*, and to prepare for a month-long tour.

The Rolling Stones had not been in America since their tour in the early summer of 1966. Since then, they had scored five albums in the Top 10, including *Between the Buttons, Flowers, Their Satanic Majesties Request*, and the landmark *Beggar's Banquet*. They had been subjected to innumerable drug arrests, gone drag in a photograph to promote a single; gone through censorship on the "Ed Sullivan Show" and through riots all over Europe; dabbled in films; and, in July, weathered the death of Brian Jones, the original leader of the group, whom the rest of the band had squeezed out just a month before.

The Stones' image had gone from bad, as in punkish, to bad, as in evil, devilish, satanic. A tune like "Sympathy for the Devil" and a death in the family—"by misadventure," at that—can do wonders to a reputation.

Weary and wary, they nonetheless ignited the city, mesmerized the media, and drew the press, as well as a press of fans, wherever they went.

While some of the Stones' entourage were put up at the Beverly Wilshire, most of the band members took over private homes. Mick and Keith stayed at Stephen Stills's house near Laurel Canyon, the kind of estate that in the late sixties could best be afforded by pop stars. Before Stills, the house had been occupied by Peter Tork of the Monkees.

On the Stones' arrival, Gram was part of the scene both at the Stills house and at the band headquarters in a house overlooking Sunset Strip.

When the Burritos played local clubs that month, the Stones were there. So were Miss Pamela and Miss Mercy. And, of course, Mick and company took note of the young women. On October 22, after a Burritos gig at the Coral, Pamela told her diary: "Gram noticed what was going on from the stage and said into the microphone, 'Watch out for Miss Pamela; she's a beauty, but she's tenderhearted.'"

A few nights later, the Burritos played the Golden Bear, a tiny club in Huntington Beach. Again, the Stones attended, along with Gram's stepfather, Bob Parsons, who commandeered a large table of personal guests. After the first set Stanley Booth, who was following the Stones on tour for a book, told his fellow Waycrossian, "You all are really going to be a success."

"I think we already are," said Gram.

Gram and Stanley went outside to the back of the club to share a joint. "They love to bust you for dope down here," said Gram, leading the way to an empty garage. Gram told Stanley how much he loved the Rolling Stones, and how much he loved love. He told Stanley about his beautiful baby girl, Polly. He sucked on what was left of the joint, exhaled, and said: "What we got to have in this world is more love . . . or more slack."

Orange County left Gram alone. But he didn't have as much luck in his own town.

The Burritos were getting ready for a gig at the Corral in Topanga Canyon. After the sound check, Gram and roadie Jim Seiter left to fetch a shirt from Hillman's house in Malibu.

On their way, a patrol car stopped the pair. As he emerged, Gram reached into the pocket of his red satin pants for a vial of cocaine, with an eye to ditching it. When one of the two cops noticed his move, Gram tore off up the road. Panicked, he still had enough wits about him to throw the cops off by faking a toss to one side while actually throwing the vial into some bushes on the other side of the road. The cops tackled Gram, cuffed him, and threw him across the hood of his car. After opening up a briefcase loaded with prescription drugs, and being uncertain of their legality, they booked Gram for possession.

In court, Gram spotted a police officer with whom he'd recently smoked marijuana on a record producer's boat. Gram waved and winked at him. The cop was not amused. "Are you queer, boy?" he asked. After a few more hours, the charges were dropped, and Gram was free.

He couldn't wait to tell his buddies how he'd duped the fuzz. Chris Hillman, for one, was mightily impressed—but he was also a careful listener. He went to the spot where Gram had been stopped, snooped around, found the cocaine, and generously gave it back to Gram.

Gram made the gig at the Corral after the bust, but while the Stones were in town, he was mostly an absentee Burrito.

Never mind that the band had hit a critical juncture. The Burritos were due to begin their second album, and they had just. lost Chris Ethridge, who was tired of playing in front of hundreds rather than thousands. According to Jim Dickson, who was hired to produce the new album, Chris was as bored as he was disillusioned. Jim, who'd worked with the Byrds early on, saw the Burritos at the Whisky-a-Go-Go. It was Chris Ethridge's last gig. The band couldn't keep time; Gram was messed up on downers. When he was up, he pranced around the stage, miming Mick Jagger. During a slow tune, Chris Ethridge nodded off. Jim was not looking forward to getting into the studios with them.

After Chris Ethridge left, Chris Hillman moved over to bass and the Burritos called on Bernie Leadon (the guitarist who'd noticed how the Burritos had everything going for them, with the exception of musical skills).

By the time Bernie joined, most of the flash was gone.

The Burritos wore random pieces of their Nudie outfits, mixed in with casual shirts and jeans. "It was like the second year at Valley Forge," said Bernie, "patched and tattered."

Bernie brought in new energy and a few new tunes, but Gram wasn't sure about the chemistry of the band. He hadn't been sure from the start, he would confess after his departure. But, he said, "I didn't know quite how to say it to Chris Hillman without getting in a fistfight. So I tried to stick it out and make it work."

However, when the Stones were around, Gram forgot all about the Burritos. As Bernie put it: "We had a working group. But—bad news for us for three months. Gram was over at Keith's house all the goddamn time and wouldn't show up for rehearsals. He just wanted to be with Keith. The music, the chicks, the drugs."

More than wanting to hang out with the Stones, said various members of the Burritos, Gram wanted to *be* a Rolling Stone.

Gram, said Bernie, was fixated on the idea of being a pop idol/tragic figure, like Hank Williams. And he wanted to mix it with the style of Mick Jagger.

Rick Roberts, who replaced Gram in the Burritos, said Chris

Hillman once told him that Gram studied Mick's moves—not his physical moves on stage, but "his conceptual ones. It made up a great portion of his panache."

In a 1970 interview with Bud Scoppa, Gram responded to the claims that he wanted to be Mick. "You can only be yourself," he said. "You can't be Mick Jagger. You can be inspired by the Rolling Stones; they're very inspiring people, great musicians, and I've taken their advice very often, like: 'Always make sure that you're yourself.'"

The flip side of the Gram-wanted-to-be-a-Stone theory has the Stones stealing Gram's music for their own.

Roger McGuinn, talking in 1976, put it succinctly: "They pulled him over and started romancing him, and they ripped him off for all he knew."

Burritos road manager Jim Seiter said the Stones had a routine on tour, setting up a studio wherever they were staying and inviting favored musicians over. One night, said Jim, Keith sang "Honky Tonk Women," and Gram followed with a countrified version on the piano. Gram's version, he said, wound up as "Country Honk" on *Let It Bleed*. When Jim told Gram that he should have received credit, he replied: "It was an honor bestowed on me."

However, Gram told one writer that "Country Honk" was recorded the way the Stones themselves composed it. He did take peripheral credit for "Honky Tonk Women." That song, he said, was a result of Keith and Mick "being with me . . . running around to a bunch of honky-tonks. . . . they had never seen it before, really." Generally, Gram once said to Judith Sims of *Rolling Stone*, "I think they've done a few country-sounding things since I got to know them."

To be absolutely technical about it, the Stones had dabbled in country as far back as 1964, when they recorded Hank Snow's "I'm Movin' On." And no biography of Keith Richards is complete without reference to his boyhood idolization of Roy Rogers. Yet Keith did agree that Gram was a significant influence on the Stones, and not just in the area of country music.

Soon after they got together in London, and then at his home in Redlands, Keith discovered the depth of Gram's musical knowledge. "He started to turn me on to certain classic tracks and certain styles of playing things—George Jones, Merle Haggard, Jimmie Rodgers. We used to sit around at the piano for ages, trying to figure out little licks, and he'd show me the different ways that Nashville will play it from Bakersfield. But not all country. That was the overwhelming impression, but also blues; Robert Johnson."

Gram's musical injections came at a crucial time. In 1968,

Keith said, his band was just being put back together again after nearly dying from the exhaustion of five years of nonstop tours and troubles, from 1963 through 1967.

"We were pretty knackered, and it was at the renaissance of the Stones, the second wind, so to speak—and one of their best winds," said Keith, that Gram entered the picture.

The Stones were working on the music that would make up *Beggar's Banquet* and *Let It Bleed*. "And Gram, with all the talent that he had, was always interesting people and getting them into music. There was a certain genuineness; he bridged certain gulfs between people. He was a very subtle man, a lovely sense of humor, a great turner of phrases."

Also, said Keith, "he kind of redefined the possibilities of country music for me, personally. If he had lived, he probably would have redefined it for everybody. But that was the other side of Gram. Did he like to get out of it, or what? Which was suiting me fine at the time. That was pretty much what I was doing."

As for what it was that Keith or the Stones were doing for Gram, Keith responded, simply: "He liked rock and roll. He was a bit of an Elvis in a way; he dug the rhinestone suits. We used to hang at Nudie's quite a bit."

The fairest assessment of the Gram-Stones relationship is that it was reciprocal. Gram said as much in 1970: "They wanted to get further into what I was doing, and I wanted to get into what they were doing." He picked up rock and roll from Keith and learned about singing from Mick.

In an interview seemingly made hazy by drugs (at one point, out of nowhere, Gram referred to "impish Keith, the gypsy"), Gram, his voice softened by nostalgia, reveled in memories of singing with the two leaders of the Stones and discovering universality in their music. "It's all the same. That's what Keith said. When the three of us sing together, it sounds like Gaelic music. Like the Incredible String Band. . . . We were doing Hank Williams songs . . . 'I was ridin' number nahne in South Caro—lah—na.' Mick's southern accent and my English accent. What does it all tell you? It's the same."

Sometimes, he said, the three combined created a fourth entity. "At the piano, with me and Jagger and Richards, we had Little Richard." Gram chuckled. "Two Georgia peaches and two English boys, stinky English kids. Fun. It's really far out. Drunk. *Drunk*."

Besides hanging out with the Stones, nothing seemed to please Gram more than to share his favorite music. Stanley Booth recalled the night, in the midst of the 1969 tour, when Gram and the Stones were sitting around listening to records. Inspired by a particular Brian Jones guitar lick, Gram suddenly left and rode off on his Harley. When he returned, he had an album by Lonnie Mack, the wonderful Memphis-based guitarist, and played it for the Stones. Charlie Watts added live drums to the record.

To many outside observers, however, the relationship between Gram and the Stones, and especially between Gram and Keith, seemed unhealthy. They didn't hear the jam sessions, but they witnessed the effects of their drug use, and they watched Gram physically transforming into a clone of a Stone.

Jim Seiter, the Burritos roadie whose job included picking Gram up at the Stones' L.A. house, said that Gram was "getting faggier by the day," and it bothered him that he was picking up the Stones' mannerisms: "Painted nails, all that effeminate shit. . . . He'd come out of the house, holding hands with Keith, skipping along. He'd come to the Palomino when it was a real truck-driver place, in these faggy outfits and the other guys would say, 'We can't go on stage with this fucker.' "

Actually, contrary to what Jim Seiter claimed, the Burritos found Gram more amusing than embarrassing.

"We sort of let it go," said Chris Hillman. "It was interesting." He quoted Emmylou Harris: "He really existed on another plane."

But Gram was hardly alone. As Stanley Booth noted, "We *all* got faggier by the day. The wonder is that by the end of the tour we weren't all wearing *dresses*. We all had to brush our hair out of our eyes every eight seconds. You never saw a more limp-wristed bunch of sissies."

The thing was, the effeminization of the Stones was meant to make them appear all the more masculine. "Mick would mince along in order to appear more macho," Stanley said. "By embracing another side of sexuality . . . androgyny is one of the most powerful forces on the globe, and I think all of us were seduced by it.

"Besides," Stanley concluded, "it made us dress better."

★

Eve Babitz thought, first of all, that Gram came to like drugs more than women. And when it came to women, he wasn't sure what kind he liked, subservient or strong-willed. Once she thought he liked bad girls until, at the Chateau, Gram told Eve he had to wait for a girl to come over with marijuana. Eve expected to see a Hell's Angels moll. "And it was this blond starlet."

In late 1969 Gretchen Burrell became Gram's kind of girl. She was only sixteen at the time, and worked as a model while attending high school at Newport Beach. Gretchen came from a Hollywood family; her father, Larry Burrell, was a well-known television news anchor and reporter who once ran, unsuccessfully, for public office. He was high profile and well connected, and his daughter got around.

In early November, a friend of Gretchen's had been hired as a driver for the Rolling Stones, and she invited Gretchen to join her at Warner Bros. studios, where the Stones were rehearsing.

It was something of an occasion. A friend of the band's—Gram Parsons—was celebrating his twenty-third birthday, and after the rehearsal the Stones hosted a party for Gram at Stephen Stills's house.

There Gretchen and Gram took their first notice of each other. It was, she said, "one of those looks-across-the-room kind of things. I thought he was the cutest thing on the planet." And when they chatted, she noted that, although he said he was from Georgia, he didn't seem saddled with southern affectations. He seemed sweet, even innocent.

After getting permission from her parents—they were crazy about Gram, she said—Gretchen moved in with Gram at the Chateau Marmont. The teenage Gretchen learned to cook from the employees at the Chalet Gourmet, a market geared toward Hollywood's upper crust. Gram, meantime, searched for his star, with the Stones, with the Burritos, and with musician buddies, jamming in his apartment or, sometimes, commandeering the baby grand piano in the lobby of the Chateau.

"He was such a show-off," said Gretchen. "Totally show-off."

★

He didn't know it, but on his birthday, besides the party and the meeting with Gretchen, Gram got a little present from *Rolling Stone* magazine.

That day, the magazine went to press in San Francisco with a lengthy interview with Bob Dylan. As ever, Dylan was enigmatic, noncommittal, and, when it came to fellow musicians, generous. When interviewer Jann Wenner asked about country rock bands, he needed some prompting on names. Jann mentioned the Burritos.

"Boy, I love them," said Dylan. "The Flying Burrito Brothers, unh-huh. I've always known Chris, you know, from the Byrds. And he's always been a fine musician. Their records knocked me out."

Dylan thought of the Burritos' "Hippie Boy" and chuckled.

"That poor little hippie boy on his way to town," he said, and laughed again.

Despite the kindnesses of Bob Dylan and the critics, *Gilded Palace of Sin* sold only about 40,000 copies and managed to reach only number 164 on *Billboard*'s album charts.

Jim Dickson, the Byrds producer who had been brought in at

Chris Hillman's suggestion, knew what was at stake with the second album. The latest word from A&M's accounting department was that the Burritos were in debt to the company to the tune of $130,000. The idea, said Jim, was simply "to try to do something to bail that out so they could keep their deal."

He had two immediate obstacles.

First, the band was in disarray, with one man out, a new one in, and the two leaders falling apart over Gram's various distractions.

Second, they had no songs.

Those days at Burrito Manor when Gram and Chris spent hours composing songs were long gone. "After that brief initial burst," said Chris, "Gram and I just couldn't seem to hook up again. *Burrito Deluxe* was written and recorded without any of the feeling or intensity of the first album, and it seemed that we were walking on different roads."

Gram admitted as much. By the time the Burritos were getting ready for a second album, Gram was elsewhere mentally. "I can't even claim to have really participated in that," he said in 1972. "I did what was asked of me, and that was it. It's a pretty lousy thing to have to admit."

The first song the Burritos presented to Jim Dickson was their attempt at Gram's funereal "$1,000 Wedding," which several of the band hated, and which dragged out to nine minutes. Jim rejected it out of hand.

Then, making the obvious connection between the Burritos and the Byrds, the producer suggested a Dylan song, "If You Gotta Go." He would regret ever doing so. The Burritos were erratic from the time they rehearsed to the time they recorded. "On 'If You Gotta Go,'" said Jim, "Chris doubled the tempo on the bass, which was very different from rehearsal, and Gram never really cared enough about it to try to phrase it well. . . . They just slaughtered it."

There were a couple of leftover Parsons-Hillman tunes that didn't make *Gilded Palace*—namely, "High Fashion Queen" and, possibly, "Down in the Churchyard." Chris wasn't certain. He did remember trying to write at the Malibu house. "We threw one or two songs together and they were terrible."

Several of the songs were finished at rehearsals and recording sessions, with Bernie Leadon pitching in. Chris or Gram would have scraps of ideas, and they'd meet with him in a projection room near the studios. Bernie remembered: "It was like, 'Here's a chord progression,' or 'How about this chord?' 'Got any ideas?' 'It's sunny outside and . . . my old lady's mad at me. . . . How am I doing?'"

Like a Rolling Stone

The rush sessions resulted in "Older Guys," which was about living in Malibu and which Bernie admitted was "a pretty stupid song"; "Cody, Cody," which pleased Jim with its Byrds-like harmonies; and the jaunty "Man in the Fog," which Bernie composed, with lyrics by Gram.

Jim and the band dug into Gram's inventory for "Lazy Days," the song he'd pitched for use in the *The Trip*. They agreed on a country standard, "Image of Me," by Harlan Howard, writer of such tunes as "I Fall to Pieces" and "Streets of Baltimore." Bernie submitted a song he'd written before joining the band—"God's Own Singer"—and sang lead on it.

The Burritos also recorded the traditional "Farther Along," for reasons unknown to Chris. "I think we were just scrambling to put together a record," he said. He thought Jim Dickson didn't know what to do with the Burritos. Gram, when he was around, was also unhappy with Jim, whose suggestions for songs evoking Dylan and the Byrds struck him as "blatantly commercial."

Gram, of course, wasn't helping much. Ironically, his friendship with the Stones, which was making life difficult for the Burritos, gave them their best song for the album.

Mick and Keith had composed a poignant ballad, "Wild Horses," and recorded it on a break from their tour in mid-November, in Muscle Shoals, Alabama. A few days later, Keith sent a copy of the tape to Gram. The Stones wanted to see if Sneeky Pete might add a pedal steel to the track.

Sneeky Pete might, but once Gram heard the song, he knew he wanted to sing it himself. Keith, busy on tour, gave permission, and before long, Gram's way with fantasy had turned "Wild Horses" into a song that the Stones had written just for him. Pamela DesBarres was in the studio when the Burritos recorded their version. Gram, she said, was ecstatic, "so happy that Mick had given him this song."

In later tellings, "Wild Horses" became not only a song the Stones had sent to Gram, but a song he'd inspired Keith and Mick to write. The more accurate story is that Keith wrote the song about his reluctance to go on the 1969 American tour, leaving his newborn son, Marlon, behind with his mother, Anita Pallenberg. Part of the song, it's been said, addresses the pressures on Mick after Marianne Faithfull's suicide attempt by drug overdose in Sydney, Australia.

No matter. And no matter that Chris Hillman didn't care much for the song. Gram jumped on it, giving the song a controlled yet impassioned reading; the Burritos, supplemented by Leon Russell on gospel-tinged piano, rode the song to victory. It was the Burritos' peak moment.

Hickory Wind

"It's a song you never get tired of," said Gram.

Despite the momentary high of "Wild Horses," Gram thought the album and the band were doomed. "After the first album I wasn't really down or anything," he said. "But the second album was a death blow to the Burritos."

Disheartened as he was, Gram felt compelled to help promote the album. In interviews, he filled his hot-air balloon to maximum pressure. He called *Burrito Deluxe* "a form of love music. It's simply a way of saying, 'Find a way to love.' We are involved in music of the spirit, or goose-bump music."

And he called on his friendship with the Stones once more to get exposure for the Burritos. In fact, he got the band its biggest audience ever by hooking it on to the Stones' last concert in the United States in 1969.

The Flying Burrito Brothers were going to Altamont.

21

A Little Woodstock

Altamont represented the Rolling Stones' answer to two things: criticism that they were charging too much for tickets to their concerts, and not having performed at Woodstock.

It was also, said Mick, a way to say "thank you" to the Stones' American audiences. And, since the Stones were having their tour filmed, a free concert in front of maybe 50,000 adoring fans would be a most picturesque and perfect ending.

Ralph J. Gleason, writing in the *San Francisco Chronicle*, called the Stones' concert ticket prices, ranging from $5.50 to $8.50, "outrageous," and said the pricing "says they despise their own audience."

At a press conference in Los Angeles, Mick, the most business wise of the Stones, begged ignorance about the going rate (the Doors, at the time, were commanding a $6.50 top ticket), and he hinted that the Stones might do a free concert toward the end of the tour.

In another chat with the press, this one at the Rainbow Grill atop Rockefeller Center on November 28, 1969, Mick committed his band, after a hectic round of negotiations among Bay Area officials, property owners, law enforcement agencies, lawyers, and Stones representatives. "We're doing a free concert in San Francisco on December 6," he said. The location was still unsecured. The show, he said, would create "a microcosm of society which sets examples for the rest of America as to how one can behave in large gatherings."

On the eve of the show, *Rolling Stone* reported that the event would attract a minimum of 200,000. "It would be a Little Woodstock," the producers expected, "and, even more exciting, it would be an *instant* Woodstock."

The Stones' management called on Chip Monck, who built and ran the stages at the Monterey Pop Festival and Woodstock. In the end, they gave him one day to get the stage and all necessary equipment together. Local bands like the Jefferson Airplane, Santana, and the Grateful Dead were enlisted. The Dead offered to bring in their friends, the Hell's Angels motorcycle club, to act as security.

Crosby, Stills, Nash, and Young would work Altamont in between Los Angeles gigs. Finally, also from L.A., there'd be the Flying Burrito Brothers, who got on, said Bernie, only after Gram begged the Stones and personally financed the Burritos' trip to the Bay Area.

The Burritos had no qualms; free concerts were the happening thing at the time. They'd get needed exposure, particularly since the Altamont concert was sure to be included in the movie being made of the Stones' tour by the highly respected documentary makers, the Maysles brothers of New York.

"We'd be crazy if we weren't involved," said Bernie.

Altamont was bedeviled before the beginning. It was announced as a definite show only four days before it took place; the site was changed just twenty hours before showtime; and Altamont raceway, an 80-acre oasis of destruction-derby entertainment amid farms, ranches, and vineyards fifty miles east of San Francisco, just off Highway 50, guaranteed a traffic jam. When it formed, it was an eight-mile doozy that inevitably became an eight-mile, four-lane parking lot, as freaks abandoned their cars and hiked to the concert, just as the people back East had done at Woodstock.

In the bowl of the property where the platform and the light scaffoldings had been erected, people could see that the stage itself was only three feet high, about the same as it had been for the Stones' very first gigs at blues clubs in 1963. And the security was left in the hands of a gang of bikers who armed themselves with

A Little Woodstock

sawed-off pool cues; who liked to combine red wine, speed, acid, and downers; and who embraced a fierce code of rules—for example, any stranger who touched their bikes was dead.

Also, they had no use for hippies or sissies.

On December 6 Miss Mercy of the GTOs checked her Tarot cards and saw nothing but death. Nonetheless, she went—she and 300,000 other rock and roll fans.

When Mick Jagger arrived that day, before he could reach the Stones' little trailer, he was punched by one young man who then shouted, "I hate you, you're so fucked!" Before day's end, Marty Balin of the Airplane would be attacked by an Angel for daring to scold them, and Paul Kantner of the Airplane would be threatened for mentioning that Balin had been knocked unconscious. Four concertgoers died—one was knifed by an Angel; one drowned; and two were run over by a hit-and-run driver.

Both Santana and the Airplane's sets had been interrupted by violence in front of the stage. The Burrito Brothers, however, managed to get through their sets without incident. The band was appropriately dressed down, although Gram, finally sharing a stage with the Stones, wore a Nudie's shirt with rhinestone Indians and thunderbirds, and suede pants.

As *Rolling Stone* reported: "Somehow the simple verities of their countrified electric music soothed the warriors. There were no fights. As luck would have it, Mick Jagger and Keith Richards chose to emerge from the backstage trailer where they'd been holed up to have a look at the stage and the audience during this period of calm. They strolled about, wound up on stage, smiling, for a bit. Then back to the trailer where, in true super-star fashion, Jagger was signing autographs."

Bernie Leadon remembered the crowd tossing what seemed like thousands of Frisbees, some of them plastic coffee can lids. Throughout the Burritos' half-hour show, he said, the vibes felt nice.

The scuffling and fighting began again during Crosby, Stills, Nash, and Young's performance, and it never really let up. Within seconds of the Stones' third song—"Sympathy for the Devil"—the Angels' stage-front thrashings caused Mick to stop and try to cool off the crowd. They started up again and got through most of the song, the crowd now quiet with unease. But the fighting started again and, as Mick peered out, there were kids staring at him in incredulous silence, mouthing the word, "Why?"

At a rear corner of the stage stood Michelle Phillips with Gram at her side. She had come to Altamont with her friend Ann Marshall. Soon after arriving, she took a swig of apple juice. "Oh, no," she groaned moments later, as she began to feel strange. After trying, without success, to throw up the LSD, she ran into Gram and begged him stay by her side.

"Everything took on a surreal quality," she said. "The fighting, screaming, hollering. . . . I saw kids on the stage picking up tabs of acid and putting them in their mouths."

Three songs later, just as the Stones had begun "Under My Thumb," a young black man named Meredith Hunter, against all wisdom and all the odds stacked against him that evening, flashed a gun. A gang of Angels took him down, and he was knifed to death.

Bernie Leadon thought he saw Hunter placed atop some flowers at a corner of the stage—"like a burnt offering." But, he said, he might have been hallucinating.

The Stones, unaware of exactly what had happened, carried on, singing songs that were ironic, in retrospect—"Brown Sugar," "Midnight Rambler," "Satisfaction," and "Street Fighting Man."

As captured by the Maysles crew, the Stones' departure by helicopter was straight out of Saigon the day the Americans pulled out of the Vietnam war.

Amid the rubble, Gram grabbed Michelle, and they just made it as the last two into the chopper. Michelle remembered the eerie silence inside the helicopter, especially when someone told Mick, apparently for the first time, that a man had been stabbed.

In the lobby of a nearby airport, awaiting a small plane to lift them back to San Francisco, Mick, Keith, and Gram railed at the Angels. "The Angels are worse than cops," said Gram. "They're so dumb. Michelle and I were standing by the side of the stage, not bothering anybody, just standing as far away as we could be and still see, and one Angel kept trying to push us back, every two minutes. Every two minutes I'd have to explain to him all over again, just like the first time, that we were supposed to be there." Moments later, the weight of the day's events seemed to have slipped off Gram's shoulders. In the limousine heading back to Nob Hill, San Franciso, and the Huntington Hotel, Gram kissed—or tried to kiss—Michelle, who was in no mood for romance.

Before the press and all the morning-after critics began parceling out the blame to the Stones, to the Angels, to the Dead (for suggesting the Angels), to the producers and planners, to the drugs, to those who peddled them and those who took them, and to rock and roll itself, the Rolling Stones knew they had blown it. Not only had they failed to re-create Woodstock in its most romanticized version—if that was ever their goal—but they had created the event that brought the Woodstock Nation to an end. They had failed its acid test.

Pamela DesBarres attended Altamont. After getting hit with a beer can she left early, before the Stones came on. Her strongest memories are of the grim, shell-shocked gathering at the Huntington Hotel afterward. "It was the most intense room to be in on earth. Everyone was high; Gram was there, leaning against the wall, nodding out. There was a whole discussion about what to do. Mick was actually thinking of quitting, retiring.

"I didn't want it to be like this," Mick said, very quietly.

The next day, bright and early, Mick was off to the airport for a nine o'clock flight to Geneva. He was carrying the Stones' earnings from the tour—some $1.2 million.

A few hours later, Gram and Michelle flew home to Los Angeles: she to Dennis Hopper; he to Gretchen Burrell and to his last, itchy months as a Flying Burrito Brother.

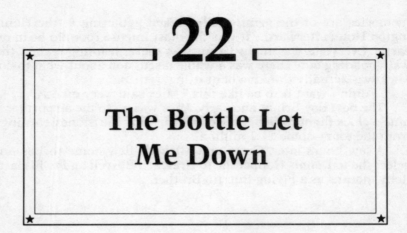

22

The Bottle Let Me Down

A&M Records knew how to make an album look good. For *Burrito Deluxe*, art director Tom Wilkes got Nudie to doll up an already handsome burrito with rhinestones. (The human Burritos, meanwhile, were dressed, for no apparent reason, in the plain white chemists' overalls used by Tony Foutz in his aborted UFO movie.)

But once A&M heard the actual album, the company knew it had a tortilla on its hands.

Jim Dickson and A&M were so certain that *Burrito Deluxe* would die a quick death that they moved to get another album— one with a specific focus on traditional country—out of the Burritos for summer release.

And so it was that Jim and the guys returned to the studios, this time to the Sound Factory in Hollywood, away from the A&M lot, to try their hand at a set of mostly country classics.

The songs included "Dim Lights," "Your Angel Steps Out of Heaven," "Close Up the Honky Tonks," "Crazy Arms," "Green, Green Grass of Home," Merle Haggard's "Sing Me Back Home" and "Tonight the Bottle Let Me Down," and Buck Owens's "Together Again."

The Bottle Let Me Down

Gram, who'd wanted to find room for some R&B in *Burrito Deluxe*, sang the Larry Williams' hit from the fifties, "Bony Moronie," and several more contemporary songs: the Stones' "Honky Tonk Women," John Fogerty's "Lodi," John D. Loudermilk's "Break My Mind," the Bee Gees' "To Love Somebody," and Bob Dylan's "I Shall Be Released."

The entire session was recorded quick and dirty—Gram's vocals and the band's instrumentals were recorded simultaneously—to give it a live feeling. In fact, Chris Hillman was certain that the Burritos were only rehearsing the songs.

But before Jim Dickson could add harmonies and additional instrumentals, the Burritos were back on the road. The album was never finished as intended, and in May, A&M grudgingly released *Burrito Deluxe*.

By that time, Gram was well on his way out of the Burritos. The others felt he had become impossible to work with. His fear of flying was at its most pronounced, and he coped with it by taking copious amounts of downers, his favorite being Tuinal. He took so many, said Chris, that he couldn't walk. "He would completely turn into a wheelchair person, breaking out in tears, and we couldn't get him on the airplane."

Once, at the Seattle airport, airline crew members refused to allow him on a flight. Hillman understood. "They'd see some guy slobbering in a chair, wearing these outlandish clothes and a top hat or something."

The Burritos would then assign a road manager to find alternate transportation and accompany Gram to the gig. At the clubs, he was often too incapacitated to perform.

It wasn't just the Burritos who couldn't rely on Gram. In the spring of 1970, his little sister desperately needed his help. "I was in an institution in New Orleans," said Avis. "I'd call him and beg him to get me out, and he could hardly talk. I think he was pretty strung out."

Not unlike Gram, Avis was constantly searching for a father figure. "And I ended up marrying one," she said. He was an older man and, she added, "He wasn't a very good choice. I can't really account for that period. It was one of utter despondency and confusion. And I was a very passive person, so I sort of let things happen to me."

Among the things that happened: Avis got pregnant, her marriage was annulled, and her stepfather committed her into DePaul Hospital, a mental institution in New Orleans, the better for him to maintain control over her life. "She didn't need to be there at all," said her uncle Tom Connor.

When Avis discovered that she was pregnant, in the summer of

1969, her stepfather tried to get her to sign her unborn child over to him. "That was because Parsons wanted to get control of her inheritance," her uncle said.

Avis's protective instincts for herself and for her unborn baby won out. She consulted with her uncle Tom and aunt Pauline, who encouraged her to keep her baby herself. When they offered to take care of the child until Avis felt capable of taking over, she accepted.

One evening in April, she pretended to be posting a letter at a mailbox at the unsecured outside gate on Calhoun Street. After faking a move to the mailbox, she jumped into a waiting friend's car, and they sped out of town.

That was as far as Avis's plans went. Fortunately, when she found herself at a bus station in Mississippi at 1:30 in the morning with no next stop in mind, and called her uncle in Nashville, he was ready to help.

The hospital had already called him about Avis's escape. Since DePaul officials were having airports and train stations checked, Tom told her to take a bus to Memphis. He arranged for a doctor friend of his to meet her there. The physician checked her health and stayed with her until she connected with a bus to Nashville. There, Tom and his wife Peggy met her (Aunt Pauline and her husband were at home, in Columbia, taking care of her ailing mother). In Nashville, Tom had arranged for another doctor friend, a gynecologist, to watch after her.

Two days later, holding onto her uncle's hand in the delivery room, Avis gave birth to a daughter, to whom she gave the star-crossed name—Avis.

A month after Avis had made him an uncle, Gram cracked up. Although he loved motorcycles—even rode one all the way to Joshua Tree with Phil Kaufman—he was never very good with bikes. In fact, Chris Hillman wrote "Wheels" ("I'm not afraid to ride/I'm not afraid to die") with Gram in mind. Gram could handle his first bike, a compact BSA, all right, Chris thought. But when he got his Harley Davidson, "He wasn't strong enough to hold it all the time. I knew he would eat it on that bike."

John Phillips remembered Gram's chopper as "pure redneck—buckskin seats, fringes hanging down." Gram seemed to work harder on looks than on getting his chops down. When his front fender loosened, he simply held it together with a coat hanger.

One day in early May, Gram and a woman friend of John's, a singer he remembered only as Maggie, were on his Harley. They were trailing John and his girlfriend, the actress Genevieve Waite. Gram gave Maggie his helmet, and as they rode out of Bel Air, north of Brentwood, at 50 mph, the hanger snapped and his bike fell apart. The handlebars came off, followed by the front tire. What was left of the Harley then smashed into a curb.

John had been riding half a mile ahead, and when he realized that he was no longer hearing Gram's bike behind him, he turned back. Gram was in the middle of the road, spewing blood from his mouth, nose, and ears. Both Gram and Maggie had been thrown from the bike. A motorist was placing a blanket over Gram, and John thought he was dead.

John knelt at Gram's side. "Gram, Gram, Gram," John called.

Gram, apparently, thought he was dead, too.

"John," he said. "Take me for a long white ride."

Instead, Gram took a long, loud ride in an ambulance and spent several weeks in a hospital, healing skin and bones. Luckily, Maggie was thrown onto a lawn and escaped with a slight concussion and multiple scratches.

Pamela DesBarres visited at the hospital. "He's so beaten up, such a mess," she wrote in her diary. "His face was blown up like a purple-and-blue balloon. God bless him and keep him through this, maybe it'll help somehow, he's been *so* high all the time, I've been calling him Gram Richards."

With time and the help of a lot of pain pills, Gram mended and rejoined the band.

On the surface, things were fine. In June, the Burritos did several dates at the Jam Factory in San Antonio. But Gram had decided, long before that night, that he no longer wanted to be in the group. Instead of leaving peacefully, however, he forced the band's hand.

Late in June, the band was at the Brass Ring, a club in the San Fernando Valley. With such friends and fellow musicians as Leon Russell and Delaney and Bonnie in the crowd, Chris Hillman would kick off one song, only to hear Gram start singing another song, in another key and tempo.

"It's pretty tricky to do that," said Chris, "and at that point you just go, 'That's it.'" Backstage, Chris told Gram he was fired and, as a twisted form of negative severance pay, grabbed Gram's guitar and broke it. He immediately regretted destroying the guitar. But, he reasoned, "It was better than hitting him in the head."

Chris drew the bottom line on Gram: "He wanted it all," he said, "but he didn't work at it. And that's what I finally realized. He didn't put his time in. Discipline was not a word in his vocabulary."

The problem may have been that, short of the stardom he desired, Gram *had* it all, at least monetarily. While Chris and most other musicians had to make a success of performing in order to make a living, Gram was set for life with his trust fund. Given that kind of edge, Chris wondered, how could Gram ever have any sense of accomplishment?

On the flip side, Gram was constantly being deserted—by his father and mother, most significantly, but also, in his view, by managers and record companies that never came through.

Gram wanted acceptance; he tried to please people. He was, at heart, a sweet man who meant no harm. But, having been left behind all his life, and having the wherewithal to buffer himself with money and drugs, he could quit his bands, drop out of Harvard, propose to Nancy, plan a wedding and forget about it, leave his sister, Avis, to fend for herself in a crisis, and feel little pain.

Life for him, after all, was a series of incomplete sentences. Why should it be different for anyone else?

Shortly after leaving the Burritos—Gram would ascribe his departure to boredom with the band—he ran into Bernie Leadon.

"Hey, Bernie," he said cheerfully, "why don't you leave these fuckers and come with me? I talked with Keith this morning and he wants you and me to come over and record with him."

Bernie didn't bite. "I'm gonna stay in town," he told Gram. "I don't have any money. You've got your trust fund, and you can run all over the fucking world if you want to."

In London, the Rolling Stones were putting together their own record label. Gram thought he might be part of it, or at least have an album produced by Keith.

When those possibilities stalled, Gram hooked up with record producer Terry Melcher. Like Gram, he was young and wealthy and surrounded himself with beautiful women and demons.

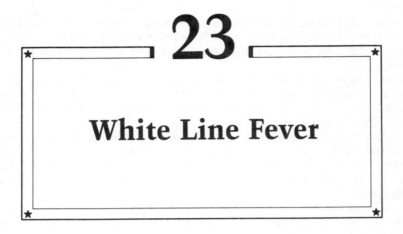

23

White Line Fever

The two had met the previous November, when Ann Marshall took Terry Melcher to a Burritos show at the Corral. The two men hit it off immediately.

"I was floored by the *Mr. Tambourine Man* album [produced by Melcher]," said Gram, "and Terry has that charisma."

Terry, in turn, loved the way Gram sang.

Within a week, Gram was spending time at Terry's house in Benedict Canyon and, after weathering the bike accident and the split from the Burritos, he began spending as much time at Terry's as at the Chateau. Gretchen sometimes joined him at Terry's, but she was busy acting in a film. By age eighteen, Gretchen had landed a role in a Roger Vadim film, *Pretty Maids All in a Row*. The film starred Angie Dickinson as a horny high-school teacher and Rock Hudson as a counselor with a thing for coeds; for loving them and leaving them dead.

The French director clearly took a liking to the slim, blond Gretchen. And, although hers was a bit part, she was pictured in a *Playboy* magazine spread. In the opening shot, she was one of five girls—nude, of course—sitting around Roger Vadim, who was, of course, clothed. Next, Gretchen got a full page. Here she looked like a frightened doe. The caption was a quote from Vadim: "Gretchen Burrell has the best figure in the cast; her breasts are just right, like a happy compromise between Jane Russell and Twiggy."

In the third photo, she was scrunched up on a throw rug with Rock Hudson hovering over her. The caption: "The first of eight girls who make love with Hudson in the film is Gretchen, the girl with the perfect body."

Once she finished work on the film, Gram shut down her acting and modeling careers. He didn't want a working woman. "I didn't get to do nearly anything I started out to do," said Gretchen. "My life sorta took a very strange turn there for a while . . . very unhealthy."

Gram himself was quite a mess, but Terry Melcher valued his companionship. Since the fall of 1969, he had been running scared from the Manson family.

Terry doesn't remember much about those days, but if he has blocked out much of what he went through, it's understandable.

He was hot stuff in the late sixties. He was the young staff producer at Columbia who got such projects as the Byrds and Paul Revere and the Raiders by default. He clicked with such hits as "Mr. Tambourine Man" and "Turn! Turn! Turn!" He also produced Taj Mahal and the blues artist/guitarist Ry Cooder at Columbia before moving on to independent production with Apple Records. He was also a producer of his mother Doris Day's TV show in 1968.

It was the connection with Apple—and thus with the Beatles— that interested Charles Manson, who, fresh out of prison, got to Melcher through a common friend, Dennis Wilson of the Beach Boys.

As he did with a dozen would-be rock stars and bands a week, Melcher gave Manson an audition; he even gave Charlie and his growing "family" $50 at one time, calling it "food money," since the communal group was known for scrounging through garbage bins for their dinners.

But Melcher ultimately wasn't interested in doing anything with Manson's music, and that's where his problems began.

When the killings climaxed with the murders of actress Sharon Tate and four others at the house Tate shared with director Roman Polanski—a house whose previous tenants had been Melcher and Candice Bergen—he thought he might have been an intended victim. If not that, the Mansons were, at the very least, sending him a message.

Melcher's suspicions were strengthened when Susan Atkins of the Family said: "The reason Charlie picked that house was to instill fear into Terry Melcher, because Terry had given us his word on a few things and never came through with them."

"The scary thing about it," he said, "was that the Family looked like every kid at every Dead or Byrds concert."

Soon after the Manson Family was captured, Melcher got what he considered as proof that they weren't after him. The DA, Vincent Bugliosi, told him that police had recovered a giant telescope from the Mansons. It had been stolen from the house Melcher had moved to, in Malibu.

They knew exactly where he lived, and they hadn't done their carnage there. But he still didn't know if something else might be going on.

Neither did the police, who gave Melcher protection by staking out his house around the clock, knocking on his door almost hourly to be sure he was still breathing, and arming him with a shotgun.

The constant police presence only made Terry more nervous. He hired a bodyguard and saw a psychiatrist. "I developed a pretty bad case of insomnia," he said.

As time passed and it became clear that he was not a target, Terry moved back into the Benedict Canyon neighborhood. He kept the shotgun and bodyguard—whom he referred to as his "house man"—but he resumed his routine.

Always looking for interesting talent, he found Gram to be a complete original.

In the middle of 1970, country-rock was still a revolutionary notion. "At that point in time, the country world was seen as a reactionary group of people, and you've got this guy dressed in Nudie suits and sounding like Hank Williams, with the attitude of the psychedelic people.

"This guy was like the white, country Jimi Hendrix."

With Gram on guitar and Terry on piano, they spent many evenings, into mid-mornings, working on songs.

"He was the sort of guy who could sit down with a guitar and do six hours and you'd never get bored. He was a real troubadour."

Soon Terry was representing himself as Gram Parsons's new producer. He approached Jerry Moss at A&M about a solo album, and Jerry agreed.

Unfortunately, neither Gram nor Terry was often in shape to make good judgments about recording.

Ginny Ganahl, Terry's secretary, lived in a guest house on the property and saw the two men from morning to night. Gram's days often began, she said, with mugs filled halfway with coffee and the rest of the way with sugar and cognac.

The refrigerator was stocked primarily with Cool Whip and Russian vodka. Around the house, Gram was more often than not on downers—mostly Seconal, but also Tuinal and Placidyl. "He just had time to kill," she said, "and that's how he killed it."

Both Gram and Terry were self-destructive, but blasé about it, said Ginny. They related to each other like wealthy outlaws. Hours were passed thinking up song and album titles. Once Gram decided to call his first solo album *Money Honey*. A moment later he came up with *These Blues Have Made a Nigger Out of Me*.

"That was one of his songs," said Terry. "That was very much his humor."

After a few weeks of jamming, Terry and Gram pronounced themselves ready to record. They rounded up a number of solid musicians, including guitarists Ry Cooder and Clarence White, pianist Earl Ball, drummer Spooner Oldham, and singers Merry Clayton and Claudia Lennear.

According to A&M's logbooks, Gram and company recorded ten songs, among them Merle Haggard's "White Line Fever," Gram's own "Brass Buttons," and the Roy Orbison hit "Dream Baby." Also recorded were an Everly Brothers song that Ann Marshall had turned him on to, "Sleepless Nights," Patsy Cline's "I Fall to Pieces," George Jones's "She Thinks I Still Care," and a reprise of "Do Right Woman" from the first Burritos album.

Once, while they were working on "White Line Fever," Ginny watched Gram fall off his stool, then attempt to sing while lying flat on the floor. Terry reportedly fell asleep once at the control board.

Jim Dickson, who produced the Burritos' second album, warned Jerry Moss about hiring Terry. He had been difficult to work with at CBS, said Jim, between his demands and his heavy drinking.

Some time later, Jim ran into Jerry, and the A&M chairman conceded that Jim had been right.

"Well," said Jerry, "Gram threw up on the piano—into the concert Yamaha." He and Terry were both drunk in the studio, and A&M was getting nothing—once again.

Terry thought Gram was in control for most of the two weeks of the sessions or, at least, "he wasn't a lot more or less stoned than anyone recording in L.A. in 1970. He knew exactly what he wanted to do." Gram overindulged in cocaine and downers, some of them acquired from one of a number of his personal physicians, a Hollywood doctor who had numerous celebrity patients.

"Excess was the order of the day," said Terry, "and he was beyond the ordinary excess."

As for himself, he confessed that he had his difficulties. But, he said, "I was a little better than Gram."

At Terry's house, Ginny remembered Gram toying with one of the weapons Terry had collected post-Manson. One afternoon, she and the bodyguard heard a blast outside the house. They found Gram standing with a sawed-off shotgun at his side. He had fired it into a hillside for no particular reason.

On other days, Gram might entertain Ginny by mimicking the sound of a vacuum cleaner and pretending to vacuum a room. But he was often as sarcastic as he was silly, she said. "When he was feeling his worst, it was just because of the way he felt about himself. He was spoiled and jaded, and chose to think he was wounded by life. He let everybody know he had been chosen to carry a heavy burden—being Gram Parsons."

Terry agreed. Gram, he said, combined a New Age fatalism and spirituality with a Neanderthal level of bitterness. "He would bear a grudge forever and waste a lot of time resenting a lot of people." Terry thought Gram saw himself as a victim, starting with his family and extending to the music business. "He thought he was too much an artist to be understood by the industry. He was such a romantic character. He was one of these people who thought it was great to die young."

It was Gram's self-destructive streak, said Terry, that led to A&M's cancellation of the album project and brought Gram's stay at Terry's to an end.

"I didn't know what to do with him. I knew he was going to die here or somewhere else."

24

Gimme Shelter

Keith Richards, talking about Gram, was being terribly nice, and he must have sensed it. "He wasn't a total angel," he felt compelled to add. At the idea of equating Gram with an angel, he unleashed a metallic cackle of a laugh. "But he was a spark."

In late October 1970 Gram went to A&M and signed out the master tapes of the ten songs he had recorded with Terry Melcher. They were never seen or heard again.

Gram stagnated. On occasion, he got involved in other musicians' projects. He was on Steve Young's debut album on A&M, playing organ on "That's How Strong My Love Is." He appeared, in various minor roles, on albums by Delaney and Bonnie, Jesse Ed Davis, and Steve Young. One night, drunk, he wound up at a Byrds session being produced by Terry and sang a faint harmony line on "All Things," a track on the Byrds' 1970 album, *(Untitled)*. Terry remembered: "I think he was drunk that night and he came in and asked to do the harmony." He played piano and sang behind Fred

Neil on "You Don't Miss Your Water," a song he'd cut with the Byrds.

In March, with Gretchen by his side, he took off for England and set up housekeeping in apartments in Kensington and Belgrave.

Gram expected that he would be working on an album for the Rolling Stones' new record label, either as a solo artist or as part of a duet with Keith Richards. He had also been asked by Rick Grech, whose supergroup effort, Blind Faith, had disbanded, to lend a hand with his solo album.

Gram and Gretchen visited Rick and Jenny Grech in Sussex, south of London on the English Channel. Rick and Gram hit the local pubs, sampled lots of barley wine, and wrote country songs.

Next, Gram and Gretchen visited Ian Dunlop and his wife, Valerie. After giving up on the first version of the Burritos, Ian had gone back to art school until 1969, when he retreated to his birthplace in Cornwall County, England, and became an organic farmer. The Dunlops lived in a fourteenth-century farmhouse in the tiny fishing village of Tregidden.

To Gram's delight, Ian hadn't given up entirely on music. He was still playing bass, writing songs, and coming up with wild names for whatever bands he could get together. One of his ensembles was called Harvey and the Sequins, consisting of Ian and an eighty-five-year-old accordion player.

"Jesus," said Gram to Ian. "Who are 'the Sequins'? "

"Well," Ian replied, "we were always looking for another guy."

Gretchen loved life around the old millhouse. "We walked and we found old Roman statues in riverbeds and we were chased by cows. It was very romantic; a very healthy time for us. It was like a whole different world all together."

Gram also loved England. Sometimes, he thought, his music could make more headway in England than in the United States. In London he found plenty of evidence that the Byrds, including the band of the *Sweetheart of the Rodeo* era, were highly regarded. "They seemed to be ready for country music," he said. "I met a lot of people who were into it, but for the main part all they ever get to hear is Jim Reeves and old Patsy Cline singles and things, and I think that's terrible."

"I always had this dream," he told Chuck Casell, "about starting a country band in England. England is so unjaded that way. They're so open-minded they're ignorant; they don't know. Maybe it's just a dream, but it seems like the perfect place to start a country music scene."

In London, looking for treatment for a minor ailment, he met Dr. Sam Hutt, a gynecologist with a love of bluesy, introspective music from a wide variety of sixties singer-songwriters. Dr. Hutt had his practice in the living room of a flat he shared with Roger Chapman, lead singer of the British band Family, and Jenny Fabian, author of the book *Groupie*. On his turntable was an album by Fred Neil.

The doctor was at his desk when Gram and Gretchen walked in. Gram was dressed in the jacket he had had on at Altamont; Gretchen's perfect body was encased in tight jeans and cowboy boots.

"Hey, that's Freddy Neil," said Gram.

Dr. Hutt was amazed that someone else actually knew about Neil.

"How do you know Fred Neil?" he asked.

"*Know* him?" Gram replied. "I *played* with him."

Gram then identified himself and learned quickly that Sam Hutt was a big fan of the Byrds, and that he hated *Sweetheart of the Rodeo*—he missed McGuinn's twanging twelve-string Rickenbacker and the spacy "mind gardens" songs. But he loved the Burrito Brothers, which, to his Rickenbacked ears, didn't sound like country.

In the doctor's office, Gram picked up a guitar and sang, never mind the doctor's distaste for *Sweetheart*, a song from that album, "You're Still On My Mind."

Gram's soulful reading immediately reached Dr. Hutt, and it wasn't long before he was splitting his time between medicine and playing traditional country music.

Dr. Hutt became "Hank Wangford," leader of a semi-comical country music band. On Gram's trips from the South of France into London, the two would get together. As he often had before, Gram pulled out his favorite George Jones sides to play for the doctor; the King of Broken Hearts had reached yet another set of ears.

Gimme Shelter, edited in a hurry to take advantage of the storm surrounding Altamont, was released before the end of 1970. As expected, it starred the Rolling Stones, the Hell's Angels, and the late Meredith Hunter.

The Burritos served as the first group in the Altamont portion of the movie. Gram was seen only briefly, shot from the side and behind. Far more camera time went to the crowds tossing Frisbees, blowing bubbles, dancing and smiling, and to the first indications of trouble.

Still, the Burritos, singing "Six Days on the Road," lasted a full two minutes and thirty seconds in *Gimme Shelter*. Gram had finally made it, as himself, in a feature film.

★

Linda Lawrence suspected it; Avis Parsons heard about it, and Dr. Hutt confirmed it: Gram was using heroin.

His use, on a casual basis, may have dated back as far as the mid-sixties. Dick Weissman, the former Journeyman, saw Gram shooting up in a New York apartment where he stayed briefly with a fledgling filmmaker. "I had never seen anybody shoot up before," said Dick. "That really startled the hell out of me." Intimates of Gram's have pointed fingers at various other intimates of Gram for getting him started. Perhaps it's most instructive to listen to Chris Hillman's reminder that Gram was a voracious consumer of all kinds of drugs. "He was going to try any of that stuff," said Chris. "No one had to push it on him."

Keith Richards didn't need to see fingers being directed at him to know that he was being accused of steering Gram wrong.

"I'm aware of those rumblings—'Oh, Gram would still be around if it wasn't for Keith Richards'—I've heard it put as boldly as that. And there is a possibility, to be totally honest, that yes, maybe hanging around the Rolling Stones didn't *help* him in his attitude toward drugs. But I would honestly say that his attitude toward those things reminded me of what was going on everywhere."

And Gram was not exactly a student at the feet of the Stones. In late 1969 Keith was in a studio in Muscle Shoals, Alabama, with the Stones, who were breaking from their American tour to cut a few new tracks. At four in the morning, he took a break and woke up an assistant to get him some cocaine. Stanley Booth, the writer, watched as Keith inhaled deeply, shook his head, and announced: "Gram Parsons gets better coke than the Mafia."

As Keith told me: "Gram was just as knowledgeable about chemical substances as I was when I met him. And he had very good taste. He went for the top of the line. I don't think I taught him much about drugs; I was still learning myself, much to my detriment. I think we were both basically into the same thing. We liked drugs and we liked the finest quality."

By the time Dr. Hutt met Gram, in 1971, Gram's use of smack had become a problem. He would be called to Gram's and Gretchen's house in London. "He'd be sitting on the lav with a needle hanging out of his arm. He'd be almost over the edge. I thought of him as someone who'd know how much people loved him by pushing himself further and further and seeing if they'd pull him back."

Sam Hutt knew right off that Gram was a junkie. When Gram talked to him about how difficult it was to come off heroin, he told him about an alternative to methadone called Lomotil.

In Gram's only known public statements about heroin, he told Jay Ehler in early 1973 that it was apathy that drove people to hard drugs. As for himself: "Sometimes I know why, sometimes I don't. To get high . . . you don't know that it'll fuck you up in the end. *You don't know!*"

Gram refused to say whether he was ever addicted. Instead, he spoke at length about how to get off heroin, talking knowledgeably about methadone, quoting from William Burroughs, Dr. Sam Hutt, and making reference to "Smithie," the nurse for the developer of the epimorphine cure.

Apparently, Gram had gone through such a cure with Keith.

"We did a couple of cures together," Keith told me. "That was ay my house in London, with a nurse called Smithie, recommended to us by Bill Burroughs."

During their cures, Keith said, he and Gram were like the Odd Couple. "We'd come down off the stuff and sit at a piano for three days in agony, just trying to take our minds off of it, arguing about whether the chord change on 'I Fall to Pieces' should be a minor or a major. And we'd get through it that way.

"We went through some intense periods together."

★

As specific as he could be on some things, Gram was a master of the opaque, intriguing remark. Once he tossed off what some referred to as his lost years—the time between his last work with the Burritos in 1970 and the release of his first solo album in early 1973—by saying, with a shrug: "I was learning how to be invisible."

But one man's low profile is another man's spotlight, and when, in February, the Rolling Stones, trapped in the 97 percent tax bracket in England and forced to flee to France, announced a "Farewell to Great Britain" tour, Gram knew where he had to be.

It was, in one sense, a business trip, since the Stones—or, at least, Keith—had an interest in Gram as part of the fledgling Rolling Stones record label. After the first album, *Sticky Fingers*, the band expected to issue solo albums by Keith and by bassist Bill Wyman, and then a coupling of Keith and Gram.

At least that's what the papers said. For some time now Gram had been telling anyone who'd listen that he'd be working with Keith and with Rolling Stones Records.

Keith didn't remember any definitive plans or any talk about a duet album. He and Gram never talked business. Instead, he said, they had an understanding that when they felt they had the songs and a record deal together, and when the Stones didn't have Keith tied up, they would work together.

"It was one of those things you looked forward to and you thought you had plenty of time for. It wasn't something he was just going to rush in and do. You figured it would happen naturally a little further down the road, but the road was shorter than we thought."

While a Keith-and-Gram project stayed on the back burner, Keith encouraged Gram to use the Stones connection whenever he felt a need to.

"He was hustled by certain people, and he would say to me, 'If you could produce this for me, that would really be a help'—a love pat—and I would say, 'I don't think it's the time; I'm going back on the road again.' He'd say, 'Can you tell them that?'" Gram was talking to Keith exactly the way he'd talked ten years earlier to Buddy Freeman, the Shilos' manager.

Keith told Gram to say to record companies that it was Keith who was interested in producing Gram. It was just a matter of getting the time.

And so it was that Gram joined the Stones on the road. He had no musical role on this ten-day, ten-town tour from Newcastle through Glasgow and Liverpool and concluding in London. In fact, Jo Bergman, the Stones' secretary, mostly remembered Gram being "pretty wrecked all the time."

He also provided, or added, several comic moments. In *Rolling Stone*, reporter Robert Greenfield documented two of them.

The first occurred after what the band considered their worst show of the tour, in Liverpool. In the midst of the misery of the dressing room, someone suggested, "What we need is a joint." Gram spoke up. "Yeah, where are the dope dealers?" He got up, went to the door, stuck his head out, and shouted: *"Dope dealers?"*

On another day—a bleary, early afternoon breakfast—Gram told Charlie Watts a little story. "Bobby Keyes played on one of Yoko's sessions," he said. "People were sniffing Excedrin and bouncing off walls. She took Bobby in a corner and said, 'Imagine there is a cold wind blowing and you are a lonely frog.'

"He just laid down his saxophone. . . . 'Lady,' he said. 'Yew shore got a strange slant on things.'"

"Yeah," Gram now added, "starting with your eyes."

Charlie laughed good-naturedly. "Fantastic," he said. "Gram . . . fantastic."

★

In April 1971, Rolling Stones Records signed a deal to have their records distributed in the United States by Atlantic Records, and the various Stones packed up and moved to France, with Keith taking over a villa in Villefranche-sur-Mer. While each Stone had a home of his own, Keith's house, known as Nellcote, would serve as headquarters and studios for the band.

After a spring occupied with Mick and Bianca's marriage in St. Tropez, the release and instant success of *Sticky Fingers*, and a Keith Richards car crash, the Stones were ready to settle in and begin what would become *Exile on Main Street*.

Nellcote was more a palace than a house. Priced at two million dollars (Keith was renting it for $10,000 a month), it overlooked the fishing village Villefranche, whose bay and harbor served both yachts and fishing boats. Its rooms were stately, designed as if for visiting royalty; the gardens were lush and abundant with fruit trees and palms.

By now Keith was addicted to heroin, and the Stones chose to make things easier on him and everyone else by going to his house to work. Beginning in July the Stones, along with Gram and a number of side musicians—many of them friends of Gram's and some of them introduced to the Stones by him—convened at Nellcote.

Gram was there as a friend of Keith's; he was not part of the recording sessions. Still, Gramophiles have spent hours listening to *Exile* and arguing over which songs he had a hand in. Some listeners have named "Sweet Virginia" and "Tumbling Dice" as songs on which Gram pitched in on background vocals; one critic called "Torn and Frayed" "Gram Parsons–influenced."

Stanley Booth once asked Keith Richards what Gram did on *Exile*. Keith replied that Gram wouldn't have presumed to work himself into the record. "He was too much of a gentleman," said Keith.

But when I told Keith that Gram once said that he'd sung along on "Sweet Virginia," he said he wouldn't be surprised. "Gram was just there. If you got lost for a harmony . . . we used to get everybody in there, and Gram could at least sing, so he probably *was* on 'Sweet Virginia' and maybe a couple more."

Gram made greater contributions to the album, said Keith, by just being around. "Usually, when I'm working with the Stones, it's very rare that anybody not involved with the job gets involved. Usually I block off and I work."

Gram was a rarity. "There's not a lot of guys in the world that you don't mind waking up and they're there—for weeks—and it's a pleasure to have them around. For me, Gram was a way of getting a bit outside of the Stones, which was getting very claustrophobic in those years. It was very nice to have another musician, a writer, just to bounce ideas over, without any sense of intrusion."

Without Gram around, picking and singing country tunes, the

Stones' more countrified songs would never have been written, said Keith. "They wouldn't have been around if it weren't for Gram. Musicians are whatever we hear, whatever we listen to."

But, Keith said, it was inadvertent. "We were just having a good time, just lying around in the sun during the day and going down to the studio at night. He'd come and listen, and during the day we'd sit around and play guitars and stuff. We just enjoyed each other's company. It was such a natural turn-on, to be with each other and play."

As far as Keith knew, none of their casual jams was ever recorded, although they sometimes talked about capturing them on tape. "We spent hours and hours, and by the end of the evening, there'd be definite plans to go and cut an album tomorrow, because we thought it was so great. And then you wake up, and you know it's impossible right now, and you look at each other kind of sheepishly and say, 'It was just another one of those nights.' "

Mick Jagger, among others, came to look on Gram and Keith's close friendship with suspicion. As Keith put it, Mick saw Gram as just another hanger-on, trying to get as much as possible out of the Stones. But Gram, Phil Kaufman noted, "could have the same dirty habits and pay his own way."

Early on, Mick expressed an appreciation of Gram, crediting him with being "one of the few people who really helped me to sing country music. Before that, Keith and I would just copy off records."

But as Keith grew closer to Gram, Mick began to feel threatened. Mick, said Keith, "is very jealous of anybody that I get close to. He's an old woman like that with me. . . . He's *very, very* possessive. Gram was special. If he was in a room, everybody else became sweet. But I noticed Mick's reaction to anybody who wanted to be a friend of mine. He was rude to Gram, and Gram did have to take a certain amount of resentment from Mick later on. But understand from Mick's point of view that Gram was pretty out of it and outrageous at the time, and in Mick's prim and proper upbringing, it was: 'This guy's being outrageous, and he's with *my* friend.' "

When Mick was rude to Gram, said Stanley Booth, Gram responded innocently, looking at him and laughing—not to mock Mick, but to say, "What do you mean?"

Gretchen joined Gram at Villefranche during the summer. The surroundings were beautiful, she said, but she had clearer memories of the tension around Nellcote. "You could cut the air with a knife all the time," she said.

It was something more than creative tension. First, there were the sheer numbers. Counting the Stones, their side musicians, their crews and their families, and assorted visitors—some of them

there, reportedly, primarily to provide drugs—the population at
Nellcote swelled at times to thirty people. Most of the musicians,
said Anita Pallenberg, stayed in the main house, "which was full of
madness."

Although the Stones hired a cook, Anita Pallenberg was still
saddled with the job of organizing a sit-down every evening—or
whenever dinner was served—for anywhere between a dozen and
thirty people.

Second, there was the work at hand. The Stones were still
getting to know their new guitarist, Mick Taylor, and often the
band was scattered, with Mick Jagger off to Paris to see Bianca, or
Keith running upstairs to put son Marlon to bed, a chore that
sometimes took an hour, "with the whole fuckin' band *thundering*
away in the basement. The strain was mostly on Anita."

Third, there were the drugs. As Gretchen recalled, "the drugs
were just incessant; the booze was incessant." The music was
interesting, and Anita was fine—"except when she'd have her
screaming fits when there was no more cocaine and stuff."

Gram wasn't in much better shape.

"He was a physical wreck, totally zonked out of his skull," said
Jo Bergman.

Linda Lawrence, former girlfriend of Brian Jones and Gram
Parsons (until she was replaced by Gretchen), was by now married
to the singer Donovan Leitch and living in Ireland. She got a call
from Keith. He asked, "Could you please take Gram? He's out of his
head and he needs to be with somebody." Linda was agreeable but
never heard again from the Stones or from Gram.

Keith vaguely recalls a time when Gram "was really going
over the edge." But instead of shipping him off to Linda, he thinks
he simply told Gram to lie low for a while.

That, however, was not Gram's style, and finally, Jo got orders
from somewhere in the Stones hierarchy. "Okay," she was told,
"you will take Gram to the airport and you will put him on a plane
out of here."

Gram and Gretchen saved Jo from having to ship them out.
They returned to England and to Ian and Valerie Dunlop's farm in
Cornwall.

There, they rediscovered the simple life, growing vegetables
and making their own wine and butter, fending off farm bats and
wasps, and taking long walks around the middle of nowhere. It
was, said Gretchen, a little bit of normalcy.

Gretchen wished they could settle in England, if not New
Orleans, which she had visited with Gram. One wish led to another, and by the time they left England for the United States, they
had decided to get married.

Gimme Shelter

While some intimates of Gram's thought his relationship with Gretchen was in trouble from the very beginning, others thought they were just fine together. David Rivkin, who wrote "How Much I've Lied" with Gram, spent many evenings at the Chateau Marmont and thought of Gram and Gretchen as a couple who loved each other. Young as she was, and erratic as he was, Gretchen had to be his mother as well as his mate, and she tried. More than once she got phone calls from club owners or a highway patrol saying Gram was too drunk to drive or ride his Harley, and she'd go to fetch him.

"You realize that this man was the love of my life," she said. "He was everything to me."

Gram never spoke in public about Gretchen, but in a letter to his Bolles classmate Frank Murphy a year after he'd married her, Gram wrote: "Yes, I'm getting along very well. One thing, though, about Gretchen—she can't seem to sew up my jeans quite as fast as I wear them out. She is a beautiful young blonde girl I met while I was being a R&R ★ & she in hi-school . . . What a drag! She still isn't 21. So, fights with bouncers, bartenders, club owners and even Gretch—when she doesn't feel wanted."

For his wedding to Gretchen, Gram entertained no Hank Williams fantasies. Except for one thing: He'd have the ceremony in New Orleans, where Hank had two of his three exchanges of vows with Billie Jean—and where his stepfather, Bob Parsons, lived.

By now, Gram had to know that his stepfather was not to be trusted.

When he called Jet Thomas to ask him to conduct the ceremony, and told him it would be at Bob and Bonnie Parsons' house, Jet knew enough to be puzzled. Maybe, he thought, it was Gram's way of coming home. Except that New Orleans had never been home to Gram.

Gretchen found her stepfather-in-law creepy, a man without scruples. Nonetheless, she said, in a way, Gram idolized him. "Bob was the flashy father figure."

"It's hard to say," said Avis, who overlooked her own derision of her stepfather to attend the wedding. "I suppose it was just one of those things where he felt like it'd be done the way he wanted it. He felt as if Bob would do it right. And why not put Bob in the capacity to which he could be used best—which was entertaining?"

As much as he could, Bob Parsons did it up right. His house was a stout, two-story brick building in a beautiful neighborhood just four blocks away from the 250-acre Audubon Park, with its zoo, golf course, and view of the Mississippi River. Just across the park was the DePaul Hospital, where Avis had been committed.

Hickory Wind

At the house Bob Parsons came through with a big, fancy wedding. But to Jet Thomas, who'd known Gram when he was talking about marrying Nancy in a star-studded mixture of wedding and rock concert, it felt weird.

The wedding party included only family and Bob and Bonnie's friends. None of Gram's friends from the South or the West Coast attended. Jet and the wedded couple felt like tourists.

25

Her Name's Emmylou

In conversation, Gram Parsons often had the sound of a soul hang-gliding through the air. His was a gentle voice with clear shades of the South, even if, as he tried to convince one interviewer, he thought he spoke without any echoes of Waycross and Winter Haven. When he was stoned, the sentences did lazy loop-de-loops getting to a point, sometimes not getting there at all.

Sitting with Chuck Casell of A&M in the spring of 1972, helping to push a live Burritos album that he wasn't even on, he was talking about the possibility, still being dangled in front of him, of working with the Stones' record label—or, failing that, maybe a smaller company. But he was distracted and let Casell know it.

"I just can't get it out of my mind," he said. "Like, I found a chick singer who's real good who I want to sing with. I've always had problems with guys who can't sing high enough. . . . And if you get a really good chick, it works better than anything, because you can look at each other with love in your eyes, right?" He laughed and looked at Gretchen, who was sitting nearby. "If my wife could put up with it, it would be the perfect solution," he said. "She's a gas. Her name's Emmylou Harris."

Hickory Wind

Gram's sister, Avis, remembered hearing from him at about this time. She was in Nashville and had been helping him look for a Louvin Brothers album he wanted. When he called for a progress report, he told her: "Oh, I've met this wonderful girl. This is the one. We just sound so good together."

Emmylou Harris had just about had it with music when Gram found her.

Born in Birmingham, Alabama, the daughter of a Marines officer, she was raised in various military bases around Virginia. In high school, she strove to be "hip and cool." A shy, self-effacing girl who was never part of the "in" crowd, she nonetheless desired attention. She sang at parties because she realized that "when I started singing, people began noticing me." As a teenager she won several beauty contests, and she played alto saxophone in her high school marching band, even though she knew being in the band was "just about the lowest thing on the social climbing ladder." A straight-A student, she was selected class valedictorian.

At the University of North Carolina in Greensboro, about the same time that Gram, one state south, was singing with the Shilos, Emmylou began to rebel against the regimentation of her childhood. She gave up her studies in drama and began singing with musicians at a local club, the Red Door. Dropping out of school after a year and a half, she gravitated to New York, where she lived at the YWCA and hung out in Greenwich Village. She was singing both folk and country music. She married, got pregnant, and made an album. Both her album and the marriage turned out to be disasters.

Emmylou moved to Nashville, where she tried singing country, then worked as a model at an art class (wearing a long gown and "holding an umbrella for *some* reason"). She was a singing waitress, and then a cocktail waitress at a Polynesian restaurant until she was so far along in her pregnancy that she had to quit. She could barely pay the rent and needed food stamps to make ends meet.

In 1970 Emmylou and baby Hallie moved back in with her parents, who now lived in Maryland. By day she handed out brochures to prospective buyers of model homes. In nearby Washington, D.C., she made friends with Bill and Taffy Danoff, who later had a big hit as part of the Starland Vocal Band ("Afternoon Delight"). They pushed Emmylou back on stage, and she began singing again, beginning with melancholy, ten-verse folk songs. After adding an acoustic guitarist, Gerry Mule, and a bassist, her boyfriend, Tom Guidera, she sang six nights a week at various D.C. clubs, including the back room of a singles bar in Georgetown called Clyde's.

She barely made a living. A big payday would be $125—for all three musicians. More often, the trio took home between $5 and $10 each. Emmylou, Tom, and Hallie shared a noisy shack on River Road—it intersected with a highway—with another couple. Once Emmylou and the other woman of the house got food stamps by telling officials that they were both married and had children.

"The people came out and we got caught," said Tom. "That's how bad it was."

But Emmylou was being heard. And while she pleased her crowds with folkie tunes, songs from the Joni Mitchell catalog, and softer sounds from the Beatles, she could also dig deeper, into bluegrass and country music.

The story of how Gram Parsons discovered her has gone every which way.

When I asked her about it, Emmylou smiled. "It was in Washington, at Clyde's," she said. "Gram used to say Baltimore because it sounds better, because we did a song called 'Streets of Baltimore.'"

It wasn't even Gram but his replacement in the Burritos, Rick Roberts, who, along with fellow Burrito Kenny Wertz, dropped into Clyde's one night in the fall of 1971. Emmylou was plowing mostly Joni Mitchell turf, but once in a while she'd do some country, and when she sang "It Wasn't God Who Made Honky Tonk Angels," they were dazzled. "She was phenomenal," said Rick, who brought Chris Hillman in the next night. He agreed with Rick's assessment, and the Burritos invited her to sit in with them at a neighboring club, the Cellar Door.

That same fall the Burritos had expanded into a seven-man band, and they were thinking about adding a female singer— someone like Linda Ronstadt would have been ideal—when Rick and Kenny spotted Emmylou. For a time they seriously considered her as the first Burrito Sister.

Chris Hillman thought about producing a record with her or singing with her, but he was occupied—not only with the Burritos but also with an offer from Stephen Stills to join a new band, Manassas.

A few weeks after the Burritos spotted Emmylou, Gram returned from Europe, hooked up with Chris, and agreed to sit in with the Burritos for a couple of concerts, including one in late October at the University of Maryland in Baltimore.

Gram had added some weight from his stay in Europe, but he was happy and appeared ready to work. Chris told him about his discovery. "You've got to go to Washington and meet this chick," he said. "She's perfect for you."

Hillman was so enthusiastic, said Gram, "that I just had to go and see her."

Gram, of course, handled things his own way.

Hickory Wind

Emmylou remembered the first call from Gram. He told her he was in Baltimore and asked her to come and pick him up. She was indignant. "Do you realize how far that is?" she said. "It's fifty miles."

Emmylou was not feeling so great when Gram called. She had just spent most of her money on her very first car—a Ford Pinto—and someone had dented her bumper. She didn't know Gram Parsons from Graham Nash. She'd had enough broken promises in her career. "It was pouring down rain and I had to work for the ten people that were gonna come into the club," she said. "I was gonna make maybe five dollars. It was that kind of a thing." So Emmylou told this Gram character that, hell, no, she would not be driving fifty miles to fetch him.

"Oh, is it that far?" said Gram, immediately apologetic. Emmylou cooled off and suggested that he and Gretchen take a train. She and Tom would meet them at the station.

A waiter, having heard about the incoming guest, propped up a cardboard sign on the window: APPEARING TONIGHT, GRAM PARSONS.

No one saw it. Emmylou drew only half of her expected crowd—there were three, plus Gram and Gretchen—in the back room. No matter. Gram was knocked out. Right away, he wanted to sing with her.

Backstage—which was nothing more than a space in the basement where musicians could sit on beer kegs—they decided to try something together, and Gram joined her on stage for the second set. Their first song together was the gospel tune "I Saw the Light."

After the show, Gram, Gretchen, and Emmylou and her musicians repaired to a house in Georgetown that served as the base for a local band, Sageworth and Drums, in which Tom Guidera used to play. In the kitchen, Gram concocted a test for Emmylou. "Okay," he thought to himself, "let's see if she can cut it or not." He thought of one of the most difficult country duets he knew, one he'd heard George Jones and Gene Pitney handle: "That's All It Took."

Emmylou, he said, "just sang it like a bird, and I said, 'Well, that's it.' And I sang with her the rest of the night and she just kept getting better and better."

Emmylou had not done much duet singing—a bit of Ian and Sylvia stuff in college—and she wasn't sure whether Gram impressed her or not with his singing. Gram, to be honest, was a little ragged.

But *together* . . . "Gram and I just seemed to *sing* together," she said simply. "I wasn't aware that I was following him; at the same time, I was. It was real natural."

As Emmylou got to know Gram, and the music he loved, her descriptions of their music became more specific and colorful.

★ 166 ★

Her Name's Emmylou

In 1976 she told *Playboy* magazine: "Gram introduced me to a vein of music I call the High Lonesome—the beautiful heartbreak harmony duets you hear in songs by the young Everly Brothers, Charlie and Ira Louvin, Felice and Boudleaux Bryant."

After their songs together, Emmylou drove Gram and Gretchen back to Baltimore. During the ride Gram threw song ideas at her, dropped Keith Richards's name, and assured her that she had a job.

But as she drove back to her home that night, Emmylou had another year of local club work ahead of her.

And it was still raining.

Back in Los Angeles, Gram scared some old friends.

Eve Babitz, whose camera had been drawn to Gram just a couple of years before, hardly recognized him. Gram looked like the stereotypical pot-bellied southern cop. Alcohol and white-trash food, she figured, had misshapen him. She stopped taking pictures of him.

After returning from England and France, "Gram had supposedly quit smack," said Chris Hillman, "and he was an alcoholic. He was this caricature, because his pants and shirts wouldn't button. It was almost like Elvis at the end when he couldn't get into his suit." Chris couldn't believe the change in his former bandmate. "Here was this very cuddly young kid, very thin, nice brown eyes, this good-looking kid who turned into this monster three years later, this overweight, loud, stupid person."

After the fact, Gram would tell an interviewer that he spent eight months getting ready for his first solo album, and that it took a lot of mental preparation.

Actually, he stumbled into it.

He had failed to come up with anything with Terry Melcher and A&M; he was still on hold with Keith Richards and the Stones' label; he was a man without either a band or a label.

He flipped through his address book, circa Burrito Brothers, and stopped at the name of Eddie Tickner.

Eddie had served as business manager of the original Byrds. He dated back to folk artists like Odetta. He was a low-keyed, deliberate sort. Still, he was connected, and that was enough to keep him employed. Two years after leaving the Byrds in 1967 he was called in by Chris Hillman to work with the Flying Burrito Brothers just before Gram's being fired. Gram barely knew Eddie, but he did know that his clients at one time or another included folk and bluegrass players like the Gosdin Brothers, Clarence White, and Gib Gilbeau.

"Trust is why he called me," said Eddie. "Gram was just a good ole country boy on one side of his brain, and Mick Jagger on the other side. Or a wealthy, sophisticated country boy on one side, and just a hillbilly on the other. And so it was trust."

Eddie met with Gram, who proceeded to talk about his being the first artist, outside the Stones, to be on the band's label, and about Keith Richards being his producer.

It took Eddie only a couple of calls to London to conclude that Gram had no immediate future with the Stones' record company. He asked Gram to come up with another label, and Gram recalled that Mo Ostin of Reprise Records had wanted him before he'd signed with A&M. Ostin invited Gram and Eddie to his offices at Warner Bros. Records in Burbank.

"I went with my hat in my hand and said, 'Mr. Ostin, sir, I sure am sorry about that deal I pulled a few years ago,'" Gram recalled in 1973. "'What do you think about doing an album now?' He said, 'Great.'"

Gram, Eddie added, also blamed the Burritos' switch from Warners to A&M on an attorney.

Before signing Gram, Ostin put him through the formality of an audition, just to check that he had some songs ready to record. Andy Wickham, a Warner Bros. A&R man who'd been assigned to oversee the company's fledgling country division, visited Gram at the Chateau Marmont.

Gram poured Andy some scotch, took out his guitar, and played pieces of half a dozen tunes. Andy needed nothing more.

"You got it," he told Gram. "I'm calling Mo now."

Eddie thought it was the Stones stardust that swayed Andy. No matter; he had a deal. Now he showed another card. His attorney represented Merle Haggard and, just as there was a chance that Keith Richards might produce Gram, so was there a possibility that Merle, who was looking for an opportunity to get behind the control boards, might like to make Gram Parsons his first project.

Gram, quite suddenly, was a bona fide solo artist.

A few phone calls from Eddie later, Gram met the man whose songs he had been singing since International Submarine Band days.

Gram and Merle spent a few days together at Haggard's home near Bakersfield. Gram watched Merle in his recording studio and marveled at the speed with which Merle, his engineer, Hugh Davies, and his musicians worked, sometimes producing two perfect tracks inside of three hours.

Her Name's Emmylou

They played with Merle's train set, drank, talked music, and agreed to work together. Merle wasn't at all like the guy who wrote and sang that slap at hippies, "Okie from Muskogee," Gram thought. "He doesn't hate long-haired people, or even moderately dislike them. He's a nice, sweet cat."

But back in Los Angeles, things fell apart.

Merle, according to Eddie, was having wife problems. That is, she left him. When Eddie went to fetch Merle at the Holiday Inn, he wouldn't come out of his room. The manager then went to the nearby Roosevelt, where he'd stashed Gram in the hope of drying him out. He told Gram the bad news, and Gram's first move was to grab a bottle.

Chris Hillman heard that Merle backed out because Gram was too drunk to work with. But years later, when Merle was asked by Mark Rose of *BAM Magazine* if Gram was too "wild" for him, he almost spat out his contempt at the notion that he could be out-wilded in any way.

"He was a pussy," he said of Gram. "Hell, he was just a long-haired kid. I thought he was a good writer. He was not wild, though. That's what was funny to me. All these guys running around in long hair talk about being wild and Rolling Stones. I don't think someone abusing themselves on drugs necessarily determines how *wild* they are. It might determine how ignorant they are."

When Gram talked about Merle in 1972, he did sound a little kittenish. "Merle Haggard is a great artist and a great person, a great human being. Great everything," he said, soft and full of concession. "He's a real hunk-a man," he added, laughing.

As for why they didn't work together, Gram was hazy. But with each sentence he seemed to make an approach to a core truth. "We were talking about the concept of him doing an album with me. He never really let on that he knew what it was, but he wanted to do it, which is saying something. And then . . . we both figured that we didn't have enough time. Because he's got his own way of doing things, and I've got my own way. And for the two to blend, it would take longer than I have the budget for, frankly. And I just don't want to stay up that much." Gram laughed again. "I need my sleep."

Without a producer, Gram disappeared into Joshua Tree for a couple of meditative weeks, and when he emerged, he himself was asked to be a producer.

In late June, he got a call from Rick Grech, who was thinking about doing an album with his friend Dr. Sam Hutt. The rock doc was deep into country music, thanks to Gram, and they were wondering, might Gram come over to London and help? Gram was delighted that two of his protégés were getting their heads to-gether, and he soon joined them, bringing along the latest George Jones record, a duet album with his wife Tammy Wynette, called *We Go Together.*

At Rick's house in Sussex, Gram told Sam and Rick that he'd found this new girl singer, and that George and Tammy were their models.

Unfortunately for the doctor, Gram also brought heroin with him, and he shared it with Rick. The good doctor declined to join them, and later wrote in his autobiography, "I could feel the dark shadow of smack blighting the air. Unsmiling. Blots out laughter." Any idea of an album, he told me, sadly, just floated away.

Rick, as Gram remembered it, decided he didn't want to make that album. "We rumbled down a few roads and wrote a few songs," said Gram. And by the time he left England, he was think-ing of having Rick help produce *his* album.

Now all he needed were some musicians.

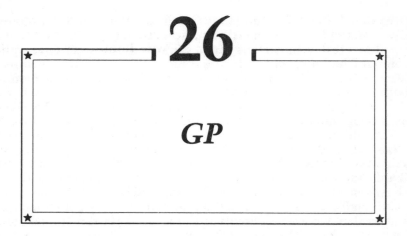

26

GP

When Elvis Presley deserted rock and roll for Hollywood in the early sixties, he lost Gram. But as soon as Elvis renewed his career with his television special of December 1968 and began to perform in concert again, Gram was right back with his main man.

Gram made several visits to Las Vegas to watch Elvis. Sometimes he'd take Andee Cohen, the photographer, along. She came to see that Gram was obsessed with the King. "The Nudie Suit thing was really Elvis, who was bizarre with the rhinestones and the Nudie stuff, and Gram was pulled into this vortex."

And now, on the eve of his first album on his own, he began to call on some friends, among them Barry Tashian, from the days in the Bronx and the earliest Burritos. Barry told Gram he'd come if he could get $100 for cross-country expenses. Done. Gram, of course, also planned to get a young woman from D.C. to come to Los Angeles.

But most of all, he wanted Elvis's boys.

Eddie Tickner had contacted Glen D. Hardin, Elvis's keyboard player and the leader of his band, to let him know of Gram's interest, and Hardin arranged for the whole party—Gram and

Gretchen, Eddie, Rick and Jenny Grech, and Barry Tashian—to see
Elvis, on the house, at the Hilton International.

The Presley musicians often worked sessions, so Gram and
company had no problem hiring three of them: Hardin, drummer
Ronnie Tutt, and guitarist James Burton, the smooth sideman to
both Elvis and Ricky Nelson.

After the show, Glen Hardin, Gram, and Rick sealed their deal
by hitting the casino at the Flamingo Sands—and hitting it hard.

As Eddie recalled, the guys tossed hundred-dollar bills at a
blackjack dealer. To shore himself up for this kind of action, he
said, Hardin usually avoided gambling while sober. And Rick
Grech was rarely sober anyway. The two of them got so loud and
abusive to the dealer that an embarrassed Gram left the table.

Glen Hardin and Rick weren't far behind. They got tossed out,
and as they were being escorted to the door, Hardin stopped and
turned to Rick. "On behalf of the entire United States," he boomed,
"let me apologize for the treatment you are getting from these
goons!"

In true rock-and-roll style, Gram had acquired a crack corps of
session players. With the Warner Bros. contract in hand and an
album on the way, Gram and Gretchen finally moved out of the
Chateau Marmont and found a cozy brown wood-shingled house
on Laurel Canyon Boulevard, which wound its way north from
Hollywood through the stars' favorite canyon.

It was time to make an album. Gram placed a call to Emmylou
Harris and sent her a plane ticket. It had been almost a year since
they met in Washington, and she was still working local clubs
when he called. She packed, but not too much. She sublet her place
in Washington and would maintain her home base throughout her
time with Gram. She had heard plenty about the fast lane, and she
wanted to make sure that it ran in both directions.

When she arrived at Wally Heider's studios in Hollywood, she
met the team that Gram had put together. With Merle Haggard out
of the picture, Eddie had recruited Merle's longtime engineer,
Hugh Davies, to run the board. Musicians, besides Barry and the
Elvis cats, now included several names from Gram's musical circles, including Popeye Goldstein, the drummer; Byron Berline, the
fiddler; and Buddy Emmons and Al Perkins on pedal steel.

The sessions for the album that would become *GP* began in a
shambles. First, Rick got sick with a kidney stone attack on the
morning of the first session and disappeared into a hospital, where
he remained most of the three weeks of recording, returning only
in time to add some bass and help mix the album. His absence left
Gram and Hugh Davies more or less in charge.

In Gram's case, it was less—at least on the first day.

GP

"The first session, Gram was loaded," said Eddie Tickner. Partly for technical reasons and partly to hide him from the session players, Eddie placed Gram, along with Emmylou, behind a baffle.

Glen Hardin counted off a song, and Gram, on his first attempted strum, missed the strings and dropped his pick. He crawled on the studio floor looking for it. Then he was ushered out of the studio to sober up. Regaining consciousness, Gram was so embarrassed to have blown it in front of some of his favorite professional musicians that he didn't have another drink—at least not before a session—for the rest of the making of *GP*. With Rick gone, he took command of the album.

But, according to Barry Tashian, Gram was still erratic. "Gretchen was there, sort of mothering him. 'Now, Gram, you're going to keep clean now, right?' "

Gram managed to avoid getting stoned in the studio, but evenings were whiled away at a neighboring restaurant, Martoni's, where spirits flowed freely. And Gram, as far as Barry could tell, hadn't shaken off the long-term effects of drug use.

"One day his voice would be pretty shaky. Other times he seemed very, very good. He shook a lot. I was ignorant about what he was putting himself through. Today I realize what the problem was. He was very sick. He had a lot of . . . devils."

Musically, the sessions went smoothly. The hired musicians did most of their own arrangements, often working them out with guitars in their hotel rooms, then bringing their ideas into the studio.

As for the vocal charts—there were none, as far as Emmylou can recall. As it had been backstage at Clyde's that first rainy night, Gram simply sang, and she added harmony, almost without thinking. "We never had to sit down and say, 'Let's phrase it this way.' We would just start singing. It was always very natural."

Emmylou knew nothing about the technical intricacies of singing harmony. "If somebody's singing a melody, I consider the harmony to be just another melody and I just sing along with it."

Although Emmylou was a little nervous at first, being the rookie in the room, she was immediately a positive, calming factor in the making of the album. During playbacks she could be found sitting in the shadows, crocheting. If asked, she knew exactly what needed to be redone. If not, she stayed quiet.

The sessions kicked off with "Still Feeling Blue." "It was so full of energy, and it gave such promise to the whole project," said Tashian. "It went down so smoothly and came out so well."

"Blue," a jump tune about a woman who walked out on him, was one of six songs Gram wrote or cowrote. Others included "A

Song for You," an abstract piece of musical philosophy ("I hope you know a lot more than you're believing/Just so the sun don't hurt you when you cry"), and "She," a picturesque song-portrait he had written with Chris Ethridge about a plain, hardworking girl who found her faith through song. Also on the album were "Big Mouth Blues," an all-out rocker in which Gram proclaimed that he was "born in a little bitty tar hut"; the confessional "How Much I've Lied," which he wrote with David Rivkin (now a producer under the name "David Z"); and "The New Soft Shoe," a heartfelt paean to, among others, the inventor of the Cord automobile.

None of these songs took hold in the American consciousness; only "How Much I've Lied" was recorded by another major artist (Elvis Costello). The most-remembered songs included the country classic "Streets of Baltimore" by Tompall Glaser and Harland Howard and a pair of tunes on which Gram and Emmylou teamed up brilliantly: "We'll Sweep Out the Ashes in the Morning," on which Emmylou danced all around Gram's melody and took her first solo; and Gram's test tune, "That's All it Took." Another stand-out was "Kiss the Children," credited to Rick Grech but echoing "Sin City" with its refrain, in which the singer eyes a shotgun hanging on a wall and sees it as a road sign leading "straight to Satan's cage."

Gram sang with passion, like a man possessed with sadness. As Gretchen noted: "He wasn't afraid to show his emotions; to be what people thought was *too* sentimental."

While Gram put all of himself into every track, he made special note of "The New Soft Shoe."

"The subject is that people use other people," he said, pausing to admire his own bravery. "Wow . . . you can get a kick out of that. These things—feelings—that are important to me are parts of people's lives. Not necessarily my own."

GP was densely layered musically, overtly personal lyrically, and saddled with Gram's imperfect, if impassioned, voice. It was more true to country than most rock stations were ready for—even with the Eagles, Poco, Kris Kristofferson, Bob Dylan, and Linda Ronstadt having breezed through their doors. When it was released, *GP* failed to get steady radio exposure, and it didn't make *Billboard*'s Top 200 albums chart.

The critics were divided over Gram's first solo effort. But those who praised him dug deep into their inventory of superlatives.

Robert Hilburn of the *Los Angeles Times* praised Gram both for his songs and his singing, which came "straight from the sentimental, George Jones heart of country music."

Bud Scoppa, in *Rolling Stone*, compared Gram with Merle Haggard. While Merle was as rugged as they came, Gram achieved

GP

"another kind of worldliness, a quieter kind of strength out of his singing. That amazing voice, with its warring qualities of sweetness and dissipation, makes for a stunning emotional experience."

Gram was unique, he added, for his ability to put to music the theme of "the innocent southern boy tossed between the staunch traditions and strict moral code he was born to and the complex, ambiguous modern world. He realizes that both are corrupt, but he survives by keeping a hold on each while believing neither."

Great. But it was a new band of country-rock hotshots, the Eagles, who were on the charts, bang-bang-bang, with "Take It Easy," "Witchy Woman," and "Peaceful Easy Feeling," and went on to become one of the most successful bands of the seventies. Gram, meantime, went nowhere.

He couldn't help being bitter. Talking to Jay Ehler of *Crawdaddy* in the early spring of 1973, he sniped at the Eagles, who, after all, followed Crosby, Stills, Nash, and Young, who followed the Byrds. "The Eagles and some others I would call bubblegum," said Gram. "It's got too much sugar in it. Life is tougher than they make it out to be."

In Chris Hillman's eyes, Gram hit rock bottom just before the album's release. In early December Chris hosted a birthday party for himself at the Chateau Marmont. "Gram was drunk and insulting to everybody. Just the obnoxious drunk. And I literally got on him. . . . I just let him have it. I whacked him across the head and I picked him up and threw him out the door. I said, 'Get out of here. You're a disgrace.'"

Chris felt terrible. "But he had gotten . . . *yuck*. A lot of junkies did that. They'd clean up and become horrible drunks. Of course, Gram got into the cocaine and stuff."

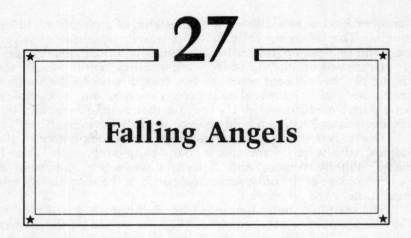

27

Falling Angels

Gram Parsons' first tour under his own name was a near-perfect reflection of his career. It had all the surface stuff: a bus with his name painted on it; a crew including not only a road manager, the one and only Phil Kaufman, but also a valet; and it had some substance: bookings at rock landmarks like the Armadillo World Headquarters in Austin and Max's Kansas City in New York. But, in reality, Gram went out with an under-rehearsed band, and his self-destruction from alcohol, drugs, and an unraveling personal life continued as they covered the miles on the leased Greyhound bus. With Gretchen along, there were lots of fights and at least one violent encounter with the police.

As the tour continued, there were a few exciting moments on stage; Gram and Emmylou learned to set off sparks in each other, and the band improved with every performance.

But years later, manager Eddie Tickner dismissed the month-long excursion as "silly." It didn't do a thing to sell copies of *GP* or to further Gram's career.

Eddie originally approached Warner Bros. with the idea of just two concerts, media showcases in New York and Los Angeles.

Falling Angels

The company decided to spend more and get more exposure: Gram would hit the road for a month.

Back in his office, Eddie pulled out a map, stuck a pin into Boulder, Colorado—he had heard that Gram could get a job there—and started calling up clubs between Boulder and New York.

While Eddie and Gram began putting the tour band together, Gram found time for a little socializing. He and Gretchen were invited to a party at John Phillips's house to celebrate the end of the Vietnam War. Emmylou, who was staying with Gram and Gretchen, went along.

John Phillips had married the actress and singer Genevieve Waite. They lived in Bel Air in a pink Italianate mansion built by William Randolph Hearst for his mistress, Marion Davies. As John recalled, the house cost a staggering $3,000 a month to rent and had fourteen-foot-high ceilings in the front entrance, a mirrored hallway, a spacious ballroom downstairs, and amid the gardens, ponds, and stone walks, a giant pool complete with a 150-foot waterfall.

Gram, Gretchen, and Emmylou toured the house and were just saying their good-byes when Gram ran into Johnny Rivers, who'd recorded Gram's song "Apple Tree" in 1970. The two rustled up a couple of guitars and commenced a session that stretched until about four in the morning.

Meanwhile, rehearsals were beginning. Eddie, after attending the first sessions, began to dread the tour. For one thing, the band didn't have a lead guitarist or a steel player yet. Barry Tashian chose not to go on the road; the Elvis guys were too expensive—band members got $250 a week—and Ed Black, who'd been hired, opted to go with Linda Ronstadt. Gram then took Emmylou's suggestion to hire Gerry Mule, her club band guitarist from Washington. For steel guitar, they got Neil Flanz, a session player in Nashville, as was bassist Kyle Tullis. For drums, Gram picked N. D. Smart, formerly with Barry and the Remains. Jon Corneal filled in until N.D. could get in from the East Coast.

The practices took place at Phil Kaufman's ramshackle house in Van Nuys. Gram ran the rehearsals the way he ran his life: laissez-faire.

But, as evidenced by a tape of one session, Gram could stay on top of things, working on details like the steel-guitar tag end for "Still Feeling Blue," scrutinizing the drumming ("That's the wrong beat," he said at one point. "Don't you know blues from bluegrass?"), and guiding Emmylou through a couple of solos.

More often than not, rehearsals were fueled by marijuana and liquor. After a couple of hours Gram would begin a medley of George Jones tunes, and work turned into play.

"Gram knew so many songs that we never finished anything," said Emmylou. "We must have gone over fifty songs, but we didn't work out a single one." Still, by rehearsals' end, she thought the band was sounding pretty good.

Now, finally, it was time for . . . yes, a *party!*

Phil Kaufman decided to host a send-off bash for the band. He hired a group called the Oily Scarf Wino Band (featuring bedpan percussion), whipped up a potload of the Mexican tripe stew known as *menudo*, and laid on cases of beer to wash it down. Among the guests was Michael Martin, an Australian who'd only recently arrived in Hollywood from a long stay in India where he'd met a friend of Phil's. He accompanied the friend to the party, struck up a conversation with Gram, and found himself hired for the tour as Gram's personal valet.

Gram didn't get his way with every whim. He thought of calling his band the Turkeys; he was vehemently voted down, and the group began to call themselves the Fallen Angels.

The next morning, the bus—with Gram's name painted on the back—took off. With a driver known as "Leadfoot Lance" at the wheel, the bus then headed through a blinding snowstorm in Arizona. There, in a motel lot, it was rammed by a truck, right where it said "Gram Parsons."

And that was before the first gig. In transit and at every stop, the band and crew got vivid reminders that, yes, they were on a rock-and-roll tour.

In Boulder, they played a club that got shut down two-thirds of the way through their three-night stand because of neighbors' complaints about the noise generated by a jazz-rock band that had preceded them.

The very first show was a disaster. Gram was out of shape and out of his mind; the incomplete rehearsals translated on stage to songs missing beginnings, endings, and arrangements. Gerry Mule, a classically trained, folk-oriented acoustic guitarist, was out of his depth.

Emmylou, working a stage with Gram for the first time, was horrified. "What have I gotten myself into?" she thought, looking out into a crowd that included members of Poco, who were also playing in town.

At one table Richie Furay sat in disbelief. "It was one of the most pitiful things I ever saw," he said. Gram looked bloated, having put on some fifty pounds since their time in the Village. With the exception of Emmylou's duets with him, the music was a mess. Embarrassed for his friend, Richie nonetheless decided to make a courtesy call backstage. He found Gram busy getting high.

Eddie threatened to shut down the tour right there. Gram promised to straighten things out—beginning with himself. For the rest of the tour, he'd confine his stimulants to liquor. He met with the band and came up with arrangements for a dozen tunes. And they decided to find a new guitarist.

Among the local musicians who'd heard about the first-night disaster was Jock Bartley, who'd been a lead guitarist in Zephyr, a now defunct band of middling renown. He attended the second night's show. The guitarist was wrong for the group, he thought. Gram was undisciplined in his singing, but he had his emotional moments. And Jock fell in love with Emmylou.

For the aborted third night, Gram got into the Pioneer Inn, a funky club in Nederland, twenty miles up the hills from Boulder. Jock Bartley sat in with the opening act at the Pioneer Inn, and Gram invited him to sit in with the Fallen Angels. Playing next to the dispirited Gerry Mule, Jock displayed solid rock-and-roll chops but also showed that he had no kinship with country music.

Gram convened the band and asked what everybody thought. Neil Flanz, the steel player, voted no; he wanted a country player. Two other band members originally sided with him, and one of them, not aware that Jock was in the room, marched in and told Gram, "Neil doesn't think that Jock plays worth a shit."

Gram smiled, looking over at Jock and back at a couple of faces quickly turning red. "I like Jock," he drawled. "He's got beautiful hands. He's got a good feel, so I vote yes."

Jock was on the bus, and Neil was the first to help him learn the band's songs. By the time they arrived at Armadillo World Headquarters, Austin's biggest rock club, the Fallen Angels were ready to kick ass.

On "Six Days on the Road," Emmylou played her tambourine so vigorously that she bruised her hand; Neil and Jock worked out their respective guitar roles and a mutual respect, and the crowd responded in kind. Neil, who was more familiar with the Grand Ole Opry than rock concerts, watched 2,000 screaming hippies crowding the skirt of the stage, reaching up to touch the band members. "It was love hysteria!" he exclaimed.

When the crowd demanded an encore, the band was stumped. They were out of rehearsed songs, and so they simply repeated songs they'd already played.

Gram and Emmylou did a radio interview at station KOKE, where they were merciless with the deejay. Gram disdained the "country-rock" label being pinned on him; he felt his music ranged widely. When the announcer asked him to define his country-rock fusion, Gram just stared at him. When the announcer turned to Emmylou for help, she followed Gram's cue, leaving the deejay with an announcer's worst nightmare: dead air. Gram also yanked the station's Emergency Broadcast System equipment off the studio wall, setting off an alarm. "Thanks for the worst interview in my life," the deejay said. As Gram boarded the bus, he opened his jacket to show a plaque he'd pilfered from the station.

From Austin the group went to Houston for a four-night stand and another peak. Gram and the Fallen Angels were booked at Liberty Hall, a converted American Legion hall. Here, he discovered a phenomenon known as the "Sin City Boys." Two high school students, inspired by the memory of a drunk who had shouted "Sin City!" at a 1971 Burrito Brothers show at Liberty Hall, began a search for the true meaning of that song. The kindred spirits grew to five young men by late 1972, and they showed up at a Manassas concert to shout "Sin City!" at Chris Hillman.

By the time they heard that Gram and the Fallen Angels were coming to town, the Sin City Boys had made up jacket patches in the style of the Hells Angels. They gave Gram his patch before the first show when they learned that the song wasn't among the few that the Fallen Angels had bothered to rehearse. No matter; they'd still attend all four nights.

The first night, most of the Sin City Boys seemed content to fall in love with Emmylou and to boogie along with a rollicking set-ending medley the Angels had worked up: "Hang on Sloopy," "Baby, What You Want Me to Do?," "Bony Maronie," "Forty Days," and "Almost Grown."

The second night, Gram again didn't sing "Sin City," but the Boys, bolstered by word of mouth and increased to thirteen members, could ogle Robert Plant and Jimmy Page of Led Zeppelin, who were in the audience of 400. And after the show, when Gram and Gretchen somehow found themselves stranded, several of the Boys gave them a lift to their hotel in an old Chevy wagon.

By Saturday, Gram had his "Sin City" patch sewed onto a jacket. And he had a surprise for the Boys, who now numbered twenty.

Throughout the first set, the contingent called out for "Sin City," and others in the packed house joined in, all to no avail. But as the opening band, a country-rock outfit called Man Mountain and the Green Slime Boys, finished their second set, Gram and Emmylou climbed the stage, accompanied by Linda Ronstadt. With Gram singing lead and the two women reading off lyrics Gram had hastily written out backstage, the trio, backed by Man Mountain, performed a ragged but much appreciated version of "Sin City." In the audience, the Sin City Boys stood in honor of the song.

Linda Ronstadt was in town with her band, on tour as the opening act for Neil Young at Sam Houston Coliseum. Linda, long a champion of country as well as rock and roll, R&B, and pop music, thought of Gram as a "brother" in their separate musical campaigns, but she had never met Emmylou. Soon after joining voices, Linda became one of Emmylou's staunchest supporters.

Sunday night, Neil Young and Linda Ronstadt joined the Angels on stage, along with five Sin City Boys, who presented Emmylou with a bouquet of yellow roses.

After the show, Neil Young sent a limo to pick up Gram and the band for a party in his suite. Jock remembered staying up until 5:00 A.M. with members of all three bands, drinking whiskey, smoking hashish, snorting cocaine, and, most of all, playing music. Gram rolled through dozens of country classics, with Emmylou and Linda doing harmonies and backups. Neil Young played an impressive steel guitar, while Neil Flanz raised the strings of a Les Paul guitar to emulate a Dobro and played through Gram's small Pignose amplifier. Drummer John Barbata kept the beat on every available surface.

Conspicuously missing was Gretchen Parsons. By now, said Jock, she'd established herself as "a downer, a whiner," and a neurotic who was constantly fighting with Gram."

"She was the most schizophrenic woman I'd ever met," said one musician who knew her. "One minute she was really warm and accommodating; the next, the picture of rage and jealousy. We all felt really sorry for Gram. I kept thinking, 'No wonder Gram drinks so much.'"

On the bus, Gram always made his way to the back, to be with the band and Phil Kaufman. "Sometimes Gram was like a five-year-old kid," said Jock, "and Phil really was a nanny."

In Texas, Gram sent a postcard to his sister, telling her that the tour was going fine. And by the way, he wrote, it looked like he and Gretchen were headed for divorce.

Gretchen blamed Gram's problems on Phil Kaufman. She never liked him. "I just knew the guy was a bum," not to mention a "snake" and a "professional creep." She blamed much of Gram's use of drugs on Phil. Gretchen, however, stood alone with her accusation.

Jock thought Gretchen hated Kaufman because he was doing his job, which was to ensure that Gram was in shape to perform every night. That, he noted, sometimes involved keeping him and Gretchen apart.

"Phil watched out over us all," said Jock. "Without Phil there, Gretchen and the whole trip that she did would've been intolerable."

As for drugs, Phil once told Barry Tashian that his job on the road was "to keep Gram straight." When he knew Gram had drugs, he said, he'd go back to the hotel during the concert, get keys from the desk, and search the rooms. He'd find drugs taped up under the sink or hidden in a shoe, and flush them down the toilet.

After Houston, Gram and the Fallen Angels faced two days on

the highways of Arkansas and Missouri to get to their next job, in Chicago. They agreed to stop exactly halfway there, and that point, as luck would have it, was Blytheville, Arkansas.

It was late at night when they pulled into the first Holiday Inn they saw. Most of the band did the wise thing and retired. Gram headed straight for the lounge, where he sat at the piano and played to the lounge crowd for two hours until Gretchen came down and loudly fetched him.

A heated argument ensued in their room, and a guest called the police. A drunken Gram opened the door and a cop forced his way in, almost hitting Gram. Gram then assumed a karate pose he'd picked up from N. D. Smart and made a feeble attempt at a swing. The police maced Gram—in the process spraying Gretchen—collared him and took him to jail. Phil bailed him out, and the next morning, the exhausted Parsonses were in the coffee shop, Gretchen hidden behind sunglasses and Gram covering his bruises and still-teary eyes under a floppy cap and shades.

Fleeing Arkansas—a matter of riding just a few miles—their first sights in Missouri were two stores: one selling liquor; the other, fireworks. Gram and Phil stocked up on beer, bourbon, and Roman candles.

Soon shenanigans rivaled music. At their Chicago hotel, the Fallen Angels did their versions of the by-now-clichéd property destruction. Gram pushed a loaded room-service tray over a ledge and into a parking lot a dozen stories below. Various Angels flung their dinner plates out their windows like Frisbees.

On stage, however, the band became tighter as the tour went on. At the Quiet Knight in Chicago, they drew a receptive audience and earned a rave review from the *Tribune*.

It may have helped, said Jock, that the volume on Gram's guitar was usually turned down. Although his vocals could go from painfully bad to painfully wonderful, his guitar playing, never a strong suit, was further hampered by alcohol. (Emmylou, on and off the bus, had at most an occasional Margarita.)

It was in Cleveland that the band first felt danger from a crowd. They played a funky biker bar called the Smiling Dog, which reminded Emmylou of something she'd seen in Robert Altman's dusty Western *McCabe and Mrs. Miller*. "I thought we were all going to get shot or knifed," she later said.

The band feared for her most of all. "It was a shit-kicking, fightin' type of bar," said Jock. The stage was even backdropped with a Confederate flag. "There were a lot of drunk bikers crowding up to the stage, leering at her, and we suddenly got very protective. Nobody tried to crash the stage, but it was rowdy and people were throwing bottles at each other. She was a trouper; she did her gig the way she did every night."

Falling Angels

The band rolled into New York to play Max's Kansas City, upstairs from a restaurant bar frequented by the kind of crowd that made New York New York. Jock remembered playing a set of country music, then going downstairs and encountering an Andy Warhol vision of New York dolls and transvestites and guys in miniskirts with heavy makeup, wearing chains and whips. But city and country mixed fine, and the Fallen Angels packed them in at Max's.

Gram and company played one of their best sets for a live broadcast over a Long Island radio station. Here Gram and company relaxed into a chat with the deejay.

The announcer asked if they'd enjoyed doing the bus tour.

"Doing what on the bus?" Gram teased. As the studio audience laughed, Emmylou piped up. *"Yeah . . ."* she said, to cheers.

Gram told the announcer about their adventures at KOKE, ripping the Emergency Broadcast System box off the wall. "He wanted to know what we thought of—"

"'Progressive country,'" Emmylou broke in. "We told him we play *regressive* country."

While Gram and Emmylou were clearly enjoying themselves, Gretchen stewed. Yes, she said, very grudgingly, by the time they got to New York, "They at least had sorta got their act together a little bit. But being in New York City, Max's Kansas City, with all those people, all those drugs and stuff—get real. It was like . . . party time."

After heading south again for Philadelphia, where they did a series of shows at a tiny club called the Bijou, they zigzagged back north to Boston for a week's stand at Oliver's. It was here that Gretchen boiled over.

The stay began with more frivolity engineered by Gram. The band was registered at the Fenway Boylston Motor Hotel, named for its location just across the street from the Red Sox's ballpark.

Gram knew he'd found the perfect launching pad for the fireworks he'd been unable to set off in New York City. When evening came, a band member spied Gram creeping down a corridor with his two sacks of explosives from Missouri, heading for the parking lot below. "We're gonna cause some trouble here," he said, giggling. One by one, the Fallen Angels gathered to watch. Gram propped the bags against each other in the middle of the parking lot, lit the edges, and scrambled back upstairs.

The musicians cheered as Roman candles shot into the sky above them, accompanied by motley explosions.

Moments later, firemen and police officers knocked on Gram's door—the management somehow suspected the rock band—but no arrests were made.

The band went on to play at Oliver's. John Nuese and Barry

Tashian stopped by. Barry joined the band to sing lead on "Cry One More Time."

At Oliver's, a shy young poet named Tom Brown approached Gram with a set of lyrics for him to consider setting to music. The potential song was titled "Return of the Grievous Angel."

Before the performance Gram had visited his freshman adviser at Harvard, and Jet Thomas had hosted a dinner for the band. Jet took note of the attention Gram paid to Dallas Hext, a youthful, music-loving 60-year-old woman who was the secretary of Addam's House, where Jet's apartment was located. Gram talked to Dallas throughout the evening, arranged special seating for her at the show, and dedicated a song to her.

At the club, Jet noticed that Gretchen was being shut out of the spotlight, and that she couldn't stand it. On stage, Gram and Emmylou's microphones were set up together, and they often faced each other while singing, the better for Emmylou to entwine her harmonies around Gram's vocals. Rev. Thomas saw Gretchen make her way to the front of the stage, where she danced and sang along with the band. "She was actually competing with the show on stage for attention."

From his place on stage, Jock saw much the same thing. "On one hand she was jealous; on the other side, she'd be singing all of Emmylou's parts . . . trying to get Gram's attention. And, of course, Gram never looked at her."

Gretchen didn't remember acting the way people remembered. She admitted to being "a little bit" jealous of Emmylou, but said that they were friends. Mostly, she said, "I was flipping out about the drug situation."

The final flip took place the next day at the motel. Feeling ignored by Gram, she went to one band member's room and asked him to hold her. After the musician led her out, she began running down the hall, crying and knocking and kicking on various doors.

When the manager—already upset over the fireworks incident—threatened to kick the entire group out of the motel, band members convinced Gretchen that it was time to go home.

To wrap up the tour, the group made an appearance on a dance-party television show. Here, bands lip-synced their records.

Backstage, several members of the Fallen Angels, led by N. D. Smart, began protesting the idea of pantomiming—especially when they hadn't even played on the album cuts being aired. After a discussion, the musicians came up with a compromise. N.D. wouldn't pretend to play drums, but he'd fake it at piano; a roadie would fill in behind the drums.

The first song to be played from the album, "Still Feeling Blue," had a fiddle on it, but the Angels had no such player or instrument. Fortunately, Emmylou had picked up a used violin in a pawn shop. It didn't have strings, so Phil stringed the instrument with white twine, grabbed a drumstick to serve as a bow, and volunteered to be the fiddler.

With Gram and Emmylou playing it relatively straight and the ensemble behind them cracking up, the semi-Angels got through two takes of the song and won a standing ovation.

After the applause died down, the tour was over. And their manager, Eddie Tickner, was right; it had been a "silly tour". In a month on the road, the Fallen Angels did only a dozen shows in eight cities, hit three radio stations, and faked their way through a local television show. Gram still wasn't a star; his album still wasn't selling.

Emmylou, in her liner notes for *Sleepless Nights,* a compilation of Gram's work with the Burritos and with her, recalled the wide world of music she learned from Gram, both on the bus and in the honky-tonks they played. And she remembered the crowds.

"The rooms were small, but the energy generated was of a special intensity," she wrote. "And they came to see this young man and to hear the voice that would break and crack but rise pure and beautiful and full with sweetness and pain." The Fallen Angels' tour was no box-office smash. But, she wrote, "There are people who will remember. . . ."

28

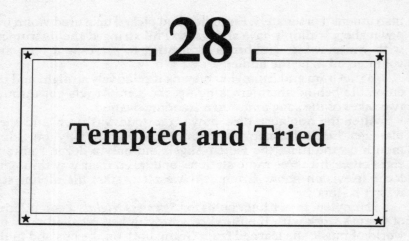

Tempted and Tried

One summer day in 1973 Emmylou was at Gram and Gretchen's rehearsing a new song. In the living room with the two singers was Emmylou's boyfriend, Tom Guidera, who'd been shipped in by Eddie Tickner as a way of rounding off the corners of the Gretchen-Gram-Emmylou triangle fixed in Gretchen's head.

It didn't work.

Gram and Emmylou were in the middle of the song, "Return of the Grievous Angel," which had been presented to Gram by Tom Brown, a poet in Boston, and which Gram had set to music. As they sang, Gretchen roared through the room, brushed by Gram, and stomped out of the house.

Gram, who'd had a few, staggered out after her, and Tom Guidera, keeping a safe distance, followed. Emmylou stopped at the front door.

Gretchen marched to the side of Laurel Canyon Boulevard, planted a foot on the road, and stuck out her thumb. Within seconds, a motorcyclist slowed down for the pretty blonde. As Gram made a clumsy lunge for her, she hopped onto the back seat and disappeared down the road.

Tempted and Tried

Gram turned around and saw Tom, shook his head, and smiled.

"God *damn!*" he said. "She's so *sexy!*"

★

Was there a love affair between Emmylou and Gram?

Emmylou never said, but she sometimes teased, as she did in the Long Island interview when she responded to the deejay's question about good times on the bus with a tantalizing, little-girl *"Yeah . . ."* Or as she did on a television show after the release of her album *The Ballad of Sally Rose* in 1985.

Some took that album as a clue. As she told Dennis Wholey, the host of "Late Night America," Sally Rose was "a young girl singer who falls in love with another singer—" She paused and offered a wry smile, then continued. "He's killed, and she carries on with his music and eventually comes to a certain peace within herself."

The host couldn't wait. "Now, here's the question," he said. "There's a lot of parallels within your own life."

"Yeah, there . . . yeah," said Emmylou, now soft and halting.

"You were at one time a protégée and sang with—"

"Gram Parsons," said Emmylou. "He died in 1973. And he did influence me greatly."

"Oh," said Dennis. "So some of the feelings are there."

"Oh, yeah." Emmylou smiled again. "I'm not denying it. I'm guilty. I'm guilty of being autobiographical."

Some thought so. Bernie Leadon once said, bluntly: "She was in love with him then; she's in love with him now." John Nuese thought Emmylou was among several women Gram saw while married to Gretchen.

Jet Thomas, who performed the wedding for Gram and Gretchen and, years later, for Emmylou and her first record producer, Brian Ahern, wasn't sure. "They had a special kind of relationship," he said, "and if there was any kind of romantic relationship, it came after the music and not before. I think the music was the most important thing to them."

Tom Guidera, Emmylou's boyfriend from 1970 through her discovery by the Burritos and her albums and tours with Gram, split with her only after she met Brian Ahern. There were times, he said, that they considered getting married.

"I know she had enormous admiration for Gram, and even love," he said, "but I'm not sure it was romantic, except that it's difficult for two people that age who are together that often not to develop some sort of romantic angle.

"But, of course, there was always Gretchen there."

For her own reasons, Emmylou, in interviews, rarely gave a definitive yes or no when she was asked about a romance with Gram. To *Crawdaddy*, she said coyly: "You know I can't talk about that." By not saying no, she was inviting a prolongation of the mystery.

When she spoke with me, she was definitive—but intriguingly so. "It's true that Gram and I were friends, and that was the extent of our relationship," she said. Case closed. But she went on: "We were very intense friends and very close friends and I think I know that I loved him very much. He's a very special person to me, but I came into his life very late . . . but at the same time he did come into my life, and he affected it and touched it."

Her words and the observations of those closest to her lead to one conclusion: She loved him and cared deeply about him, but the passion was musical. Given her own commitment to Tom and the obvious traumas Gram was going through with Gretchen, anything beyond a musical connection would have put the relationship with Gram in jeopardy.

On more cynical notes, various people who knew Gram said he was in no shape to be carrying on much with women at all, and that Gram tended to be attracted to women he could dominate. Emmylou was an artistic equal, and that set her apart from almost every other woman Gram knew.

Gram and Gretchen's marriage was doomed, but in the spring of 1973, neither was quite ready to give up. They had been invited by Bob and Bonnie Parsons to sail to the West Indies and decided to go in an attempt to salve their relationship.

But the journey was cut short by yet another trauma.

On the sailboat, Bob started drinking and talking. He told Gretchen and Gram that he had been instrumental in Gram's mother's death. "He was despicable," said Gretchen. "He admitted that to Gram and me. He said that, inside his suitcoat, he took in little airline bottles of vodka while Gram's mom was in the hospital. He made her one last martini, and . . . she never came out."

"It was not long after that that he died, actually," said Gretchen. Bob Parsons died, ironically, of an alcohol-related illness in 1974. "I guess," said Gretchen, "he wanted to clean up his act."

Gram was traumatized by the sudden disclosure. He and his stepfather were in tears by the end of Bob's confession. "He was never the same, ever," said Gretchen about Gram. "That's when his seizures started. He just wasn't mentally there anymore. He would just [slows down] t-a-a-lk like th-i-i-s. . . . It scared the shit out of me."

They were like epileptic seizures, she said, except that after the speech slowdown, Gram's body would slow down as well.

Gram woke up from his first seizure with absolutely no recollection of it. Gretchen, hysterical, had called paramedics, and when Gram regained consciousness, he asked, "What are these people doing here in my house?"

As the seizures continued, she said, Gram began to blame her for them. "He was going, 'What are you trying to do here?' And that made it even worse."

After a stay at St. Joseph's Hospital in Burbank, Gram improved, and soon he was back to music. He had another tour to do with Emmylou, and she flew out from Maryland for rehearsals. They ran through some songs in her room at the Sportsmen's Lodge Hotel in North Hollywood; practices that required a piano took place at Gram and Gretchen's house in Laurel Canyon.

Gretchen was in Hawaii in June. She constantly called Gram—at their home and at Emmylou's hotel. Gram was annoyed by Gretchen's unending suspicions and accusations, but when he tried reasoning with her, she'd hang up on him.

Gram and Emmylou were preparing for a trial, three-date tour set up by Warner Bros. Records. The idea was to have a caravan of country acts—Country Gazette, the Kentucky Colonels (featuring Clarence, Roland, and Eric White, with banjoist Alan Munde), and Gram and Emmylou. Gene Parsons, by now a solo artist on Warner Bros., along with Chris Ethridge and Sneeky Pete, completed what the label billed as a traveling "country rock festival."

With so much talent on board, the stage was bound to be overcrowded, and at one of the shows—this one in Annapolis, Maryland—it was. It was the electric set, the highlight of a day- and night-long show. It was after midnight when Gene, Chris, and Sneeky Pete, joined by Clarence White, climbed onto the stage with Gram and Emmylou.

As Gene recalled it, the song had reached the place where lead guitarist Clarence White would take his solo break. Clarence was considered by many of his peers the best country guitar player going. Clarence was not a great admirer of Gram's; the word was that he'd been considered for the Byrds in 1968 when Gram got the job.

Now here was Gram playing to the crowd by motioning for Clarence to turn down his volume. If Gram was no longer sashaying like Mick Jagger, he was still putting on superstar airs. Soon he was motioning for the whole band to turn it down, even confiscating Gene's drum sticks, leaving him to play with his hands.

Hickory Wind

When Clarence stopped playing his solo entirely, Gram didn't appear to notice. All he knew was that the crowd seemed to enjoy his antics. Clarence picked up again and finished his solo, and the electric set ended. But the show continued backstage.

Clarence, who was almost a foot shorter than Gram, grabbed him by the neck, pulled him off to one side, and shouted: "Listen, you son of a bitch, I've played more country music than you've ever played, and I know more about it than you'll ever know. Just remember: you're not the only fucking star around here."

Gram talked back, but without much energy or conviction. It was nearly three in the morning now, and through a haze of drink and drugs, Gram managed to understand that he had been out of line. His southern manners came back and he managed an apology. "I didn't mean to offend," he said.

Clarence accepted the apology, and they became close friends for the few days remaining on the tour.

A month later that friendship and the tight circle that was Los Angeles country and country-rock suffered a tragic blow. Late one night in the middle of July, Clarence was killed by a drunk driver. He and his brothers had just finished a show in the flatlands north of the San Fernando Valley and were loading equipment into a car. Roland suffered a dislocated shoulder; Eric witnessed the accident. Clarence left behind a wife and two young children.

On July 19 more than a hundred mourners—family and friends, most all of them musicians, gathered for services at St. Mary's Catholic Church in Palmdale.

A few months before Clarence's death, Gram had talked to *Crawdaddy* just before setting off on tour with the Fallen Angels. The previous summer, Brandon deWilde had died in an automobile accident in Colorado; in the winter of 1972, Miss Christine of the GTOs died.

"Death is a warm cloak," he said. "An old friend. I regard death as something that comes up on a roulette wheel every once in a while. It's sad to lose a close friend. I've lost a lot of people close to me. It makes you a little bit stronger each time. They wouldn't want me to grieve. They would want me to go out and get drunk and have one on them."

On the occasion of Clarence's death, Gram got good and drunk. But he couldn't help grieving; Chris Hillman remembered Gram crying and hanging all over him. Gram stayed away from the memorial service; he sat outside, then joined the procession to the Joshua Memorial Park in Lancaster.

The priest finished his ceremony at the graveside, and a clumsy silence ensued. No one knew what to do next.

Finally, a voice rose in a tentative hum, searching out a mel-

ody. Within seconds, another voice joined in, and humming gave
way to song:

> Tempted and tried we're oft made to wonder
> Why it should be thus all the day long
> While there are others living about us
> Never molested though in the wrong

It was the traditional gospel song, "Farther Along," well
known in bluegrass circles, and the voices were those of Bernie
Leadon and, by his side, Gram Parsons. The two had sung the song
on the Burritos' second album in 1970, and Clarence had recorded
the song with the Byrds the same year.

As they sang, a few more joined in, singing in ragged, spur-of-
the-moment harmony.

> Farther along we'll know more about it
> Farther along we'll understand why
> Cheer up my brother
> Live in the sunshine
> We'll understand it all, by and by . . .

Afterward, Roland White, one arm in a sling, approached
Bernie to express his family's appreciation for the musical send-off.

Chris Ethridge remembered singing along to "Farther Along"
and to "Amazing Grace." And he remembered one other thing. At
graveside, he heard Gram and Phil Kaufman talking while the
priest was sprinkling water on the casket. Gram turned to his
trusted nanny.

"Phil," he said, "if this happens to me, I don't want them doing
this to me. You can take me to the desert and burn me. I want to go
out in a cloud of smoke."

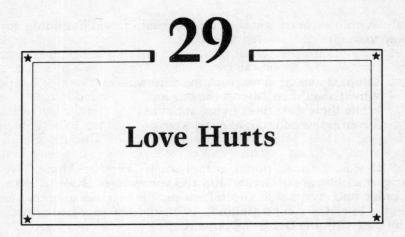

29

Love Hurts

The last time I felt like this
I was in the wilderness
and the canyon was on fire
And I stood on the mountain in the night
And I watched it burn

Even from 3,000 miles away in Maryland, Emmylou could feel the storm clouds gathering over Gram. "You wondered if the stars were colliding," she said.

From their last time together, for the country-rock festival tour, she knew that Gretchen and Gram could not stay together long. What she didn't know was that it would be neither her raging jealousy nor his deteriorating health that would come between them.

In late July 1973, just two weeks before Gram was scheduled to begin work on his second album, his house in Laurel Canyon burned down.

Love Hurts

Around Gram's circle of friends, one story had Gram in a deep sleep when the fire started late at night. Gretchen ran outside to seek help and locked herself out. Gram woke up and, thinking he was fleeing out the door, ran into a closet, where firefighters found him, asleep or unconscious, under a pile of his clothes. It was the weight of his Nudie outfits, this story went, that saved his life.

A more widely told story was a simpler one: that the fire might have been started by Gram smoking in bed, and Gram and Gretchen escaped after Gram threw a telephone through a plate glass window. Gram was also said to have grabbed a few song-lyric sheets.

Gram was briefly hospitalized for smoke inhalation, and the couple moved into Gretchen's father's spacious home on Mulholland Drive in Laurel Canyon, many winding roads above Hollywood.

They did not stay together long. Because Gretchen barred Phil Kaufman from visiting Gram at her father's home, Gram went off to Phil's.

With album sessions having begun, Phil resumed his job as executive nanny and, once again, sheltered Gram from his wife.

★

Somehow Gram managed to watch the stars collide and make music out of the dust.

Just as his walkout on his own wedding plans gave him "$1000 Wedding," and failed romances inspired "Still Feeling Blue," "Kiss the Children," "How Much I've Lied," and many others, now death moved him to write a song called "In My Hour of Darkness."

Around the same time that Clarence White was killed, Sid Kaiser, a familiar face in the Los Angeles rock scene, a close friend of Gram's and, not so incidentally, a source of high-quality drugs, died of a heart attack.

Within a prayerlike song, Gram offered a farewell to Sid, Clarence, and to Brandon deWilde, giving each man his own verse. Brandon was the young man driving through the night, the victim of a "deadly Denver bend." Clarence was the man who "safely strummed his silver string guitar." And Sid was "kind and wise with age/and he read me just like a book/and he never missed a page."

Because Gram never lived to see through the details of the album, including the order of songs and the cover artwork, "Darkness" was placed at the end of the second side, partly because it made sense, and partly because it could easily be read as a song about Gram himself, in particular the lines he wrote for Clarence:

Hickory Wind

Some say he was a star
But he was just a country boy,
his simple songs confess
And the music he had in him,
So very few possess

Emmylou received a cowriter credit on "In My Hour of Darkness," but later she demurred. Gram wrote the song, she said. It was just that, as a writer, he invited—even needed—input from others. She simply stood by the piano and helped sing pieces of the song as it was being put together. Gram told her, firmly, "I'm giving you half the credit on this song."

The song, however, was Gram's only brand-new set of original lyrics. Gram had a hand in the composing of six of the ten songs on *Grievous Angel*, but most of his work came from his files. There was "Brass Buttons," which he had sung as a folk song in 1965; "Hickory Wind," from the Sub Band days of 1967; "$1000 Wedding," which had been recorded unsuccessfully by the Burrito Brothers; and "Ooh Las Vegas," half-credited to Rick Grech, which came from their work toward the first solo album.

Finally, there was the song for which the album was ultimately named. "Return of the Grievous Angel" sounded like pure Parsons with its conversational tone, its crisp descriptions evoking the South and "the truckers and the kickers and the cowboy angels," its Dylanesque reference to a meeting with "the King/on his head, an amphetamine crown," and its swooping chorus tailor-fit for Gram and Emmylou's hand-held harmonies.

The words, given to Gram by poet Tom Brown in Boston, were among the sheets of lyrics Gram salvaged while escaping his burning house.

The song chronicled Brown's romance with his wife, but he said he had Gram in mind, too. The title was inspired by a photo he'd seen of a sad-looking Gram; the king with the head full of speed was Gram.

"Grievous Angel" became the album's signature song. It also served to show how resourceful Gram was when he needed to be, as he applied the perfect, lilting melody to Brown's words. Whether he did it by design or out of desperation, Gram's resulting set of original songs was brilliant, a dossier of life lived and deeply felt.

To this he added four more songs. "Hearts on Fire" was another perfect torch-song vehicle for Gram and Emmylou; one that she had been singing since her nights in D.C. The song was originally written by Walter Egan of Sageworth and Drums as a

Love Hurts

tongue-in-cheek takeoff of country music; his lyrics had to do with gastric heartburn. Tom Guidera, Emmylou's boyfriend, bandmate, and a former partner of Walter's, rewrote the song into a standard unrequited love ballad, and Emmylou successfully pitched it to Gram.

"Love Hurts" was originally recorded by the Everly Brothers in 1960 (it was written by Boudleaux Bryant, who, with wife Felice, accounted for numerous Everly Brothers hits), and Gram and Emmylou gave it a loving adoption. And, just for fun, they added "I Can't Dance," a Tom T. Hall stomper, and the Louvin Brothers' "Cash on the Barrelhead."

Acting as his own producer, Gram took out some insurance by hiring Hugh Davies to engineer again, and by calling back many of the key session players from *GP*. James Burton, Glen Hardin, and Ronnie Tutt—the Elvis contingent—returned, with Glen Hardin once again acting as musical director. Fiddler Byron Berline also returned. Bernie Leadon played various stringed instruments on three cuts; Herb Pedersen from the Dillards helped out on guitar, Al Perkins from the Burritos played pedal steel, and Emory Gordy, whose credits ranged from country artist Joe South to pop star Neil Diamond, played bass.

Glen Hardin orchestrated the musicians' parts; Hugh handled the controls; and Gram seemed content to oversee. Having gotten the hint about his guitar work, he focused on his lead vocals and on refining the songs.

The concentration reaped obvious benefits. On dramatic love songs like "Love Hurts" and "Hearts on Fire," he became absolutely intense. Except for a couple of tracks on the International Submarine Band album, he never sounded better.

Emmylou loved what she was hearing. "Our singing came together on two songs, 'Love Hurts' and 'The Angels Rejoiced,'" she said. ". . . I finally learned what I was supposed to do. . . . Each night we'd get mixes of what we'd done and we'd take them back and listen to them over and over again. We'd get so excited, dancing around. His singing was so much better after a year on the road. I felt like Gram was on his way to getting himself under control."

Gram showed that he knew how to balance an album, inserting up-tempo numbers like "I Can't Dance" and "Ooh Las Vegas" at the right spots and, in mid-show, staging a mock "live" concert in a make-believe barroom, with a studio crowd whooping and hollering as if they were at the Smiling Dog in Cleveland. Gram threw bottles at buckets to simulate the sound of guns being fired. For this little show, Gram and Emmylou opened with "Cash on the Barrelhead," then segued into Gram's third—and finest—version of "Hickory Wind," with Emmylou's harmony lines making all the difference.

In one of the post-session playbacks, Gram pointed to the speakers when "Hickory Wind" reached its last line, and Emmylou scaled a high note. "That note right there," he said. "It's gonna make you famous!"

The sessions, which ran only two weeks, also yielded three tracks that didn't make the final cut. The songs were "Brand New Heartache" and "Sleepless Nights" by Felice and Boudleaux Bryant, and "The Angels Rejoiced Last Night." These would have to wait several years to see the record store racks, as part of the *Sleepless Nights* album.

To most observers in the studio, Gram was in charge, not only of the sessions but of himself. Phil Kaufman kept Gram away from the bottle for two weeks before the recordings began. He made sure the caterers provided plenty of fresh fruits for meals. Once the recording began there was no way to keep Gram from the occasional drink. But Kathy Miles, Phil Kaufman's girlfriend, was at the studio every day and heard nothing but harmony. "Everybody got along well," she said. "Gram was really happy with the work."

In fact, Gram made phone calls to various friends to tell them he'd finally made the album he always wanted to make.

Gram also called his sister, Avis, in Virginia. He told her first off that he was in good health and that he wasn't drinking. Over the phone, Avis heard a dog barking. "I'm calling from Phil's," said Gram. He explained why he was staying at his road manager's house.

"I just filed for divorce," he said. He was matter-of-fact, knowing that Avis wouldn't be surprised.

And, of course, he plugged his new album. *"GP's* okay," he said, "but *Sleepless Nights"*—that was what he was planning to call the new record—"is a lot more like what I want to accomplish."

Good old cocky Gram, Avis thought. With what they'd each gone through, she was happy to hear him sounding like the old brother she'd always known.

This time around, Gram thought, he'd do a *real* promotional tour. Warner Bros. already had him and Emmylou booked for another round of country-rock festival shows that would take him to Europe. But that would be in October, a whole month away.

Gram had time for a vacation, and he knew the perfect spot.

30

Oh Lord, Grant Me Vision

"He was always anxious to go there. It was nothing exciting . . . but he knew every bar and saloon in the area."

—Eddie Tickner

"Nobody gets Joshua Tree yet. Joshua Tree represented a spiritual quest, climbing the mountains. Like an American Indian kind of thing, you're doing it for your higher self, and that's what we were all doing. It wasn't about running out to the desert, trying to get loaded. It was searching for a meaning to all of it."

—Andee Cohen

On Monday, September 17, 1973, Gram headed east for the high desert. He had booked two rooms at the Joshua Tree Inn for four nights for himself and three friends. With him was Michael Martin, his erstwhile valet, who took the place of Phil as a sidekick/attendant. Michael's girlfriend was Dale McElroy, a wealthy young woman from Chula Vista and a friend of

Phil's. With Gram was Margaret Fisher, a woman Gram had known in high school days in Jacksonville. She moved to San Francisco, where she did a bit of everything, from waiting on tables to dancing with the Cockettes, a transvestite theater troupe. Several friends recalled her voracious appetite for sex, drugs, and rock and roll. One called her "the ultimate groupie." She listed among her conquests a Beatle, a son of Timothy Leary, and fellow Floridian Gram Parsons. She and Gram had run into each other in Los Angeles several months before, and now Gram invited her to visit, sending her a telegram: PSA PLANE TICKET PAID AND WAITING. CALL PHIL'S COLLECT. LOVE GRAM.

Gram and Margaret rode out in his Jaguar; Dale drove her 1960 Cadillac hearse, which Michael had convinced her to buy for camping purposes.

During their first day in town, Gram and his friends had just enough of a good time that Michael had to make his trip back to Los Angeles for more marijuana.

The events of Tuesday—Gram's last day of life—are tangled up in conflicting stories from various eyewitnesses, or people claiming to have been eyewitnesses.

Most press reports told of Gram being left in his room, asleep, in early evening while Michael, Dale, and Margaret went to Yucca Valley, six miles away, to get something to eat. Frank Barbary, who owned the motel with his wife, told *Rolling Stone*'s Patrick Sullivan that the group came knocking on his window late that night, saying that they couldn't revive Gram.

In her statement to the investigating coroner of San Bernardino County, however, Margaret Fisher left Michael (who, after all, was in Los Angeles) and Dale out of the picture, saying that she left around 8:00 P.M. to get something to eat, and that when she left, Gram "did not look well." Around 11:00 P.M., she said, she called the motel to have "some friends" check in on Gram, and when she couldn't locate them, she rushed back to find him "not breathing at 11:45 P.M."

After the resuscitation effort in Room 8, Gram was taken by ambulance to the Hi-Desert Memorial Hospital in Yucca Valley. He arrived at 12:15 A.M., cold and blue, with his pupils fixed and dilated, with no oxygen in his system, and with no pulse. The emergency room staff made three quick attempts to get his heart started again, but he was dead.

The press was told that Gram Parsons died of heart failure due to natural causes. But after an autopsy, Dr. Irving Root listed the official cause of death on Gram's death certificate: "Drug toxicity, days, due to multiple drug use, weeks."

Many of Gram's friends spread stories—later repeated in newspapers, magazines, and books—that got so wild that they just *had* to be true.

They ranged from the merely inaccurate—that he died sitting in a turquoise Naugahyde chair—to the impossible—Gram died after drinking heavily, going home, and making love with Gretchen. Then, of course, there was the conspiracy theory: Gram was murdered.

There was poetic justice in the way the story of Gram's death— a simple enough tale of an overdose—so quickly approached mythical proportions. Just as Gram toyed with the facts of his own life, and mixed truth and fantasy in song, so his last hours on earth are rendered into the fabric of what could be, in the proper hands, another great Gram Parsons song.

There were eyewitnesses. Margaret Fisher spoke to the coroner's investigators, but she has since disappeared. Michael Martin was last heard from in his native Australia. Dale McElroy Millman, who now lives in Santa Fe, New Mexico, told her story to me.

In her telling, she was the last person to see Gram alive. She made attempts to keep him alive, but he was dead by the time Margaret and, soon afterward, ambulance crewmen arrived.

But that leaves out several people who said they were at the death scene: the Barbarys, the family who owned and operated the motel: Frank (since deceased), his wife, Margaret, and their son, Alan, a self-described "social director" at the motel.

When they spoke to a magazine writer in 1976, they had little to protect. The motel was not liable for any damages. And when Alan Barbary spoke to me, he had even less reason to shelter details, because the motel no longer existed.

Still, father's and son's stories clashed. Frank said that "the girls"—Margaret and Dale—went to a Mexican restaurant, then came knocking on the windows of his apartment. Around the same time, Al showed up, and they found Gram in bed. "Like he was asleep, you know? He looked good, really." That's not what his son thought or remembered.

Alan Barbary, a Vietnam vet who had seen death close up, thought Gram was gone by the time he got to him, which he thought was around 10:00 P.M.

The following is Alan's story: He sat around that afternoon with Gram, drinking tequila and shooters. Alan then went to a swap meet and suspected that Gram scored some morphine while he was gone.

His mother, he said, spotted drug users on sight. "She knew I'd done drugs; she'd done drugs; we smoked weed together. And she spotted this chick. She knew this lady—it was this lady that had one arm. She came and went. The place was clean as a whistle."

When he came back from the swap meet, he "caught some weird vibes." He looked toward the office and saw his parents approaching Gram's room.

"What's going on?" he shouted.

"Something happened to Gram; he isn't breathing," his mother said.

Alan ran into the room and saw Gram in bed. His parents went off to call an ambulance, and Alan returned to the room. "When I got there," he said, "there was a chick on her knees *jerking him off*, saying his name and shit, trying to revive him. She was probably in love with him. She was spaced out so bad that she was spaced out two days later until someone took her away."

Alan shouted at her: "Get away from him." He began mouth-to-mouth and almost got sick. "I've seen a lot of dead people . . . and he'd been dead a little while. I almost gagged . . . from the poison that came out of his body, right out of him, into me. . . . You take morphine and booze, and you get morphine poison."

"That," said Dale McElroy in a quiet, even voice, "is a crock."

Dale, after all, was the "chick" Alan claimed to have seen. She considered herself neither a fan nor a friend of Gram's, and was doing nothing more than trying to get him breathing.

She never saw a man enter the room until an ambulance attendant rushed in. And Margaret Fisher was in no condition to have straddled Gram. Dale said Margaret was only gone an hour or so and was still high from the heroin she'd taken with Gram. When she got to the room and saw Gram, she was hysterical, and she'd fled to get help.

And there was no woman who remained "spaced out two days later until someone took her away." Dale and Margaret both left for Los Angeles within two hours. As for Alan Barbary's diagnosis of morphine poisoning, at least one medical authority that I contacted disputed it, basing her opinion on the autopsy reports. "Unless (Gram) had a needle and syringe in his arm at the time," said Dr. Margaret Greenwald of the San Francisco Coroner's Office, "you wouldn't be able to tell just by doing mouth-to-mouth. He may have been able to smell the alcohol, but there's no way to smell the morphine."

Morphine poisoning would be indicated by high levels of morphine in the blood; tests on Gram's blood showed an alcohol level of 0.21 mg%, but no morphine or barbiturates.

A urinalysis showed traces of cocaine and amphetamines, and more than traces of morphine, at 166 mg%. Liver and bile tests indicated morphine at a 228 mg% level.

Dr. Greenwald considered those figures meaningless. Yes, they were high, but drugs can accumulate in urine and in the liver over a long period of time. "That just indicates he'd been using [those drugs] for a long period of time," she said.

Because the necessary technology did not exist in 1973, there was no data on how much, if any, cocaine was in the blood. If the cocaine level in the blood was high, the doctor said, "it might have answered the question of how long the cocaine had been in the person's system."

To Dr. Greenwald, descriptions in the autopsy report of encrusted needle puncture wounds over the back of the left hand, and of other abrasions in front of and in the left elbow, indicated chronic usage of drugs as well as some relatively recent usage.

(Gretchen Parsons told the coroner's investigator that Gram had been taking medication for nerves, but she "knew of no other medications or drugs he might be taking." Phil Kaufman said Gram had been using heroin "several years ago but had kicked the habit" and did not know if he was taking any other drugs.)

While Dr. Greenwald could not say that Gram's was a clear-cut case of toxicity, she thought the coroner had come to a proper conclusion.

Gram's sister, Avis, said that Gretchen Parsons told her that she thought some people left Gram to go into town for dinner; that when they returned, he was dying; that "they freaked out because they had some junk on them" and delayed calling for help because "they couldn't get it together to get rid of the junk. So they let him die."

Gretchen wasn't alone in making such accusations. Rick Grech, saying that "Gram was in a crazy state because of his separation" and "was out on a binge," said he thought that Gram was left alone to die. "When he got *heavy*, they *split*. They left him. They got afraid and let him go." Even without Gretchen's or Rick's charges, there were questions that not only remain unanswered to this day but that might never have been asked. At Hi-Desert Memorial Hospital, according to Dale, the police looked with suspicion on Margaret, who was wearing sunglasses for some reason at midnight. Dale suggested they call Phil Kaufman, and he promised to be there in an hour and a half. The women were then released on their own recognizance and escorted back to the Joshua Tree Inn, where they were told to "stay put."

As promised, Phil got into Joshua Tree as quickly as his van could get him there. But he did not go to the hospital or the police station. He went to the Joshua Tree Inn, packed the women into his vehicle, and headed straight back to Los Angeles.

The police never contacted them again.

Which leaves a few questions.

Alan Barbary said he returned to the motel around 10:00 P.M.

and that "vibes" led him directly to Gram's room. Why was it midnight before the ambulance arrived? (Alan insisted that the ambulance came well before midnight, but the autopsy protocol listed Gram's time of arrival at Hi-Desert Memorial Hospital as 12:15 A.M.)

How did Margaret Fisher take two to three hours to get food in a town six miles away? (Dale said Margaret never went to Yucca Valley; that she went to a local coffee shop and was actually gone less than an hour. Dr. Gene Schoenfeld, who knew Margaret before and after her time with Gram, said she told him that while Dale stayed with Gram, she left "to look for some stimulants.") If Margaret was concerned for Gram, why did she wait between two and three hours, according to her own story, before calling the motel?

Dr. Greenwald raised a brow. She, too, had been bothered by Margaret's testimony.

The doctor scanned the report again. "She goes out. She calls the motel a couple of times. Why is she so suddenly concerned about him, if he drank four whiskey sours—which would be something he would do normally? Or was he already in difficulty?

"It doesn't say what condition he was in when she left. I would suspect he was kind of out of it and unresponsive and almost in a coma at that point, that those drugs had been in the system for a few hours. . . ."

Dr. Greenwald tapped the sheaf of papers from San Bernardino.

"If I had the case in here and that was the story I heard, it would raise my suspicions."

Oh, but she hadn't heard anything yet.

31

Night Moves

Gram said, 'Please let my spirit be released in the Joshua Tree,'" Nancy Parsons remembered. "That was a request. . . . There was nothing weird about it, except Phil Coffin." She sat upright and exploded in laughter. *"Whoahh!* a slight slip of the lip!"

Dickey Smith, Gram's schoolmate at Williams Heights, was living in Athens, Georgia, when his parents in Waycross sent him a clipping from the *Journal-Herald* about Gram's death.

"It was such a waste. I hate to relate drugs and musicians, but Gram could have had everything he wanted. If he didn't go into music, there was money, opportunity, and everything else in the family business. Gram just took another route."

Patti Johnson, Gram's high-school girlfriend who almost eloped with him in 1963, was in Florida when she got word of his death. Along with sadness, she felt anger.

"It's not like he was forced to do a lot of things," she said, "but I felt the people who were around him weren't helping him any." She mentioned Keith Richards; she mentioned Gretchen Parsons. And she sighed. "Or it was just the times."

Avis Parsons was angry at people who may have let Gram die.

But, she said, Gram may have subconsciously been getting ready to go. At times *Grievous Angel* sounded to her like a suicide note. "He wanted to go out in a great flash of glory rather than fading away. Look how beautifully he got himself together for that last album. Son of a bitch. I'm really pissed at him."

Rick Grech was angry at himself. He felt a guilt, explicable only by partnerships forged in the kinds of drugs they had shared.

"The way I see it, if Gram and I had been together, it wouldn't have happened—because whatever was done, we *split* it. And when it happened to Gram, there was nobody around to *share* it."

Emmylou had gone home after the sessions. She was at her parents' house in Clarkesville, Maryland, just north of Washington. Tom Guidera, who'd rejoined Sageworth and Drums after Emmylou began working with Gram, was with her. They were in the kitchen with Emmylou's mother, Eugenia, when the phone rang. Eugenia answered and, seconds later, told her daughter that it was Eddie Tickner calling.

Emmylou accepted the news in silence. She did not cry or break down, and she was not in shock. Sure, Gram had managed to control himself for the two weeks it took to make his album, but control was not the story of his life. She had seen the storm clouds gathering a long time ago, it seems, and from all the way across the country. Now, here she was, 3,000 miles away again, and it was pouring everywhere.

Bob Parsons was in a hospital in New Orleans when he heard about Gram. He acted fast. In the coroner's report, Gram was listed as a resident of Hollywood and a native of Florida. That was bad news for Parsons.

He hurried out of New Orleans. He had to get to Los Angeles and claim the body.

The reason was simple: The state of Louisiana's Napoleonic Law stipulates that male survivors are the sole inheritors of any estate. Apparently Bob wanted a body to help him establish a New Orleans residency for Gram.

Avis remembered Bob telling her that "Gram would have wanted to be buried in the South, under a big live oak tree."

Why not Waycross, then? Or Columbia, Tennessee? Or Florida? Between the Snivelys and the Connors, someone must have known what Bob Parsons was doing.

"Well," said Avis, "I think maybe we had to go through the actual shock and grief before we started to say, 'Wait a minute.'"

Without consulting Gretchen, Bob began arranging a funeral for Gram. When Gram's friends asked about services, they were told that they would be in New Orleans, and they received strong hints that it was going to be for family only.

Night Moves

Gram's buddies sensed that they were being left out and this may have been what prompted the wild episode that followed.

Also there had been the pact; Chris Ethridge heard it during the funeral services for Clarence White. Others remembered Gram and Phil Kaufman talking at a drunken wake afterward, about how they didn't want a straight, religious service. They loudly promised each other that whoever died first, the survivor would take care of business. Gram, sitting with Phil, Kathy Miles, Michael Martin, and a few others, proclaimed that he wanted to die in Joshua Tree. He wanted to be cremated there, too, and he wanted his ashes spread around Cap Rock.

On Thursday, with Bob Parsons heading into town to claim Gram's body, Phil Kaufman and company sat around his kitchen table, drinking beer and vodka, smoking dope, and getting angrier by the minute.

"Gram wouldn't want this," said Phil. "He would be really pissed off. He wouldn't even go to his own funeral if he knew what they were doing."

Then someone mentioned the pact.

To fulfill it, all they had to do was get the body. In mid-afternoon, Phil went to work.

In an interview published by the British music paper, *Melody Maker*, Phil told what he did. "I found out which airline was due to ship the body and called them up. They said the remains were there and I almost hung up. Then something made me ask them to check the name. They said, 'Emma Goldberg.' I nearly stole an old Jewish lady! I could just imagine getting to the desert, opening the casket, and . . . 'Oh, Gram! You look *terrible!*' "

After learning where Gram's body was going to be, he and Michael prepared to go to Los Angeles International Airport. Phil put on a suit, but Kathy thought he looked all wrong in such formal wear—especially in his drunken state—and Phil switched back to his casual clothes. He and Michael put on cowboy hats and their Sin City jackets, souvenirs from the Fallen Angels' Houston gig. They borrowed Dale's old black hearse and stocked it with a case of beer and a couple of fifths of Jack Daniels.

Phil and Michael arrived at the loading dock around 5:00 P.M. Just then, the hearse bearing Gram's body pulled up. Phil approached the driver while he was still behind the wheel.

"I'm from the mortuary," he said, waving a few sheets of paper around. "The family has changed its mind. They want to use a private plane." The body was now being shipped out of the Van Nuys airport, he said.

The driver gave Phil the once-over. He'd noticed the old hearse, which had broken windows and no license plate. He was skeptical.

"Look, fella," said Phil, "we're on overtime and we've got a date with a couple of hot broads. Give us the stiff; we want to get out of here."

The driver shrugged and even offered to help carry the coffin. Phil signed a slip of paper by scribbling the name "Jeremy Nobody" on it, loaded Donna's hearse, and took off.

On the way out the car stalled, and a motorcycle cop pulled up and frightened Phil. "They weren't looking for me, but I thought they were—because I was drunk and paranoid! So I just said to the cops, 'Isn't this a shitty job?'" The cop nodded, dismounted, and gave the hearse a push.

Phil sped toward Joshua Tree, sweating, swearing at Gram, yelling, "You bastard! Why'd you have to go first?" On the long ride, he and Michael also drank from the liquor stash, toasting their passenger.

Phil remembered stopping at a gas station along the way. He handed a five-gallon tin can to the attendant.

"Do you want regular or ethyl?" he asked.

"Regular," said Phil. "I don't want him to ping."

The attendant didn't know what he was talking about.

"Private joke," said Phil.

The pair then drove out to the Joshua Tree Monument and six miles into the preserve, to Cap Rock.

Just off the main road, they unloaded the hearse, and Phil opened the casket to be sure he had stolen the right body. It was Gram, all right; and Phil, ever the joker, couldn't resist one last, stupid joke. He touched Gram's chest; then, as if Gram had looked down, flicked his hand up at his face.

Phil then placed a can of beer into the box, doused the body with gasoline, and lit a match.

"You aren't supposed to have open fires in national parks," he was quoted saying in *Melody Maker*, "and this one created an unbelievable fireball, which was seen by some forest rangers. They chased us, but we were unencumbered by sobriety, so we got away."

In their escape they ran other motorists off the highway. But, as it turned out, the forest rangers must have been a drunken hallucination of Phil's. The smoldering remains of the coffin weren't spotted until early the next morning, when campers reported to park rangers that "a log was burning" near Cap Rock.

Meanwhile, in Los Angeles, police detectives, led by Gretchen's father, Larry Burrell, knocked on the door at Phil's house. It was just past midnight. A detective shouted through the door to Phil's girlfriend Kathy Miles: "We're looking for Gram Parsons."

Kathy began to cry. "He's definitely not here," she screamed, "and I think that's a pretty sick joke."

Night Moves

After looking around the outside of the house, the party left.

By the time they—and the rest of the world—learned what had happened, Phil had done his job.

One Associated Press account quoted a policeman saying, "It looks like something out of Transylvania, out of the legend of Count Dracula." Another cop called the cremation "ritualistic," which the newspapers were only too happy to quote.

People who knew Gram knew what had happened, and they knew who had done it, and why. But, while the detectives were tracing leads, and while Gram's remains were finally being shipped out to New Orleans, the craziness continued at Phil's house.

Before Gram's death, a film company had arranged to use the property for a scene in director Arthur Penn's movie, *Night Moves*. The cast and crew, including the star, Gene Hackman, were there on the night of September 26 when police arrived with warrants for the arrests of Phil and Michael. Since there were no laws on the books in California covering the theft of a dead body, the charge was grand theft—for having taken the *coffin* from its rightful owner.

Phil wasn't there when the police arrived, but Kathy was. The cops chose to wait around awhile, and moments later Phil called. She told him about the police.

"Tell them not to pull any guns," he said. "I'll go with them peaceably. I'll be there in twenty minutes."

Kathy told the police, and they promised to keep things cool. She also told Arthur Penn and the crew what Phil had done. Sure enough, Phil showed up and left with the police.

As the police drove off, Arthur Penn turned to Kathy.

"I think we're filming the *wrong movie*," he said.

The day before Phil Kaufman was arrested, Gram Parsons was buried in New Orleans. On September 25, 1973, services were conducted at the House of Bultman, not far from Bob Parsons's home. Avis, entering the funeral parlor, thought she'd walked onto a Hollywood set of a saloon, whorehouse, or some combination of the two. It was all red velvet and crystal lamps, and rickety to boot. "Every time a streetcar would pass by, the prisms would tinkle and shake and tremble."

Among the fifty people who attended were Aunt May Snively from Florida and Uncle Tom and Aunt Pauline Connor from Tennessee. Tom Connor found the service impersonal and stayed close by Avis and her new husband, Robert "Beau" Johnson. Avis thought the funeral was "empty," and Beau worked to keep her away from Bob Parsons.

The only people who made it in from California were Gretchen and a friend, Claudia Lennear, who was an Ikette behind the Ike and Tina Turner Revue. "They made a wonderful, grand entrance, and they clung to each other through the whole thing," said Avis.

"Thank God for her," Gretchen said about Claudia, adding that she feared for her safety while she was in town. "There was a lot of infighting with Bob about money and stuff like that." She even had the Parsonses drop them off at one hotel, then sneaked off and registered in another one.

And how was the stepfather in this time of grief?

"I can't tell you how thrilled he was," said Gretchen, dripping sarcasm.

Whatever Parsons' reason for claiming Gram's body for burial in New Orleans, he derived no profit. He may have wanted to show that Gram, dead or alive, was a resident of Louisiana, but, as Avis recalls, a Florida court squelched his plans. In the year of life left to him, Bob Parsons made no money off his stepson.

While most of Gram's family was upset with what Phil Kaufman had done in Joshua Tree, Tom Connor understood. "Gram didn't want to be put through a funeral home, a service like that," he said.

"In fact, I don't think that's a bad idea. It's like the Indians. For them, cremation is the way. I see nothing wrong with that."

Bonnie Parsons called Phil's actions "just a morbid publicity stunt." Gram might have wanted to be buried in Joshua Tree, she said, "but I don't think he would have made a big deal over it. You know, 'When I'm gone put me anywhere.'"

Keith Richards saw Phil not long after Gram's death. He hugged the executive nanny and told him: "Nice one, Phil, you took care of Gram."

"I don't think Gram wanted much to do with the New Orleans group," Keith told me. "He had a real affection for his father. He used to talk about his old man a lot—his real father—as opposed to the Parsons family."

At least one other musician endorsed Phil's private service. Years later Elvis Costello said of Gram's death: "His exit was perfect."

★

Emmylou Harris, who would later employ Phil Kaufman as her road manager, stayed neutral about the bizarre end to Gram's time on earth. "All I know," she said, "is that Phil Kaufman was Gram's best friend. What he did, he did for Gram."

From the first, Phil was handled like some kind of folk hero. When he was booked at the police station in Venice, just north of the L.A. airport, one of the cops told him, "We had the damndest time trying to figure out what to charge you with," and kidded with him about having committed "Gram Theft Parsons."

"I was only gone about three or four hours," said Phil. "I went right back to the house and the movie crew cheered when I walked in."

Michael Martin surrendered the next day.

In West Los Angeles Municipal Court, the two men pled guilty to misdemeanor theft charges. They were given thirty-day jail sentences, which were suspended; they were fined $300 each, and they were ordered to pay Larry Burrell, Gretchen's father, the $750 he had paid for Gram's coffin.

It was November 5. Happy birthday, dear Gram.

To cover the fine he had to pay, Phil staged a combination wake for Gram and a benefit for himself. He called it the Gram Parsons Funeral Party. At Phil's house on a Sunday in November 1973, he charged $5 admission and made up Gram Parsons T-shirts and had bottles of beer relabeled "Gram Pilsner—A Good Stiff Drink for What Ales You"—on sale. Jonathan Richman and the Modern Lovers (a group Eddie Tickner was managing) played; so did a guy doing a Johnny Cash imitation, and so did Bobby "Boris" Pickett and the Cryptkickers, doing "Monster Mash" for half of their eight-song set.

About 200 people showed up and bought enough mementos to net Phil about $800.

Pamela DesBarres attended, reaching out for anything or anyone who had something to do with her beloved Gram. She found herself repelled by Phil's demented humor; the Cryptkickers performing amid papier-mâché tombstones; the peddling of souvenir T-shirts and beer. But she couldn't resist buying. Today she still uses the Gram Pilsner beer bottle as a candle holder.

There was one other gathering for Gram. After he got the news, John Nuese called a few friends and arranged for a weekend at a summer house Barry and Holly Tashian were renting in the northwest corner of Connecticut.

There, in a cabin heated only by a wood stove, Emmylou and Tom, Barry and Holly, John Nuese, and Bill Keith, the banjo and pedal steel guitarist, got together for a long day of songs and the occasional reflection about Gram.

And it was there that Emmylou cried for the first time. She had brought a reel-to-reel tape from the sessions for *Grievous*

Angel, a tape of some songs she hadn't yet heard in their final mixes. The Tashians had a machine at the house and played the tape.

The song was "Brass Buttons," written by Gram in 1965, when he was nineteen. It was sung by Gram alone, at his gentlest, with keyboards, steel guitars, and drum brushes discreetly trailing behind him:

> My mind was young until she grew
> My secret thoughts known only by a few
> It was a dream much too real to be leaned against too
>   long
> All the time I think she knew . . .

After the song, Barry said something about that voice no longer being around, now that Gram had "graduated."

Emmylou and Tom looked at each other and burst into tears. Emmylou rushed out of the house.

As she would write and sing to him in "Boulder to Birmingham," "Well, you really got me this time. And the hardest part is knowing I'll survive."

32

Grievous Angels

$\mathbf{O}$n November 3 Pamela Des-
Barres drove to the Joshua Tree Inn "to give Gram the good vibe."
She asked Frank Barbary for Gram's room. "I was really into a
specific Japanese religious thing," she said, "where you channeled
the light to the spirit to help them realize they're gone."

She looked around in the room at the things that had surrounded Gram in his last hours. Thinking that he had died in a
Naugahyde chair, she sat and chanted into the night, *Nam myo ho
ren ge kyo*, envisioning Gram slim and happy again, and telling him
he was on his way to better things. "It was intense," she said.

After this ceremony, Pamela slept in the bed in which Gram
had died—just to be closer to him.

★

Gretchen Parsons did not go to Joshua Tree; did not chant; did not
have any interest in getting closer to her dead husband.

Blaming not only his death but their breakup, as well, on
"irresponsible friends," she went on mini-rampages, legal and
physical. She destroyed all their mutual possessions she found in
the bungalow he'd been staying in behind Phil's house. She threat-

ened to sue the shipping company that released Gram's coffin to Phil, and she hired an investigator to establish her husband's monetary worth.

In December, as Warner Bros. Records prepared *Grievous Angel* for release, Gretchen, through her father, put a stop to plans for a cover photo of Gram and Emmylou astride his Harley, with Emmylou's arms resting on Gram's shoulders. Joe Smith, president of the record company at the time, chose to "respect the family's wishes," and Emmylou was relegated to a back-of-the-cover credit, and no photo.

John Nuese visited Gretchen a month after Gram's death. "She was vehement with hate for Nancy and Emmylou," he remembered. "Any woman who had anything to do with Gram, she was just livid with hate for. He had just died, and she was beside herself."

Emmylou Harris, through the years, remained a model of restraint when it came to talking about Gram's personal life. Only once did she let her guard down.

The *Washington Post*'s Sunday magazine visited the hometown girl in Los Angeles in the fall of 1975, on the eve of her first solo album. The writer, Marion Clark, asked Emmylou about her first husband.

Emmylou said she didn't want to talk about her ex in print, and then she told Marion, "I can't talk about Gretchen, either. She shouldn't be written about. She needs help. She's been on the L.A. scene since she was fourteen years old, and all she ever cared about was looking good and being known as Mrs. Gram Parsons."

Emmylou had just done a concert in South Carolina, she said, when she saw Gretchen. "I hadn't seen her since he'd died, and she comes over and she acts like nothing ever happened. Can you believe it? *Like nothing at all ever happened!*

"I told her I couldn't talk to her."

★

A few weeks after Gram died, Emmylou took a half-step forward. She and Tom formed a band, the Angel Band, and began playing around D.C. clubs.

When she was discovered all over again—this time as a solo artist—she was signed onto Gram's last label, Warner Bros. When she began doing interviews to promote her first album, she found herself being connected with Gram again. Headlines read HAUNTED BY GRAM; EMMYLOU'S FIGHT AGAINST TRAGEDY; and GRIEVING ANGEL.

In the interviews themselves, Emmylou was the picture of calm and reason, always taking care to put the music first and their friendship second. But she couldn't deny or hold back her pain.

Grievous Angels

"When Gram died, I felt like I'd been amputated, like my life had just been whacked off," she told Alanna Nash. "I never realized what kind of music was inside me . . . until I met him."

To Cameron Crowe in *Rolling Stone*, she said: "Gram's death was like falling off a mountain. It was a very hard year between his death and the recording of my [first] album. A year of throwing myself into a lot of work that my heart wasn't really into. There was a lot of stumbling involved. I was playing quite a few bars and was in a real vulnerable position. People felt that they could come up and ask me anything. I used to get hostile. It hurt. I didn't want to get emotional around some perfect stranger who had the goddamn gall to come up and ask me something that was none of his goddamn business."

Years later, talking to me for the same magazine, she explained why every story about her inevitably took a turn to the grievous.

"What I was doing musically had a lot to do with him. . . . He turned me completely around . . . and I did have a lot of feeling for him and what he had done, so it's impossible for me to talk about my music, or myself, without talking about Gram."

Being Gram's partner and having what she called "the freedom of being restricted" to singing tenor were joyous. "I still think back on that period of time that I worked with him as probably my happiest time as a performer. I got something out of it that I just have never gotten again and probably shouldn't. I never will forget him," she said. "I suppose I think about him as much and still care about him and love him just as much."

It wasn't simply emotional ties that drove Emmylou to mention Gram. She was on a crusade; she wanted to spread the word about Gram's music. "I thought that if the world just heard him once, they'd be touched by his voice in the same way that I was."

Emmylou was realistic enough to know that not everyone would be so deeply affected. As she told Robert Hilburn in a 1975 interview, "He cut straight through the middle with no compromises. . . . He was never afraid to write from the heart, and perhaps that's why he was never really accepted. It's like the light was too strong and bright, and people just had to turn away . . . because it was all too painful. It could rip you up. Not many people can take music that real."

When *Grievous Angel* was released in January, Emmylou was proven right.

Rolling Stone raved; the *Los Angeles Times* applauded. When the *Village Voice* polled two dozen critics on the best albums of

1974, *Grievous Angel* placed in the Top 15, and the critics were joined by artists like Johnny Cash, Elvis Costello, and Tom Petty. Petty named *Grievous Angel* his favorite album.

But, consistent with Gram's previous efforts, *Grievous Angel* never sold, just denting the lower rungs of the album charts for three weeks before falling off.

The album made one other chart: Paul Gambaccini's book *Critic's Choice: Top 200 Albums*, published in 1978. Gambaccini surveyed forty-eight rock and pop tastemakers, and *Grievous Angel* ranked number 179.

★

Emmylou never tried to fill Gram's shoes. But by dedicating herself to serving as a continuum, of sorts, for Gram Parsons, she did change. She became a star.

Once Warner Bros. heard her singing lead vocals, the company committed itself. It gave her the financial resources to back her up with some of the best musicians she'd met through Gram— $125,000 just to get James Burton and Glen D. Hardin into the studio and on tour with her. Others who worked with her, early on, included Elvis's drummer Ron Tutt; Bernie Leadon; Herb Pedersen; Little Feat's Bill Payne; Willie Nelson's harmonica player, Mickey Raphael; and Linda Ronstadt.

Brian Ahern, the producer Warner Bros. hired for her, made her comfortable by hooking up his recording studio—built into a converted semi-truck trailer—to a rented house in the hills above Beverly Hills, so that she could record in a living room. After their third album together they married in 1977, in ceremonies conducted by Jet Thomas. (The marriage ended in 1984 and in late 1985 Emmylou married Paul Kennerly, a songwriter who succeeded Ahern as her producer.)

The various forms of support brought out the best in Emmylou. She applied her voice to an encyclopedic range of music, based on traditional country but ranging from the Louvin Brothers and Merle Haggard to the Beatles, Chuck Berry, the Drifters, and Bruce Springsteen. On stage, her shyness was offset by a natural spunk. And, supported by a music press eager to hear her story as well as her music, she launched a career that met with immediate success.

While Gram's albums peaked with sales of about 40,000 copies, Emmylou's debut, *Pieces of the Sky*, sold 130,000 by the end of 1975, and reached 250,000 the next year. A quick follow-up, *Elite Hotel*, sold 300,000; and *Luxury Liner*, issued in 1977, gave her her first gold record, for sales over 500,000.

Grievous Angels

In the sixteen years between 1975 and 1990 Emmylou produced seventeen albums, not counting two "best-of" packages. Throughout her prolific recording career, she has remained true to her stated goal of keeping Gram's music and spirit alive.

The first album included "Sleepless Nights" and the song she and Bill Danoff wrote for Gram, "Boulder to Birmingham." The second album had "Sin City," "Wheels," and "Ooh Las Vegas." Her version of "Together Again," which Gram had cut with the Burritos, hit the top of the country charts. *Luxury Liner*, named for one of Gram's songs from his Sub Band days, also contained Gram's "She."

Emmylou sang "Hickory Wind" on her 1979 album, *Blue Kentucky Girl*. She included "Hot Burrito #2" in *Evangeline*, one of two albums she released in 1981. A live set, *Last Date*, in 1982, featured "Grievous Angel," "We'll Sweep Out the Ashes (in the Morning)," "Juanita," and "Devil in Disguise." Her album with Linda Ronstadt and Dolly Parton, *Trio*, included "Farther Along." In *Bluebird*, in 1988, she brought back "I Still Miss Someone," which Gram sang with the Sub Band.

In 1990 she issued *Duets*, a compilation of partnerships with, among others, George Jones, Willie Nelson, Neil Young, Roy Orbison, the Band, the Desert Rose Band (led by Chris Hillman), and Gram, for "Love Hurts."

In concert Emmylou not only kept the torch lit but her selection of musicians for her Hot Band introduced her listeners to numerous talented singers and songwriters who, along with Emmylou, represented a generation of more adventurous country musicians who became known as "new traditionalists."

Her first was Rodney Crowell, a superb songwriter and singer she found through a demo tape of his songs.

Rodney, who liked *Grievous Angel*, with all of its "kinfolk singing," could tell that Emmylou was trying to fill a void. "I was sensitive to the fact that there was a deep wound there that was in the process of healing." Rodney, a rock and roller with a gentle soul, made Emmylou instantly comfortable.

Because he wrote songs and sang duets with Emmylou, the rock press, right away, called Rodney "the new Gram Parsons."

He wasn't much bothered. "You can understand how people would draw that conclusion, but I never felt it on stage." But there were a few people he couldn't understand, some kooks who moved from Gram to Emmylou. "In one case, one guy was gonna rub me out because I couldn't replace Gram Parsons. And another crazy guy, I think it was in Long Island, had decided that I was Gram Parsons' ghost."

By the time bluegrass picker and singer Ricky Skaggs replaced Rodney in 1978, the fringe had quieted down. Still, Barry Tashian, who took Skaggs's place in 1980 and played in the Hot Band for almost a decade, was sensitive to members of Emmylou's audiences who were clearly fans of Gram's.

They were not banner-bearing fanatics, but in every city, it seemed, there was a core group. Emmylou, who had a repertoire of some 125 songs, kept a half dozen Gram Parsons tunes rehearsed, and did at least one a night, with "Sin City" and "Wheels" most likely to come up.

For all of her success—the number one singles and albums, the gold records, the Grammy and Country Music Association awards, and the sellout concerts—there was one album Emmylou performed on that didn't sell.

It was *Sleepless Nights*, the Burrito Brothers compilation that included three achingly gorgeous duets between Gram and Emmylou—on "Brand New Heartache," "Sleepless Nights," and "The Angels Rejoiced Last Night."

Released in 1976, after Emmylou had already had five number one country singles, the album barely moved off the racks.

"I don't think any of Gram's albums have sold," said Emmylou, looking resigned to the destiny assigned to certain artists.

She chose to believe that, in the case of Gram's audiences, it was quality, not quantity, that really counted.

"People who buy Gram's albums have a certain amount of special feeling for the music," she told me. "I like to think of it as being that way.

"His music is in the hands of appreciative people."

33

Calling Me Home

Few rock stars, dead or alive, have many songs written about them. The Beatles had at least a couple dozen, most of them novelty attempts to cash in on Beatlemania; Buddy Holly had four tributes; Elvis Presley had a handful, mostly by Elvis imitators, of course; Otis Redding had one; and so did Brian Jones. Among dead musicians the champ, until Gram came along, was Hiram Williams, better known as Hank. His death triggered a slew of musical (in most cases) tributes, from attempts at the sublime—"Hank Williams Will Live Forever (in People's Hearts)" by Johnnie and Jack—to the ridiculous: "(I Would Like to Have Been) Hank's Little Flower Girl" by Little Barbara.

At last count, by Thor Martinsen, who counts such things, Gram Parsons was the inspiration for about twenty songs, among them "My Man" by Bernie Leadon, "Artists and Poets" by Johnny Rivers and "He Had That Sweet Country Sound" by John Phillips.

Years ago, Richie Furay expressed amazement that there were more songs about Gram than about Brian Jones. But Richie had added to the inventory himself with "Crazy Eyes," recorded on the same album on which Poco cut "Brass Buttons."

Almost from the instant he passed from this life, Gram became a cult object.

There were the songs about him, followed by lengthy newspaper and magazine pieces. There was talk about books and movies. As country-rock took hold, by way of bands ranging from the Eagles to Alabama, Gram Parsons received various posthumous awards and honors.

In 1981 "Sin City," as recorded by the Burritos, was included in the Smithsonian Collection of Classic Country Music. In 1983, "Love Hurts," from a live album of the Fallen Angels' Long Island radio concert, was nominated for a Grammy. In 1984 the Franklin Mint Society included the Submarine Band's performance of "I Still Miss Someone" in a compilation album, and in 1986 the Country Music Foundation in Nashville selected two Submarine Band tracks, "Luxury Liner" and "Blue Eyes," for inclusion in *The Greatest Country Music Recordings of All Time*, part of its official archive collection. The foundation's Country Music Hall of Fame, on which Emmylou Harris served as president of the board, accepted from her a Martin guitar that Gram had used on tour, and it is on display.

And in Holland, Poll-Gala's award, presented to outstanding country artists, was renamed the Gram Award, in the form of a sculpture of Gram Parsons, sitting and wearing a casual denim cap, jacket, and jeans.

"Gram would've sure dug it if he'd known he was gonna be this hot after he died," said Roger McGuinn.

The main link for Gram's appreciators around the world is the Gram Parsons Memorial Foundation, started by Mark Holland in Tampa, with inspiration from Thor Martinsen in Norway.

Thor, a banker, was a Byrds fan who discovered Gram through *Sweetheart of the Rodeo*. Both Thor and Mark were Gram Parsons fans from before his death; both were collectors of Gram's records, articles, and facts about his life. And they both knew there had to be others like them.

Mark started up the foundation, not as a fan club but as an organization devoted to preserving, protecting, and perpetuating Gram's music and name. Mark wanted Gram memorialized by way of a statue in Winter Haven, a plaque at Joshua Tree, and by induction into the Country Music Hall of Fame. He spent several years putting together a video documentary of Gram, the idea being to reach a younger generation of musicians. "I think Gram's music is going to be perpetuated through somebody that is younger, the way the Stones picked up Robert Johnson's 'Love in Vain' and took the songs into another generation," he said. "Gram's music is never-ending."

Calling Me Home

Mark became known as "that fanatic in Tampa," and some of Gram's peers—notably Emmylou Harris and Chris Hillman—avoided him.

Mark admitted to being obsessive about Gram, but he made no apologies. Besides, he and Thor were right. There were hundreds of Gram Parsons fans around the world, and within a few years, the group sprouted a newsletter that became a magazine, *Cosmic American Music News*, devoted not only to Gram but to artists deemed to be carrying on Gram's music or what he once called "cosmic American music." They included Dwight Yoakam, Tom Petty, Vince Gill, Tom Russell, Marty Stuart, Steve Earle, Steve Forbert, Joe Ely, Jason and the Scorchers, the Long Ryders, Nanci Griffith, Highway 101, and Lyle Lovett.

The sincere appreciation of a wide range of roots music made the Gram Parsons Memorial Foundation something more than a time-warped cult devoted to a dead musician. The majority of the magazine was devoted to interviews with musicians who played with Gram (or in associated bands). News items ranged from reissues of Gram's music and its inclusion in such movie sound-tracks as *Planes, Trains, and Automobiles* (but, the correspondent noted, the credit read "Chris Hillman and Graham Parsons") to calls for a campaign to get Gram into the Rock and Roll Hall of Fame.

Members wrote about their devotion to Gram, their memories of Burritos or Fallen Angels concerts, their meetings with other GP fans around the world, and their own efforts to keep his music alive.

Advertisements offered Gram's records and other memorabilia through mail auctions. Although original copies of the International Submarine Band album were getting more than $100 in the collectors' market, rare Sub Band and Burritos singles might be obtained for as low as $15. In a personal ad, a Nudie leather jacket once owned by Gram was offered for a minimum bid of $2,500.

The Foundation and various of its members also staged tributes to Gram, beginning with a birthday show at the Lone Star Cafe in New York in 1983. Since 1986 a Nashville pedal steel player, Argyle Bell, has produced an annual tribute to Gram and Clarence White, the most recent concerts being fund-raisers for MADD (Mothers Against Drunk Driving). The shows have drawn such participants as Rodney Crowell, the Nitty Gritty Dirt Band (with Bob Carpenter, husband of Gretchen Parsons), the Kentucky Colonels (with Roland White), Barry and Holly Tashian, and Michael Clarke.

The 1988 tribute at the Cannery nightclub was packed with fine cosmic American music from the Colonels (Roland was joined by Doug Dillard and two emerging stars, Vince Gill and Marty Stuart); from Jason Ringenberg of Jason and the Scorchers; from Foster and Lloyd; and from Bobby Bare, whose versions of "Streets of Baltimore" and "Miller's Cave" in the early sixties inspired Gram to cover them.

That concert included the first public appearance of Gram's twenty-one year-old daughter, Polly. With her mother, Nancy, and half-sister C.C., in the audience, Polly thanked the audience for "helping me realize how truly incredible my past, present, and future really are." She concluded: "I love you, Daddy, wherever you are."

Holly Tashian and Chris James, the house band's keyboard player, then serenaded Polly with "Hickory Wind."

C.C. stared at Polly, then turned to her mother.

"Mommy, do you see him?" she asked. "Do you see him right next to her?"

Nancy looked, and she saw Gram.

"Does anybody else see him?" C.C. asked.

"That doesn't matter."

"Mommy, why is he so sad?" C.C. asked, tears welling.

As Nancy watched, Polly appeared to turn, reaching for something, and the apparition disappeared. "I felt him," Polly said. "I definitely felt him."

★

Gram's life and death were so confused, no one even knew where to go to pay respects. In Waycross, everyone who knew Gram and his family told me that the house had been burned down or blown up that election eve in 1968. Dickey Smith and Henry Clarke had driven me to the house that now stands at 1600 Suwannee Drive. As far as they knew, the Connors home had disappeared, just as the Connors had.

They didn't know that the house had been only moderately damaged, and that a Wendell Dixon, whose business it is to move entire houses, had purchased the building from Sheriff Robert E. Lee, sliced it into four parts, moved it to the outskirts of town, and put it back together.

Wendell now lives in the house, and he offered a tour. In the living room he pointed out a couple of changes he'd made, turning the fireplace around and moving the location of the garage. But I saw the Florida Room in which Gram hosted his Saturday parties, and from which he and his friends went "promming." I looked into Coon Dog's gun closet, with its special shelves and brackets still intact. I went into Gram's bedroom and saw the walk-in closet he had used as a toy chest.

And outside was the front porch stoop on which Gram first tried to make himself into Elvis.

I videotaped what I saw and rushed back to show it to Dickey. As he peered through the camera's viewfinder, he looked ashen, as if he'd seen a ghost. In a way, he had.

More than a few fans of Gram Parsons were led to the house at 916 Piedmont Drive in Winter Haven, a handsome home with a driveway on which the names "Gram" and "Avis" were etched into the concrete. Here, they were told, was where Gram spent his teenage years. Gram or Avis—or someone else—may have written his name into the cement, but they actually lived across the street, at 941.

And then there's Joshua Tree National Monument, considered by most of his fans and by some of his own family as his true resting place. Visitors have made their way to Cap Rock, where they've found a small, cave-like opening in which some of the rock remains charred. In front of the area, which looks directly onto the main road, is a homemade concrete plaque on the ground. Through the years, various messages have been scrawled and painted in the area. Today all that remains is the plaque, on which someone wrote the title of Gram's album with the Submarine Band: SAFE AT HOME.

But Gram's admirers who have gathered here have also been misled.

Phil Kaufman, who should know, told me that he and Michael never carried the coffin that far in from the highway. The spot in which he set off the flames was not the one that has been pictured in articles about Gram, he said. "Somebody must've had a barbecue there," he commented.

Which leaves us, for better or worse, in New Orleans, where Gram was buried in an unlikely-looking place—the Garden of Memories, a modest cemetery located off Airline Highway, a tacky highway that rolls, none too quickly, past motels offering $10 rates and adult movies.

Here, under a round bronze marker, lies Gram.

And here, on a small marble bench nearby, his admirers can sit, knowing they actually have found Gram safe at home, and contemplating what might have been.

Some think he was too talented not to have become a star eventually. Others are less certain. Gram, they think, was ultimately too spoiled, too undisciplined, too comfortable, too stubborn, too disillusioned with the group concept and the business side of making music to do the things necessary to get the industry behind him. The Gram Parsons Memorial Foundation conducted an informal poll of members on the question, and half of them, according to the group's newsletter, "felt he was too real and honest to become a superstar."

Given his history, it's likely that if commercial success and stardom had found him, he would have found a reason, and a way, to desert it.

For most of the people who knew him, and for the thousands who discovered him after he was gone, he was a star. Jim Carlton, his buddy from Florida, was just one of many who used the word "charisma" to describe Gram. Tom Guidera, Emmylou's boyfriend, thought fate had touched Gram, affording him a magnetism few possessed. And when he combined his inner triumphs and tragedies with his music and his free-wheeling sense of showmanship, he affected people in the way only stars and lovers do.

He may never have been treated with all the recognition due him, but as long as people are drawn to music that comes from somewhere between the heart and the cosmos, Gram Parsons will be heard.

Elvis is in Graceland, a world unto itself. Thousands of fans visit him daily. Hank is in Montgomery, Alabama, his home since he was fourteen, and has the company of a monolithic monument, with clouds, sunbeams, and various of his song titles carved into a slab of white Georgia marble. Gram is in some godforsaken cemetery in New Orleans, under a simple marker on which is engraved GOD'S OWN SINGER, which was neither a Gram Parsons composition nor a song about him.

But yes, Bob Parsons did find the burial spot that he said Gram might like. Just yards away from him stands a tall, handsome oak tree. And when the quiet chug of a train from the Yazoo & Mississippi Valley railroad line punctuates the air, the more romantic could take any breeze that comes along and pretend that it's the hickory wind that called him home.

That, however, is for the romantic. When Pauline Wilkes, Gram's aunt in Columbia, Tennessee, heard about where Gram was buried, she was shocked. All these years, she'd had no idea.

And New Orleans simply did not sound right to her. Florida, yes. Georgia, yes. Tennessee, yes. But *New Orleans?* Out by *Airline Highway?* Out by one of those motels where the Reverend Jimmy Swaggart was caught with a girl?

Pauline frowned over this latest chapter of a sad, sad story. And then she spoke.

"Maybe we ought to have him moved," she said.

★_____ DISCOGRAPHY _____★

The following is a selective discography of Gram Parsons' recordings released in the United States. It is largely based on information compiled by Thor Martinsen in Norway. Those interested in seeing Mr. Martinsen's complete discography, including international releases, bootlegs, and Gram's compositions covered by other artists, should write to him at N-2140 Sander, Norway.

With the Shilos:
(Gram Parsons, vocals, guitar; Joe Kelly, vocals, bass; Paul Surratt, vocals, banjo; George Wrigley, vocals, guitar)
Gram Parsons: The Early Years 1963–65, Sierra/Briar SRS 8702, February 1979; rereleased July 1985 as Sierra SP 1963 (with additional songs)

With the International Submarine Band:
(Gram Parsons, vocals, guitar, piano; John Nuese, vocals, lead guitar; Ian Dunlop, vocals, bass, saxophone; Mickey Gauvin, drums)
"Sum Up Broke" (Parsons-Nuese)/"One Day Week" (Parsons), Columbia 4-43935, 1966
"The Russians are Coming" (Mandel)/"Truck Driving Man" (Terry Fell), Ascot 2218, 1966
(Gram Parsons, vocals, guitar; John Nuese, vocals, lead guitar; Bob Buchanan, vocals, guitar; Jon Corneal, vocals, drums):
Safe at Home, LHI Records LHI-12001 (monaural); LHK-S-12001 (stereo), 1968; reissued as *Gram Parsons*, Shiloh SLP-4088, 1976 and Shiloh SCD-4088 (CD reissue), 1987
"Luxury Liner" (Parsons)/"Blue Eyes" (Parsons), LHI 45-1205, 1968 "Miller's Cave" (Clement)/"I Must be Somebody Else You've Known" (Haggard), LHI 45-1217, 1968.

Discography

With the Byrds:
(Gram Parsons, vocals, guitar; Roger McGuinn, vocals, guitar, banjo; Chris Hillman, vocals, bass, mandolin; Kevin Kelley, drums)
Sweetheart of the Rodeo, Columbia/CBS CS 9670, August 1968
"You Ain't Going Nowhere" (Dylan)/"Artificial Energy" (Hillman-McGuinn-Clark), Columbia 44499, 1968
"I Am a Pilgrim" (Arr. McGuinn-Hillman)/"Pretty Boy Floyd" (Guthrie), Columbia 4-44643, 1968
The Byrds, Columbia/Legacy C4K 46773, October 1990 (Four-CD set includes eleven songs from the *Sweetheart of the Rodeo* sessions, among them outtakes and "lost" tracks featuring Gram on lead vocals: "Reputation," "The Christian Life," "You Don't Miss Your Water," "One Hundred Years From Now," and "Lazy Days.")

With the Flying Burrito Brothers:
(Gram Parsons, vocals, guitar, piano; Chris Hillman, vocals, guitar, mandolin; Sneeky Pete Kleinow, pedal steel guitar; Chris Ethridge, bass, piano; Jon Corneal, Sam Goldstein, Eddie Hoh, Popeye Philips, drums)
Gilded Palace of Sin, A&M SP 4175, February 1969
"The Train Song" (Hillman-Parsons)/"Hot Burrito #1" (Ethridge-Parsons), A&M 1067, 1969
(Gram Parsons, vocals, guitar, piano; Chris Hillman, vocals, bass, mandolin; Sneeky Pete Kleinow, pedal steel guitar; Bernie Leadon, vocals, guitar, dobro; Michael Clarke, drums):
Burrito Deluxe, A&M SP 4258, May 1970
"If You Gotta Go" (Dylan)/"Cody, Cody" (Parsons-Hillman), A&M 1166, 1970
"Older Guys" (Parsons-Hillman-Leadon)/"Down in the Churchyard" (Hillman-Parsons), A&M 1189, 1970
Close Up the Honky Tonks, A&M SP 3631, July 1974
(Two-record compilation includes five outtakes from the Burrito Brothers with Gram: "Close Up the Honky Tonks," "Break My Mind," "Bony Maronie," "Sing Me Back Home," and "To Love Somebody.")
Sleepless Nights, A&M SP 4578, May 1976
(Compilation of outtakes of the Burrito Brothers in 1970, after the *Burrito Deluxe* sessions, and by Gram, circa *Grievous Angel*. The Burritos songs include "Tonight the Bottle Let Me Down," "Your Angel Steps Out of Heaven," "Crazy Arms," "Together Again," "Green, Green Grass of Home," "Dim Lights," "Sing Me Back Home," and "Close Up the Honky Tonks.")
Farther Along: The Best of the Flying Burrito Brothers, A&M CD 5216, 1988
(Includes outtakes and unreleased tracks, including "Just Because," "Six Days on the Road," an alternate version of "Sing Me Back Home," a partial tape of "I Shall Be Released," and four tracks issued on *Close Up the Honky Tonks*.)

Gram Parsons Solo:
GP, Reprise MS 2123, February 1973
"She" (Parsons-Ethridge)/"That's All it Took" (Edwards-Grier-Jones), Reprise 1139, 1973

Discography

"Cry One More Time" (Wolf-Justman)/"Streets of Baltimore" (Glaser-Howard), Reprise PRO-557, 1973

Grievous Angel, Reprise MS 2171, January 1974

"Love Hurts" (Bryant)/"In My Hour of Darkness" (Parsons-Harris), Reprise 1192, 1974

Sleepless Nights, A&M SP 4578, 1976
> (Compilation of outtakes by the Flying Burrito Brothers and by Gram for the album that became *Grievous Angel*. The tracks featuring Gram and Emmylou are "Brand New Heartache," "Sleepless Nights," and "The Angels Rejoiced Last Night.")

"Return of the Grievous Angel" (Brown-Parsons)/"Hearts on Fire" (Egan-Guidera), Warner Bros. WBS 50013, 1982

Gram Parsons and the Fallen Angels—Live 1973, Sierra Records GP 1973, February 1982

More Gram Parsons and the Fallen Angels, Sierra GP/EP 104, 1982
> (EP not for sale; included with mail orders for the *Fallen Angels* album. Includes a live medley of "Bony Maronie," "Forty Days," "Almost Grown," a deejay interview with Gram, Emmylou, and other Fallen Angels, and "Hot Burrito #1" performed by Gene Parsons. The medley is included in the CD version of the *Fallen Angels* album, Sierra SECD 4222. Sierra Records, PO Box 5853, Pasadena CA 91107.)

"Love Hurts" (Bryant)/"The New Soft Shoe" (Parsons), Sierra 105, 1983
> (A single from the Fallen Angels album, released after the live "Love Hurts," was nominated for a Grammy for "Best Country Vocal by a Duo or Group.")

GP/Grievous Angel, Reprise 9 26108-2, 1990

NOTES:

The International Submarine Band's "Luxury Liner" and "Blue Eyes" were included in Record #98 of *Country Music Foundation's Official Archive Collection: The Greatest Country Music Recordings of All Time.*

The Flying Burrito Brothers' "The Train Song" was included in *The A&M Bootleg Album*, A&M SP 8022, a 1969 limited release.

The Flying Burrito Brothers' "Sin City" was included in *The Smithsonian Collection of Classical Country Music* (Smithsonian Records RO25-P8-15640, 1981).

The Flying Burrito Brothers' *Last of the Red Hot Burritos*, A&M SP 4343, 1972, is a live album of the Burritos after Gram Parsons's departure, but its liner notes include an interview with him by Chuck Casell.

BIBLIOGRAPHY

Babitz, Eve. *Eve's Hollywood.* New York: Seymour Lawrence, 1972.

Balfour, Victoria. *Rock Wives.* New York: Beech Tree Books, William Morrow, 1986.

Bonanno, Massimo. *The Rolling Stones Chronicle: The First Thirty Years.* New York: Henry Holt and Company, 1990.

Booth, Stanley. *Dance with the Devil.* New York: Random House, 1984.

Burr, Josephine G. *History of Winter Haven, Florida.* Winter Haven, Florida: Larry Burr Printing Company, 1974.

Chant, Christopher; Bidwell, Shelford; Preston, Anthony; and Shaw, Jenny. *World War II.* London: Treasure Press, 1986.

Charone, Barbara. *Keith Richards.* London: Futura Publications Limited, 1979.

Crane, Robert David and Fryer, Christopher. *Jack Nicholson Face to Face.* New York: M. Evans and Company Inc., 1975.

Dalton, David, ed. *Rolling Stones.* New York: Amsco Music Publishing Company, 1972.

Dalton, David, ed. *Rolling Stones: The First Twenty Years.* New York: Alfred A. Knopf, 1981.

Dellar, Fred; Cackett, Alan; and Thompson, Roy. *The Harmony Illustrated Encyclopedia of Country Music.* New York: Harmony Books, 1986.

DesBarres, Pamela. *I'm With the Band.* New York: Beech Tree Books, William Morrow, 1987.

Encyclopaedia Britannica and Dictionary of Arts, Sciences, and General Literature. Edinburgh: Adam and Charles Black, 1987.

Felton, David, ed. *Mindfuckers.* San Francisco: Straight Arrow Books, 1972.

Flippo, Chet. *Your Cheatin' Heart.* New York: Simon and Schuster, 1981.

———. *It's Only Rock 'n' Roll.* New York: St. Martin's Press, 1985.

Bibliography

Frame, Peter. *Rock Family Trees*. New York/London/Tokyo: Quick Fox, 1980.
———. *Rock Family Trees: Volume 2*. London/New York/Cologne/Sydney: Omnibus Press, 1983.
Frith, Simon. *Sound Effects*. New York: Pantheon Books, 1982.
Gambaccini, Paul, compiler. *Critic's Choice: Top 200 Albums*. London: Omnibus Press, 1978.
Gitlin, Todd. *The Sixties*. New York: Bantam Books, 1987.
Griffin, Sid. *Gram Parsons*. Pasadena, California: Sierra Records and Books, 1985.
Hutt, Sam. *Hank Wangford, Volume III: The Middle Years*. London: Pan Books, 1989.
Leary, Timothy. *Flashbacks*. Los Angeles: Jeremy P. Tarcher, Inc., 1983.
Lewisohn, Mark. *The Beatles Day by Day*. New York: Harmony Books, 1987.
Malone, Bill C. *Country Music USA*. Austin and London: University of Texas Press, 1968.
Marcus, Greil. *Mystery Train*. New York: E. P. Dutton and Co., Inc., 1975.
Mason, Michael, ed. *The Country Music Book*. New York: Charles Scribner's Sons, 1985.
Matschat, Cecile Hulse. *Suwanee River: Strange Green Land*. New York: Literary Guild, 1938.
Morthland, John. *The Best of Country Music*. New York: Doubleday and Company, 1984.
Nash, Alanna. *Behind Closed Doors*. New York: Alfred A. Knopf, 1988.
Obst, Linda, ed. *The Sixties*. New York: Random House, 1977.
Pareles, Jon and Romanowski, Patricia, editors. *The Rolling Stone Encyclopedia of Rock and Roll*. New York: Summit Books, 1983.
Parris, Thomas, ed. *The Simon and Schuster Encyclopedia of World War II*. New York: Simon and Schuster, 1978.
Phillips, John and Jerome, Jim. *Papa John*. New York: Dolphin Books, Doubleday and Company, Inc., 1986.
Phillips, Michelle. *California Dreamin'*. New York: Warner Books, 1986.
Riese, Randall. *Nashville Babylon*. New York/Chicago: Congdon and Weed, Inc./Contemporary Books, 1988.
Rogan, John. *Timeless Flight*. London: Scorpion Publications/Dark Star, 1981.
Rolling Stone, Editors of. *The Rolling Stone Interviews*. New York: Paperback Library, 1971.
Rolling Stone, Editors of. *The Rolling Stone Record Review*. New York: Pocket Books, 1971.
Rolling Stone, Editors of. *The Rolling Stone Record Review, Volume II*. New York: Pocket Books, 1974.
Romanowski, Patricia, ed. *Rolling Stone Rock Almanac*. New York: Rolling Stone Press/Macmillan, 1983.
Roxon, Lillian. *Lillian Roxon's Rock Encyclopedia*. New York: Grosset and Dunlap, 1971.
Sanchez, Tony. *Up and Down with the Rolling Stones*. New York: Morrow Quill, 1979.
Sanders, Ed. *The Family*. New York: Signet/New American Library, Penguin Books USA Inc., 1990.
Sarlot, Raymond and Basten, Fred E. *Life at the Marmont*. Santa Monica: Roundtable Publishing, 1987.

Bibliography

Selvin, Joel. *Ricky Nelson: Idol for a Generation.* Chicago: Contemporary Books, 1990.

Shestack, Melvin. *The Country Music Encyclopedia.* New York: Thomas Y. Crowell Company, 1974.

Vellenga, Dirk and Farren, Mick. *Elvis and the Colonel.* New York: Dell Publishing, 1988.

von Schmidt, Eric and Rooney, Jim. *Baby, Let Me Follow You Down.* New York: Anchor Press/Doubleday, 1979.

Woodward, Bob. *Wired: The Short Life and Fast Times of John Belushi.* New York: Simon and Schuster, 1984.

Zach, Paul, ed. *Florida.* Singapore: APA Publications; New York: Prentice-Hall Press, 1988.

Index

Index

Index

childhood, 25
death of, 197–202
motorcycle accident, 144–45
and music, 24
seizures, 188–89
and women, 26–27, 132
Parsons, Gretchen, 2, 211–12
on Gram's drug problems,
181–82
marriage difficulties, 188–89,
192–93
marriage to Gram, 160–61
meeting with Gram, 132–33
in Vadim film, 147–48
Parsons, Polly, 84, 220
Parsons, Robert Ellis, 128, 188
Avis (stepdaughter) and, 143–
44
Gram's funeral and, 204–05
Gram's wedding and, 161–62
marriage to Avis, 35–36
relations with Gram, 49–50
Snively family lawsuits and,
54–56
Payne, Bill, 214
Pearl Blossom, 108
Pedersen, Herb, 195, 214
Perkins, Al, 172, 195
Peters, Mercy, 104–05, 139
Phillips, John, 48, 144–45, 177,
217
Phillips, Michelle, 1, 125
at Altamont, 139–41
Phillips, Popeye, 107
Poker, 117, 123
Presley, Elvis, 24–25, 171
Protest songs, 109

R

Raphael, Mickey, 214
Rascals, 69
"Return of the Grievous Angel,"
184–86, 194
Richards, Keith, 1, 3, 92, 95–96,
98, 128–32, 135, 209

at Altamont, 139–41
and heroin, 155–60
Rivers, Johnny, 177, 217
Rivkin, David, 174
Roberts, Rick, 165
Rolling Stones, 92, 116–17,
127–32, 156–60
at Altamont, 137–41
Ronstadt, Linda, 180–81, 214
Rosser, Skip, 36–37
Ross, Nancy Marthai, 71–73,
82–85, 107, 112–14, 121–22,
220
Rumors, 38
Russell, Leon, 78, 122, 135
"Russians Are Coming, The," 69

S

Safe at Home, 80–85
Shapard, Van, 15–16
"She," 174
Shilos, 42–45, 48–51
"Sin City," 105
Sin City Boys, 180
Sixties, 64–65
Skaggs, Ricky, 215–16
Smart, N. D., 177
Smith, Dickey, 22, 55–56, 203
Snively, Dorothy DeHaven, 10–
11
Snively, Evalyn, 32–33, 54
Snively, John Jr., 17–18, 54–55
Snively, Papa John, 10–11, 21
Snow, Tom, 60, 66
South Africa, 95–96
Spector, Larry, 84, 87, 100
Stafford, Jim, 37–38
"Still Feeling Blue," 173
"Strong Boy," 82
"Sum Up Broke," 69
Surratt, Paul, 43–45, 48–49
Sutherland, Rick, 115
Sweetheart of the Rodeo, 86–98
"Sweet Virginia," 158

Index

T

Tarp, Maurice, 107
Tashian, Barry, 67, 77, 171, 209
  and Emmylou Harris, 215–16
Thomas, James E. "Jet," 57
Tickner, Eddie, 167–69, 171,
  178, 204
"Train Song, The," 119, 122
"Truck Driving Man," 69
Tullis, Kyle, 177
"Tumbling Dice," 158
Tutt, Ronnie, 172, 195, 214

U

Usher, Gary, 94–95

V

Van Tassel, George, 125
Village Vanguards, 39
Vosse, Michael, 115–19

W

Waycross, Georgia, 19–25
Weissman, Dick, 48

Wertz, Kenny, 165
"Wheels," 106
White, Clarence, 59, 122, 150,
  189–90
  and Byrds, 88, 96
  and Flying Burrito Brothers,
  100
White, Roland, 190–91
Wickham, Andy, 168
"Wild Horses," 135–36
Wilkes, Tom, 102
Williams, Hank, 113
Williams, Larry, 122
Winter Haven, 11–12
Woodstock, 126
Wrigley, George, 43–45, 48–
  49

Y

Young, Neil, 181

Z

Zahariah, 48
"Zah's Blues," 51–52

★ 236 ★